THE HITLER TERROR

THE BROWN BOOK OF
THE HITLER TERROR
AND THE BURNING OF
THE REICHSTAG

*Prepared by the World Committee for the
Victims of German Fascism*

With an Introduction by
LORD MARLEY

LONDON
VICTOR GOLLANCZ LTD
14 Henrietta Street Covent Garden
1933

First published September 1933
Second impression September 1933
Third impression September 1933

Printed in Great Britain by
The Camelot Press Ltd., London and Southampton

CONTENTS

CONTENTS

LIST OF ILLUSTRATIONS

FOREWORD

I₮ IS ALWAYS difficult to secure authentic information as to what is happening under a well-organised terror. Even experienced journalists find it difficult, in spite of their training, to get anything like the truth. Special credit is due to a few of the Foreign Press correspondents in Germany who, at the risk of losing their posts, have contrived to get so much of the truth across the frontier.

Many authentic documents have been placed at the disposal of the World Committee for the Victims of German Fascism : some by journalists, others by doctors and members of the legal profession, to whom special means of discovering the truth were available, but who did not dare and indeed were unable to publish their information in Germany. Other documents have been sent by the tortured and martyred victims themselves. For the greater part of the material the Committee has to thank its own reporters, who have been working in Germany at the risk of their lives.

We have not used the most sensational of these documents. Every statement made in this book has been carefully verified and is typical of a number of similar cases. We would have been able to publish even worse individual cases, but we have not done this, just because they were individual cases. Not a single one of the cases published in this book is an exceptional case. Each case cited is typical of many others which are in our possession or in the hands of the National Committees.

These manifestations of Fascism are appalling. But the memory of the public is short, and public opinion is unfortunately only too ready to reconcile itself to a *fait accompli*, as in the case of Italy.

This book aims at keeping alive the memory of the criminal acts of the Nazi Government. It is a contribution to the fight against Hitler Fascism. This fight is not directed against Germany ; it is a fight on behalf of the real Germany.

MARLEY,

Chairman of the World Committee
for the Victims of German Fascism.

House of Lords,
*London, S.W.*1

CHAPTER I: THE PATH TO POWER

THE " German Labour Party " was founded in Munich
in January 1919. In July of that year Adolf Hitler, at
that time " Education Officer " in the Reichswehr, joined
this party. He was the seventh member of what later developed into the National Socialist German Labour Party.

Who were the founders and first members of this party?
From what sections of the population did they come, and
what interests did they represent? In the first place, they
consisted of soldiers and officers who had come back from
the war completely disillusioned. For four years they had
honestly believed in the chauvinist slogans with which they
had been fed. They had staked their lives in the struggle for
a Greater Germany. They believed in the legend that
pacifist and Social Democratic traitors had stabbed the
German Army in the back and brought about its defeat.
These men who came back were deeply embittered by
what they thought was the weakness of the ruling class,
the treachery and flight of the Kaiser and of the deposed
princes, and the failure of the generals of the Great War
to strike down the " November criminals."

These deeply disillusioned soldiers and officers could no
longer find a place for themselves in civil life. To a great
extent the professions which they had once practised now
no longer existed. This was true particularly of the professional soldiers, military cadets and a number of categories
of officials. They were joined by members of the uprooted
nobility, students who had been torn from their studies by
the war, and declassed and radicalised members of the
middle classes who now began to feel the ground giving
way under their feet. All of these elements, who at that
time also flocked into the many other military bodies which
arose at that time—the Einwohnerwehr, the Stahlhelm and
the Ehrhardt Brigade—formed the first basis of the young
National Socialist German Labour Association, as the party
first called itself officially.

For two years after its formation the National Socialists were quite an insignificant group. The November revolution of 1918 had been beaten down, and the capitalist system had got a new lease of life. The Social Democrat Friedrich Ebert became the first President of the Weimar Republic. The old forces of finance-capitalism consolidated their rule again. The trade union leaders had concluded an agreement with the employers, based on negotiations in November 1918 between Hugo Stinnes and the president of the General Committee of the trade unions, the Social Democrat Karl Legien. What at that time could Hitler do for the leading groups of German capitalists ? At that period they were not yet in need of the National Socialists. Hitler's Association therefore remained without any significance. He himself continued in the service of the Reichswehr until April 1920, giving political lectures to the soldiers. On instructions from the Reichswehr he also " observed " political organisations and meetings, bringing in reports and information. This was how Hitler first came into contact with the " German Labour Party."

Not long afterwards the political importance of the party began to grow. The political situation in Germany began to change rapidly under the effect of the dictated Peace of Versailles and the losses of the War. Milliards of marks were demanded in reparations and had to be paid. Important industrial areas were lopped off ; Alsace-Lorraine, Upper Silesia, the Saar territory, Posen and West Prussia— the so-called Polish corridor—Danzig and Eugen Malmedy. The German market was still further restricted by the loss of a considerable portion of its European and oversea connections in addition to the German colonies. The cost of demobilisation and of putting the war industries on to a peace basis was a terrific burden on the smaller taxpayers, as the dominant circles of German monopoly capital were continuously devising new methods of transferring the reparations payments and all other losses on to the shoulders of the workers and the middle class.

This development reached its highest point in the inflation

which had begun during the war but was only widely felt
among the population in the course of 1921 and 1922.
In the autumn of 1923 it reached the point of catastrophe.
It had brought about still further impoverishment of the
workers, and had transformed a considerable section of the
middle classes into proletarians. Millions of the poorer
sections of the middle class were literally robbed of everything they had by the inflation. The State paid the banks
and heavy industry concerns 600,000,000 gold marks as
compensation for the occupation of the Ruhr by the French,
and these concerns also made enormous profits.

The economic chaos produced far-reaching political
disturbances. Erzberger and Rathenau fell victims to the
bullets of Nationalist murderers. Among the working class
a process of radicalisation was taking place. The Spartacus
struggles in Berlin in January 1919 were followed by the
rising of the workers in the Ruhr during the Kapp *Putsch*
of March 1920, and the workers' revolt in March 1921.
The workers began to leave the Social Democratic organisations, making their way first to the Independent Social
Democrats, then, after the autumn of 1920, to the Communist Party. Great demonstrations culminated in the
Hamburg rising of October 1923.

The 25 points of the Nazi Programme.   In 1920 the
National Socialist German Labour Party first began to
develop importance. In February of that year Hitler himself, at a meeting in Munich, put forward the programme
of the party, the so-called 25 points. These are a hash of
theses and demands which in parts are self-contradictory.
The political practice of the Nazi Party has at no time
followed the principles laid down in the 25 points. Nor
did it matter to Hitler and his vassals that at the end of the
programme the following passage occurs :

" The leaders of the party undertake, if necessary at the
    risk of their own lives, to work unceasingly for the carry-
    ing through of the points enumerated above."

This was not the only promise which the Nazi leaders gave and failed to keep. In a general meeting of the party in May 1926, a resolution was once again adopted stressing the " unalterable character " of the party's programme. Gottfried Feder, the joint author of the 25 points and theoretician of the party, in his commentary on the programme laid stress on the fact that :

" There must be no tampering with the basis and fundamental conceptions of this programme. There must be no twisting and turning on any opportunist grounds, there must be no hide-and-seek with the present State, economic and social order of things, and there must be no weakening of our principles. . . . Those who in the Jewish question, in our fight against high finance, against the Dawes Pact and the policy of impoverishing Germany, or in other questions on our programme, cannot see eye to eye with the irrevocable aims and methods which we have laid down ; those who believe that the freedom of the German nation can be ' bought ' through the League of Nations or Locarno by compromise and cowardice—such people need have nothing to do with us ; let them remain outside of our party."

But all these magnificent words cannot hide the fact that the National Socialist leaders have repeatedly repudiated and betrayed their own half-hearted and compromising programme. Their treachery to their programme begins with the first two points : point 1, " the union of all Germans on the basis of the right of self-determination of peoples, to form a Greater Germany " ; point 2, " The equal right of the German nation with all other nations, and the cancellation of the Peace Treaties of Versailles and St. Germain." Neither of these two points in his programme prevented Hitler, both before and after his seizure of power, from concluding compromises with the signatories of the Versailles Treaty, and sending envoys to negotiate with the League of Nations, France, Poland, England and Italy.

Nor did either of these points make him hesitate to betray the South Tyrol to Mussolini. In the first edition of Feder's Commentary on the programme the following passage occurs: "We shall not give up a single German in South Germany, in Alsace-Lorraine, *in the South Tyrol*, in Poland, in Austria, the colony of the League of Nations, and the succession States of what was formerly Austria." *In the second and all later editions, the words " in the South Tyrol " were omitted.* It may be noted in passing that in his foreword to the fifth edition Feder remarks "The only alterations which have been made are in the case of a few stylistic expressions and passages which might have led to misunderstanding."

It is the same with other points of the programme, particularly the demands of an economic and social character, such as " the abolition of income derived without labour and effort," " abolition of the domination of interest " (point 11) ; " the complete confiscation of all war profits " (point 12) ; " the taking over by the State of all concerns which have already been trustified " (point 13) ; " participation in the profits of large concerns " (point 14) ; " a considerable extension of provision for old age " (point 15) ; " the creation and maintenance of a healthy middle class ; the immediate municipalisation of the large stores, and the leasing of them at low prices to small tradespeople ; close control of all small tradespeople in their sales to the Reich, to the constituent States of the Reich, or to the local authorities " (point 16) ; " land reform suited to our national needs, the establishment of legislation to provide for expropriation of land without compensation where required for public purposes, abolition of the land tax, and measures to prevent speculation in land " (point 17). It is not necessary to examine each of these points in the programme in detail. Some of them will be dealt with in later chapters, as for example the points relating to the Jewish question (points 4–8 and 23).

At this stage, we are concerned only with indicating the general basis of the National Socialist programme and with showing how the leaders of the National Socialist Party have unscrupulously betrayed their own programme. The demands themselves are in part reactionary, lower middle-class demands, as for example " the creation and maintenance of a healthy middle class." Here too, we have half-heartedness and contradiction such as is characteristic of the programme throughout. For how is the middle class to be maintained if the capitalist economic system, which necessarily destroys the middle class and brings them into the ranks of the working class, is also to be maintained? This is also true of the point dealing with agrarian policy. How can Hitler save the peasantry if he maintains private property intact, if he repudiates any expropriation of the big landlords in favour of the landless peasant ? In April 1928 Hitler expressly stated that the National Socialist Party was determined to protect the private ownership of the means of production with all the strength it could command. In an explanation of the phrase " expropriation without compensation " in point 17 of his programme he stated that this only referred to legislation authorising the expropriation, where necessary, of land which was not being properly used from the standpoint of the welfare of the people ; and that this passage was in the first place directed against Jewish land-speculation companies.

On the other hand the National Socialist programme also contained demands which had previously been the stock-in-trade of Liberal parties, and also demands embodied in the Weimar Constitution. Point 13, the taking over of the trusts by the State, is stolen straight out of the programme of the German Democratic Party of 1919. Other points are unfulfilled promises made in the Weimar Constitution. Examples of this are : point 15, " extension of provision for old age " ; point 20, " full opportunities for ability " ; compare with the Constitution and the Welfare Act of 1924 ; point 21, " improvement of the health of the people and protection for mother and child " ; and point 24,

The Gate of Lies is wide open : HITLER speaks !

PLATE NO. I.

" public service before private interest "—compare paragraph 156 of the Constitution.

The Growth of the Nazi Movement.   Hitler appeared in the first great meetings organised by the Nationalist Socialist Party to put forward this programme. At that period, the agitation against the Versailles Treaty was put in the forefront of the Nazi agitation. The more the middle class was affected by the continuous inflation, the more popular the Nazi demonstrations became. It cannot however be disputed that in the middle class it was not only the material losses they suffered through reparations, inflation and the occupation of the Ruhr which affected their outlook but also the blow to national sentiment which was inflicted by the dictated Peace of Versailles and the entry of French troops into German territory.

In February 1921, soon after the reparations negotiations, a great National Socialist demonstration was held in Munich with the slogan " Germany's future or extinction." For the first time motors carrying swastika flags passed through the streets of Munich, advertising the demonstration. Posters were put up everywhere with the demagogic text :

"If sixty million Germans, young and old, declare their united determination : ' We will not pay,' then the will of these millions will at least secure the respect which is not given to those who kiss the lash which whips them. We are men, not dogs. The sixty million Germans must tell the Government clearly that whoever negotiates will be overthrown ! "

This demonstration was a great success for Hitler. The National parties and associations which had been using old pre-war methods of propaganda ridiculed the " young man " when he came to them proposing the organisation of giant demonstrations against the Government's " policy of fulfilment," and still more when, on their refusal, he himself undertook the task with his own tiny party. But the programme of the Nationalist parties, which was that of the Junkers and big capitalists, was not suitable for the middle classes, who however were carried away by the twenty-five points and Hitler's unscrupulous agitation.

The failure of the Kapp *Putsch* had shown the weakness of the Junkers. The *putsch* was based on the support of the big landlords and parts of the Reichswehr and the higher grades of the civil service, besides a few military groups ; but it was completely out of touch with the discontent in the middle class. It was therefore beaten by the working class within twenty-four hours.

The Stahlhelm too could never win more than a very limited influence, chiefly among peasant and urban youth and the most backward sections of the workers—members of the Yellow Unions and agricultural labourers. But the National Socialists were different. They put forward their imaginary fight against " international Jewish banking and speculative capital " and their slogan of the " national union " in which all sections of the population would live at peace with each other under a strong State, and with this programme they were able to penetrate widely different groups, including large numbers of the middle class. In 1921 the membership of the National Socialist Party grew from 3,000 to 6,000 ; but its sphere of influence at that time was almost exclusively limited to Bavaria. In North Germany the movements under Graefe, Wulle, Henning and Count Reventlow were very much stronger.

In 1920 the first congress of the National Socialist Party was held in Salzburg. This congress was attended by members of the Austrian National Socialist Party, which dated from before the war. It had been formed in 1904 as a " German Labour Party," and in May 1918 this joined with other groups to form the National Socialist Party of Austria. National Socialism dates therefore from the early years of the century. It developed first in Bohemia, where the national question played a particularly important rôle. Hitler, an Austrian by birth, had taken a great deal from their programme. But he was unable to reach an agreement at Salzburg with Jung, the leader of the Bohemian Party.

The next congress was held at Reichenhall in 1921. *This congress was held jointly with Russian and Ukrainian White Guard associations.* Hetman Skoropadski was among the speakers. In conjunction with the National Socialist Alfred Rosenberg, whose family came from the Baltic provinces and who later became editor of the *Völkischer Beobachter* and Nazi expert in foreign politics, the White Guard emigrants developed their plans of intervention against the Soviet State, which had just driven out the last of the troops of intervention. Already at that period Rosenberg had developed connections with Deterding and the German industrial employer Rechberg, both of them violently hostile to the Soviet Union. It is interesting to note that in the *Völkischer Beobachter* Rosenberg wrote his first anti-Bolshevik articles— which were pro-Polish !

In a manifesto issued in connection with the congress of the party in Munich in January 1922, Hitler, who had still to win his position as sole dictator of the Nazi Party, stated that it was necessary to purge the movement, as it had become a breeding-ground for well-meaning fools, who were all the more dangerous because of their good intentions. This was evidently directed against the other founders of the party, including Anton Drexler and Körner, who were not prepared to follow Hitler in his new and unscrupulous methods. High and influential officers in the Reichswehr at Munich had for a considerable time given support to the movement ; among them were some of Hitler's former colleagues of 1919 and 1920. With their help he set up, alongside of the party organisation proper and the Press and propaganda department, a third organisation, which in the following years and later on served as his main fighting weapon : the storm troops.

In the summer of 1920, the National Socialist Party, under the pretext of protecting their meetings against attacks by the " Reds," had set up what they called a " corps for maintaining order." But this was too small and

weak for Hitler, who in August 1921 set up his own protective organisation : the storm troops. These formed the
terrorist section of the National Socialist Party and were
brought directly under the political leadership of the
party.

Who Financed Hitler?

Not long after this period, a
number of capitalists, particularly in South Germany,
began to take an interest in Hitler and the National Socialist
Party, with a view to drawing them in to support their own
reactionary politics. They realised the value of the National
Socialist movement as a weapon against the militant
sections of the working class, and they were therefore prepared to support the Nazis, particularly with finance.

In the Hitler-Ludendorff trial of 1924 it was proved that
Hitler had received considerable sums of money for his
party from Aust, the director of the Bavarian Employers'
Association ; Bechstein, the piano manufacturer ; Maffei,
an industrial employer in Munich ; and Hornschuh of
Kulmbach, and Grandel of Augsburg, two manufacturers.
Hitler also gave lectures on his aims in the select clubs of
bankers, landlords and big employers of labour. In return,
he received contributions in support of the National
Socialist Press, and for similar purposes. Hitler also received
subsidies from Borsig, a large industrial employer of Berlin,
who was chairman of the Union of German Employers'
Associations. An agent of Hitler's in Switzerland, Dr.
Gausser, is also said to have secured for Hitler finance from
Henry Ford and also from French capitalist groups who
were speculating on the Bavarian separatist movement.

It is probable that the full sources of Hitler's finance will
only become known when the archives come into the hands
of the German workers. But political proof of the source of
his finance is already clear. The whole policy of the National
Socialist Party and the declarations of sympathy for it
made by important capitalist groups, such as Thyssen and
Schacht, are proof of the great interest necessarily taken in
the Hitler movement by the ruling class. Hitler's debts, and

the immense expenditure on propaganda and for the maintenance of the storm troops, were factors which played a
certain rôle in bringing him into action in 1923.

The *Putsch* of November 9th, 1923.   The Munich *Putsch*
of November 9th, 1923, was the highest point and also the
end of the first upward movement of the National Socialist
Party. All through 1923 Hitler had been urging his allies
in the Bavarian Government and the Reichswehr to take
action. Early in November he mobilised the fighting
associations, and in a great demonstration of patriotic
associations in Munich, announced the formation of " the
National Republic." He announced the deposition of
Ebert, appointed himself Chancellor, Kahr his vice-consul
for Bavaria, Pöhner, the chief of the Munich police, Prime
Minister, and Ludendorff Minister of the Reichswehr. The
Bavarian Ministers were arrested, but released by Ludendorff a few hours later on parole. At first Kahr supported
Hitler's proposals, but in the evening went with General
von Lossow and Colonel Seisser to the barracks of the 19th
Infantry Regiment, from which they declared in a broadcast that they repudiated the Hitler *Putsch*. Kahr stated that
his consent had been obtained from him by the threat of
force. He also announced the compulsory liquidation of the
National Socialist German Labour Party as well as the
fighting associations " Oberland " and " Reichsflagge."
This report and the order for the dissolution of these
organisations were published in the Munich papers on
November 9th.

Hitler and Ludendorff made a despairing effort to take
power, although Hitler had given his word of honour a few
months earlier to the Bavarian Minister of the Interior that
he would not make any attempt at a *putsch*. They marched
with their fighting organisations through the streets. The
Reichswehr maintained an attitude of neutrality. It would
not fire on the marching troops. Bavarian police awaited
Hitler's approach in one of the public buildings. The police
fired one volley : fifteen of the Hitlerites fell dead. Hitler

himself fled and was arrested in the villa of a princess before he was able to cross the Austrian frontier. Goering fled to Italy and later to Sweden. Ludendorff was not arrested.

The trial of the *putschists* of November 9th took place in the spring of 1924. The judges were merciful and sympathetic : for the accused were " nationally minded " people who had acted " with the best intentions." The accused were : Hitler ; Field Marshal von Ludendorff ; Frick, a police official, who was to become Minister of the Interior in 1933 ; Captain Röhm ; Lieutenant Pernet, Ludendorff's stepson ; and a few others. Nazi historians record that the accused were in cheerful mood, and were smiling and cracking jokes. Hitler was sentenced to five years' detention in a fortress—subject to being released on parole when he had served a portion of the sentence. A few months later, in December 1924, he was released from the Landsberg fortress. Röhm, Frick and Brückner got away with only three months' detention. Ludendorff was released without punishment, on the ground that he had been carried away in the excitement of the moment. Hitler, then still an Austrian citizen, was not expelled but was allowed to continue to reside in Germany.

The Nazis disappear from the scene.   The failure of the 1923 *putsch* formed the close of the " insurrectionary " period of the Hitler movement. The time of plans for armed uprisings against the " Jewish government in Berlin " had now passed. The German economic situation had reached a certain stability, and the position of the middle class was improving. Hence for some years the National Socialist Party virtually disappeared from the scene. The united People's and National Socialist parties, which in the Reichstag elections of May 1924 had obtained 1,900,000 votes and 32 seats, in December of that year secured only 840,000 votes and 14 seats. They sank down among the " splinter parties," while the German Nationals secured over 100 and the Social Democrats 120 seats.

The following years were marked by internal struggles

within the Nationalist and National Socialist parties. In the summer of 1925 the German People's Freedom Party split, and a large section of its former supporters went over to Hitler. In the meanwhile, the employers continued to take back from the workers the concessions they had won in 1918. In January 1925 a government was formed of the reactionary parties under the leadership of the German Nationalists. Three months later Field Marshal von Hindenburg was elected by the combined forces of the Right to succeed Ebert as president of the Reich. The National Socialists, who in the first ballot had supported the hopeless candidature of Ludendorff, in the second ballot voted for Hindenburg ; this was the beginning of the transformation of the National Socialist movement.

The Nazis support the Princes.   In 1926, in connection with the referendum for the expropriation of the princes, the National Socialists joined the chorus of all the reactionary parties from the German Nationalists to the Centre and the Democrats in shouting : " The expropriation of the princes is robbery of well-earned wealth ! " Moreover, the Nazis have never changed their line in connection with this question. The leader of the Nazi fraction in the Reichstag declared, in connection with a Communist motion for the expropriation of the princes and the discontinuance of payments to the Kaiser and the nobility :

> " A sense of justice makes us reject the Communist motion for the expropriation of the princes. German Socialism must also recognise the rights of the Hohenzollerns."

The German princes and former nobility have rewarded the Nazis for this attitude by putting millions of their " compensation " money at the disposal of the Nazis. We refer particularly to Prince August-Wilhelm, son of the ex-Kaiser ; Duke Karl Eduard of Saxe-Coburg-Gotha ; Prince Wilhelm von Hessen, whom Goering appointed president of Hessen-Nassau in 1933 ; Prince Christian of

Minister of Lies in the " Third Empire " :
Dr. Josef Goebbels

PLATE NO. 2.

Schaumburg-Lippe ; and recently the former Crown Prince has joined the Motor Corps of the Nazis. The National Socialists have not been in a position to deny that the ex-Kaiser Wilhelm II has also helped in the financing of the storm troops.

Hitler then tried the policy of drawing closer to the reactionary parties in order to win back the confidence of the capitalists, which he had lost through the Munich *Putsch*. He attempted to win legal positions, because he realised that this was the only way to win the favour and support of the ruling class. Once again he began lecturing in the employers' clubs, in order to persuade the big capitalists that his ideas were not at all dangerous, and to explain to them how much better they could work with the National Socialists than with the unpatriotic Social Democrats. But now the " leader " did not restrict his activities to South Germany. He went to the western areas, to find the industrial barons in their citadels. In 1926 he spoke twice to specially invited audiences in Essen and Königswinter ; and again in 1927 at the Krupp Hall in Essen. The organ of heavy industry, the *Rheinisch-Westfälische Zeitung*, records the applause with which Hitler's remarks were greeted.

Strasser and Goebbels speak of " Socialism."   In the same period—and this is typical of the double-faced, unscrupulous propaganda of the National Socialists—Gregor Strasser, one of Hitler's lieutenants, toured through North and East Germany with " socialist " slogans of the " German revolution." At that time also Josef Goebbels comes on the stage ; he was a young Catholic writer from the Rhineland. In October 1925 Strasser started the *National Socialist Correspondence*, which became as it were the " theoretical " organ of the " left " National Socialists. Goebbels, at first editor of this journal, then went in 1926 to Berlin as district leader ; up to then the movement had made little headway there. From July 1927 he published a weekly called *Der Angriff*, with the pseudo-socialist mottoes : " For the oppressed ! Against the exploiters ! "

Gregor Strasser, with his brother Otto, formerly a Social Democrat, started a small press in Berlin, the "Kampf-Verlag." It produced three daily papers : the *Nationaler Sozialist* (NS) in Berlin, the *Märkischer Beobachter* for the Brandenburg province, and the *Sächsiger Beobachter*. At that time these were the only Nazi daily newspapers in Central and North Germany. The Kampf-Verlag also published three weekly papers and a number of books and pamphlets. There is no doubt that at that period Gregor Strasser attempted to rival Hitler in North Germany ; he had certain differences with Hitler, and only made these up later. But he continued to carry out an independent policy and eventually, at the end of 1932, Hitler relieved him of his functions, when he had become too closely associated with General Schleicher.

In all the publications of the Kampf-Verlag a very " radical " tone was used, which was intended to make the reader believe that he was being spoken to by a " friend of the workers " and even a " class-fighter." " National or International Socialism," a pamphlet published by the Kampf-Verlag, asserted that " The National Socialist Party is the class party of creative labour." The author of this pamphlet was Jung, first president of the Austrian Nazis. Gregor Strasser's motto was " Freedom and Bread," and his trade-mark is a hammer and sword.

Goebbels uses the same tactics in his pamphlet : " The Nazi-Sozi : Questions and Answers for Nationalists."

" There can surely be nothing more hypocritical than a fat, well-fed capitalist who protests against the pro-letarian idea of class struggle. . . . Who gave you the right to throw out your chest, swollen with national responsibility, in indignation against the class struggle of the proletariat ? Has not the capitalist State for some 60 years been an organised class State, which brought with it as an inevitable historical necessity the proletarian idea of class struggle ? . . . Are you not ashamed, you well-fed Central European, to fight the class fight against underfed, hollow-eyed, hungry, workless proletarians ? Yes, we call ourselves the Workers' State. This is the first step. The first step away from the capitalist State. We call ourselves a Labour Party, because we want to set labour free, because to us creative labour is the progressive element in history, because labour means more to us than property, education, rank and bourgeois origin. That is why we call ourselves a Labour Party. . . .

" We call ourselves socialist, as a protest against the lie of capitalist social compassion. We want no compassion, we want no social outlook. We despise the rubbish which you call ' social legislation.' It is too little to live with and too much to die with. . . . We demand a full share of what heaven gave us and of what we create with our hands and our brains. That is socialism ! . . . We protest against the idea of the class struggle. Our whole movement is one great protest against the class struggle. . . . But at the same time we call things by their right names : if on one side 17 million proletarians see their only salvation in the class struggle, this is because, from the Right side, they have been taught this in practice for 60 years. How can we find any moral justification in fighting against the class struggle, unless the capitalist class State is first absolutely torn in shreds and abolished, through a new socialist organisation of the German people ? "

These words were written not so very long ago by the man who later became Reich Minister for Enlightenment and Propaganda. It is quite a different tone from that used in the 25 points, in which the word " socialism " does not occur. Compare Goebbels' demand for the tearing in shreds of the capitalist class State with the official organ of the Nazi Party, which in point 25 says :

" For the carrying through of the above (the whole programme) we demand : The creation of a strong central power in the Reich. The absolute authority of the central political parliament over the whole Reich and all its organisations. The formation of chambers of trades and professions for the carrying through in the separate States of the Reich of the general measures laid down by the Reich."

By the side of the policy as put forward by Goebbels, the Hitler programme of 1920 seems colourless, conventional, philistine and liberal. Goebbels' manifesto against the " fat, well-fed capitalist " provides a Fascist programme which is much more suitable for industrial areas than the 25 points of Hitler.

New Defeats in 1928.

Nevertheless, neither Hitler with his lectures to the " well-fed capitalists " of the Rhineland and the Ruhr, nor Strasser and Goebbels with their demagogy, could succeed in extending the mass influence of the National Socialist Party. It is true that a certain internal consolidation of the party took place during this period. The membership rose from 17,000 in 1926 to 40,000 in 1927. Two Congresses were held : Weimar in 1926 and Nürnberg in 1927. The storm detachments were re-established. The party got rid of " well-meaning, but for that reason all the more dangerous, fools " ; the " racial specialist " Dinter in Thuringia was among those expelled. Moreover, in order to make the party presentable in drawing-rooms, the infamous murderer Heines was expelled ; although his bloody record did not prevent Hitler from taking him back again later and appointing him police president of Breslau and head of the storm detachments of the whole of North and East Germany. In May 1928 the National Socialist Party again suffered a heavy defeat at the polls, securing only 12 seats in the Reichstag. The objective situation for the growth of the Fascist movement had not yet developed. The years 1924 to 1927 had brought a certain restoration of Germany's economic life, and this had resulted in easier conditions for the middle

class generally and also for some sections of the working
class.

The Economic Crisis in Germany.   The illusory economic
prosperity however reached its zenith. Germany was the
first European country to be affected by the developing
world crisis. Production fell, and unemployment rose. In
the winter of 1930 there were already over three million
unemployed in Germany. The employers began a general
attack on wages. According to estimates made by the Berlin
Finanzpolitische Korrespondenz the average weekly wages of
industrial workers fell as follows : in the summer of 1929,
they were 44.60 Reichsmarks ; in March 1930, 39.05 Rm.
The average weekly wage throughout the year, which in
1928 and 1929 was 42 and 45 marks, fell to 37 marks in
1930 and 30 marks in 1931. Under the Papen-Schleicher
Government the average weekly wage was reduced to fifty
per cent of what it had been in 1928 and 1929 : it fell to
20.80 marks in August 1932, and since then it has fallen
still further. The *Finanzpolitische Korrespondenz* estimates the
total wage reductions of workers and employees in Germany, from July 1929 to July 1932, at approximately
38,000,000,000 marks (at par, about £1,900,000,000).

Together with the wage and salary reductions there was
also a tremendous rise in unemployment. According to the
official figures of the Reich Ministry of Labour, unemployment rose to over six million. The official *Trade Research
Institute* however showed that these official figures were not
comprehensive, as they covered only those workers who
were reporting at the Labour Exchanges ; that in addition
to the " visible " unemployed, there were also many
" invisible." On the basis of the Health Insurance statistics,
which cover all employed persons, the " invisible " unemployment amounted to approximately two millions. While
therefore the Ministry of Labour figures showed close on
six million unemployed in the winter of 1931–32, and five
million in the summer of 1932, the Institute estimated the
figures at eight million in the winter of 1931–32, and over

seven million in the third quarter of 1932—the best season.
But even these figures did not accurately reflect the position.
They did not include the hundreds of thousands of persons
who had been unemployed for several years and were
walking the streets of the towns as beggars or wandering
through Germany as tramps ; nor did they include the
destitute children and the young unemployed who could
find no work when they left school. They did not include
the hundreds of thousands of small merchants and tradespeople, of people who had formerly been " independent "
and professional people, who were living on the verge of
starvation and were in fact unemployed. The real number
of unemployed at the end of 1932 must be put at somewhere round about nine million.

The position of the middle class was increasingly getting
worse. The specific weight of this section of the population
in Germany is considerable. According to a statistical
enquiry made by Theodor Geiger (" Die soziale Schichtung
des deutschen Volkes," Stuttgart, 1932), the percentage
proportion of the various classes in the total number of
occupied persons is : Capitalists, 0.84 per cent ; " old
middle class " (small proprietors) 18.33 per cent ; " new
middle class " (officials, employees, etc.) 16.04 per cent ;
" proletaroids " (workers on own account, small traders,
etc.) 13.76 per cent ; proletariat, 51.03 per cent. The proportion of the proletariat may be put too high, but the
general distribution is probably correct.

The crisis brought wide sections of the middle class down
into the proletariat. The number of bankruptcies rose.
Compulsory sales became more and more frequent. The
small tradespeople of the towns and the small peasants were
particularly severely hit. And the crisis hit sections of
people who had hitherto not been affected, and whose
position had improved during the preceding period of rela-
tive stabilisation. Unemployment began to creep into the
most privileged sections of intellectual workers. The
standard of living of teachers, engineers, doctors, lawyers,
writers, artists, fell lower and lower. A quarter of the

university lecturers could find no posts. Of eight thousand graduates from the technical colleges and universities in 1931–32, only 1,000 found employment in their professions ; 1,500 continued their studies "provisionally," suffering great privation ; 1,500 found temporary work as street-hawkers, waiters, etc. ; but 4,000 remained totally unemployed. An investigation undertaken by the Hartmann-bund, the officially recognised doctors' association, showed that in 1932 seventy per cent of the German medical profession were earning less than 170 marks a month (at par, £8 10s. 0d.). The German legal association found that its members were in much the same position. According to a statement issued by the Prussian Minister of Education, of 22,000 teachers who completed their training in the previous year, only 990 found posts, and even these were only temporary and auxiliary teaching posts. And these figures cover Prussia only ! The number of unemployed engineers and chemists increased five times between April 1930 and April 1932, while unemployment among technical staffs doubled, and among all employees rose by $1\frac{1}{2}$ times, during the same period. The position of those university lecturers who were still employed got worse from year to year. Hours were lengthened. Salaries were rigorously cut. In addition, there was an increase in short time working : many industries worked only 3 to 5 days a week.

The immense burden of reparations sharpened the crisis. The promises and hopes of the Dawes Plan and the Locarno Treaty were not fulfilled. The Young Plan of 1929 made a new " regulation of debts " which brought fresh opportunities for the German capitalists to transfer the burden to the workers. A new wave of radicalisation passed through the workers. After the electoral success of the Social Democrats in May 1928 the working class began again to turn towards the Communist Party. Sections of the middle class which had hitherto been indifferent to politics now began to become active. The peasants were roused. In North Germany in 1929 they were in a state of revolt, resisting by force the bailiffs sent to rob them of their last cow. There were conflicts with the police. Then came one bomb attack after another. In Schleswig-Holstein attempts were made to blow up government offices.

In 1928 a " great coalition " government was formed, reaching from the German People's Party (the party of heavy industry) to the Social Democrats. Hermann Müller, president of the Social Democratic party, became Chancellor. In addition to him there were three Social Democrats in the Government : Severing (Minister of the Interior), Hilferding (Minister of Finance) and Winell (Minister of Labour). Stresemann, leader of the German People's Party, became Foreign Minister, his friend Dr. Curtius Minister of Economics, and the Democrat Gessler (now a Fascist) Minister of the Reichswehr. It was under Müller's Government that the Young Plan was put through. The chief delegate at the Paris Young Plan conference was Schacht, president of the Reichsbank, who was removed from his post in 1930 and restored to it again in 1933 as a follower of Hitler.

The Brüning Period.   In December 1929 Hilferding was removed from the Government, and his place as Finance Minister was taken by Professor Moldenhauer, a member of the board of control of the great German chemical trust, the I.G. Farbenindustrie. A few months later, in March 1930, the Müller cabinet was replaced by the Brüning Government. The Social Democratic Party was manœuvred out of the Government. Nevertheless, the Brüning-Groener-Stegerwald Government, which did not have a majority in the Reichstag, was willingly supported and " tolerated " by the Social Democrats. At the same time, this Government was already thinking of bringing in the National Socialists. In the Gereke trial in June 1933, the former Minister Treviranus explicitly stated that at that time Brüning had the intention of bringing in the Nazis. The Social Democrats represented to the workers that the Brüning Government was " a lesser evil " than a government which was purely Fascist and capitalist. The Social Democratic Prussian Government

Bт

of Braun and Severing firmly supported the Brüning Government of the Reich.

The period of " democracy " came to an end amid the difficulties which the economic crisis brought to Germany's financial, industrial and agrarian capitalists. Brüning ruled Germany with Article 48 of the Weimar Constitution, which in fact suspends the constitution. But it was not the first time that the rulers of the German republic had had to " correct " a political development which was beginning to get dangerous, by the introduction of the state of siege and the suspension of democratic rights. During the years 1919 to 1923, when the Social Democrat Ebert was president of the Reich, Article 48 made it possible to prohibit strikes in so-called vital industries, to organise strike-breaking corps for technical assistance in emergencies, to send the Reichswehr to Saxony and Thuringia in 1923 " to restore constitutional conditions," and to appoint General von Seeckt as military dictator for the prohibition of the German Communist Party. Zörgiebel, the Social Democratic police president of Berlin and a former trade union leader, prohibited the working-class demonstrations of May 1st, 1929, and when the workers broke through his prohibition and demonstrated, he sent police against them, killing 33 Berlin workers. A few days later Severing prohibited the Red Front organisation, which was the anti-Fascist defence organisation of the revolutionary workers, while in Prussia the Nazis were allowed to continue legally building up their fighting organisations.

The Reichstag was side-tracked by Brüning. The Social Democrats gave their consent to this, and Brüning ruled with emergency decrees on the basis of Article 48 of the constitution. He decreed the reduction of unemployment payments, the lowering of the miserable pensions of the victims of the war, of the sick, of old people, widows and orphans. He decreed new taxes on the masses : the poll tax, the crisis tax, the bachelors tax. He decreed increases in import duties, and thereby increases in the price of food. He put an end to the rent protection legislation. Banks and industrial concerns received millions in subsidies. The great land-lords were able to put themselves right at the expense of their workers. They received millions out of the so-called " aid for the east." And the police presidents, of whom more than half were members of the Social Democratic Party, put down with intense severity the defensive movements of the workers, prohibited the Communist Press and forbade working-class demonstrations.

Through this policy the Social Democrats not only actually helped forward the development of the reactionary and Fascist forces in Germany, but also gave the National Socialists the pretext for their demagogic campaign against the failure of the " Marxist system." The Social Democrats tolerated the Brüning government, which increased the burdens of the workers until they became intolerable, and ruled by dictatorial methods, preparing the way for the summoning of the National Socialists to Government power.

During this period the second revival of the National Socialist Party began. Together with Hugenberg, the spokesman of the reactionary wing of German heavy indus-try and of the landlords, and with the support of the Stahl-helm and other nationalist organisations, the National Socialists demanded a referendum against the Young Plan. It was conveniently forgotten that in 1925 Hugen-berg's German National People's Party had set aside one-half of their fraction in the Reichstag to help to secure the acceptance of the Dawes Plan. The gigantic propaganda apparatus of the Hugenberg concern, with its hundreds of newspapers and its telegraph agency, the *Telegrafen Union* (TU), was now at the service of the National Socialists. The referendum came to nothing, but the National Socialists could record definite successes in the elections for the Diets of Saxony and Thuringia and in the Prussian local elections.

In 1930 Frick became Minister of the Interior and of Education in Thuringia—the first National Socialist Min-ister in Germany. In Thuringia they joined a coalition with all the parties of the Right including the German People's

Party, which at that time was in the Reich coalition with the Social Democrats. Only a year earlier Goebbels, in his *Small ABC of National Socialism*, had called the German People's Party a representative of the interests of big capital.

Hitler Shows his True Colours.   One section of the " socialists " in the Nazi Party, under the leadership of Otto Strasser, considered that they could no longer follow the legal tactics then used, and in May 1930 left the Party under the slogan : " The Socialists leave the National Socialist Party." Before this Strasser had a long discussion with Hitler, who told him :

> " The great mass of the workers wants nothing more than bread and circuses. It has no comprehension of any ideals, and we shall never be able to count on ideals to win the workers in large numbers. We want a selection from the new master class (!), who are not guided as you are by a morality of sympathy."

Strasser asked Hitler : " If you took power to-morrow, what would you do the day after, for example with the Krupp concern ? Will everything remain just as it is now for the shareholders and the workers in regard to ownership, profits and management ? " Hitler replied :

> " But of course. Do you imagine I am so crazy as to destroy trade ? The State would only step in when people were not acting in the interests of the nation. But for this no expropriation is necessary, nor any joint share in control, but the power of the strong State, which alone is in the position to let itself be governed entirely by wide viewpoints without consideration of individuals. . . . The expression socialism is in itself bad, but above all it does not mean that these concerns *must* be socialised, but only that they *can* be socialised, if they conflict with the interests of the nation. So long as they

do not do this, it would be simply a crime to interfere with trade. .... In this connection we have a precedent, which we can adopt without further question, namely, Italian Fascism ! Just as the Fascists have already put this into effect, in our National Socialist State also employers and workers will stand alongside each other with equal rights, while the decision in disputes is left to the State, which takes care that economic struggles do not endanger the life of the nation."

With this guarantee to the capitalist economic system Hitler once again recommended himself to the ruling groups of German finance capital. He showed them that, as in the case of the Italian Fascist programme, so the nationalist economic programme only aimed at guaranteeing the reconsolidation of capitalism. He has kept the promises which he then gave.

The Reichstag elections of September 1930 gave the National Socialists their first great electoral success. They secured 6,400,000 votes and 107 seats, becoming the second strongest party, after the Social Democrats. The Communists won 600,000 votes. The German Nationalist Party lost half their seats, the German People's Party one-third. The National Socialists owed their success to propaganda aimed at winning the radicalised middle-class elements. This propaganda offered unlimited promises to all sections, and it was conducted with gigantic resources supplied by capitalist donors. The Nazis promised the workers higher wages, the employers higher profits, the tenants lower rents, the house-owners higher rents, the peasants higher prices, the middle class cheaper food. But they did not succeed in effecting any real penetration of the working class. They merely attracted large sections of former voters for the capitalist parties.

Should Hitler be Chancellor of the Reich ?   Brüning continued in office, and issued new emergency decrees. The Social Democrats supported him in carrying through this policy. And with the growth of the National Socialist Party the question of openly calling it to power became more and more frequently raised.

In April 1932 Hindenburg was elected a second time as President of the Reich, with the votes of the Social Democrats, who issued the slogan : " A vote for Hindenburg is a blow at Hitler ! " In May 1932, at the instigation of the East Prussian Junkers, Chancellor Brüning was overthrown, and a Papen-Schleicher Government took his place.

The new government started to bring in even more severe dictatorial measures. On July 20th, 1932, Papen was appointed Reich Commissioner for Prussia. A captain with three soldiers of the Reichswehr sufficed to break the " resistance " of the Social Democratic ministers of Prussia. For a short time martial law was in force in the Berlin-Brandenburg area. The Social Democrat leaders offered no resistance, although they still had under their control the whole of the police in Prussia and in several of the other States of the Reich, and although the Social Democrat police officers were urging armed resistance. On the contrary, the Social Democrat leaders denounced the Communists, who were calling on the workers for a general strike, as " provocators." They weakened the working-class forces, and abandoned their positions, in order to be able, as they thought, to save at least something from the wreck. And so the Prussian " home of democracy " fell into the hands of the reactionaries without a struggle.

In August 1932, after a second electoral success for the Nazis (13½ million votes and 225 seats in the Reichstag), the appointment of Hitler as Chancellor began to be discussed. Hindenburg still hesitated. But the demand for Hitler's appointment grew more insistent. The *Deutsche Führerbriefe*, a private bulletin of the Union of German Industry, published an article which disclosed the plans of the dominant capitalist groups, under the title " The social re-consolidation of capitalism." It contained the following passages :

" The problem of consolidating the capitalist régime in
post-war Germany is governed by the fact that the
leading section, that is, the capitalists controlling industry, has become too small to maintain its rule alone.
Unless recourse is to be had to the extremely dangerous
weapon of purely military force, it is necessary for it
to link itself with sections which do not belong to
it from a social standpoint, but which can render it
the essential service of anchoring its rule among the
people, and thereby becoming its special or last defender. This last or ' outermost ' defender of bourgeois
rule, in the first period after the war, was Social
Democracy.

" National Socialism has to succeed Social Democracy in
providing a mass support for capitalist rule in Germany.
. . . Social Democracy had a special qualification for
this task, which up to the present National Socialism
lacks. . . . Thanks to its character as the original party
of the workers, Social Democracy, in addition to its
purely political force, also had the much more valuable
and permanent advantage of control over organised
labour, and by paralysing its revolutionary energies
chained it firmly to the capitalist State. . . .

" In the first period of re-consolidation of the capitalist
régime after the war, the working class was divided by
the wages victories and social-political measures through
which the Social Democrats canalised the revolutionary
movement. . . . The deflection of the revolution into
social-political measures corresponded with the trans-
ference of the struggle from the factories and the streets
into Parliament and Cabinets, that is, with the transformation of the struggle ' from below ' into concessions
' from above.'

" From then onwards, therefore, the Social Democratic
and trade union bureaucracy, and with them also the
section of the workers whom they led, were closely tied
to the capitalist State and participation in its administration—at least so long as there was anything left of

their post-war victories to defend by these means, and so long as the workers followed their leadership.

" This analysis leads to four important conclusions :

1. The policy of ' the lesser evil ' is not merely tactical, it is the political essence of Social Democracy.

2. The cords which bind the trade union bureaucracy to the State method " from above " are more compelling than those which bind them to Marxism, and therefore to Social Democracy ; and this holds in relation to the bourgeois State which wants to draw in this bureaucracy.

3. The links between the trade union bureaucracy and Social Democracy stand or fall, from a political standpoint, with parliamentarism.

4. The possibility of a Liberal social policy for monopoly capitalism is conditioned by the existence of an automatic mechanism for the creation of divisions in the working class. A capitalist régime which adopts a Liberal social policy must not only be entirely parliamentary, it must also be based on Social Democracy and must allow Social Democracy to have sufficient gains to record ; a capitalist régime which puts an end to these gains must also sacrifice parliamentarism and Social Democracy, must create a *substitute* for Social Democracy and pass over to a social policy of constraint.

" The process of this transition, in which we are at the moment, for the reason that the economic crisis has perforce blotted out the gains referred to, has to pass through the acutely dangerous stage, when, with the wiping out of these gains, the mechanism for the creation of divisions in the working class which depended on them also ceases to function, the working class moves in the direction of Communism, and the capitalist rule approaches the emergency stage of military dictatorship. . . . The only safeguard from this acute stage is if the division and holding back of the working class, which the former mechanism can no longer adequately maintain, is carried out by other and more direct methods. In this lie the positive opportunities and tasks of National Socialism. . . .

"If National Socialism succeeds in bringing the trade unions into a social policy of constraint, as Social Democracy formerly succeeded in bringing them into a Liberal policy, then National Socialism would become the bearer of one of the functions essential to the future of capitalist rule, and must necessarily find its place in the State and social system. The danger of a State capitalist or even socialistic development, which is often urged against such an incorporation of the trade unions under National Socialist leadership, will in fact be avoided precisely by these means. . . . There is no third course between a re-consolidation of capitalist rule and the Communist revolution."

These paragraphs give the key to an understanding of the political situation.

The Papen-Schleicher Period. The Papen-Schleicher Government was a further stage on the road to a Hitler dictatorship. Its emergency decrees were models for Hitler to follow : the death penalty for high treason ; the death penalty for " political acts of violence " ; the establishment of emergency courts which imposed long sentences of imprisonment for minor " offences." But this Government of big capitalists, Junkers and generals had no mass following. The Stahlhelm and the German National People's Party were entirely inadequate. Papen's much advertised economic programme of September 1932 laid new burdens on the workers and gave new millions to the rich. Powerful anti-Fascist demonstrations under the leadership of the Communist Party, which was carrying on the only serious extra-parliamentary fight against Fascism, were broken up. These reached their highest point in the Berlin traffic strike of November 1932, which demonstrated the helplessness of the Government in face of the determination of the workers.

At this period, too, National Socialism was passing through a serious crisis. In the November elections it lost almost two million votes. The total vote for the Communist Party reached six millions.

At the end of November Papen fell, and Schleicher succeeded him early in December. Behind the scenes negotiations were carried on, in one direction with the trade unions and also with a view to the drawing in of Hitler. No government can sit on bayonets. Schleicher hesitated, did nothing, and merely modified some of Papen's emergency decrees. On January 22nd the National Socialists staged a provocative demonstration in front of the Communist Party headquarters, the Karl Liebknecht House. General Schleicher sent the whole police force to protect the Nazis from the workers' counter-demonstrations.

The situation grew more and more acute. General Schleicher was considering the immediate proclamation of a military dictatorship. Papen worked against Schleicher's plan by negotiating with Hitler and Hugenberg. At last the ruling groups of Germany, as the *Deutsche Allgemeine Zeitung* put it, tried a leap in the dark. On January 30th, 1933, Hindenburg, the candidate for the presidency who had been supported by the Social Democrats, appointed Hitler Chancellor of the German Reich.

Chapter II: "THE REICHSTAG IS IN FLAMES!"

Months of intrigue in President Hindenburg's palace had preceded the fall of General Schleicher. Papen's "cranking-up" of industry had come to nothing. The economic difficulties were increasing. At every step Schleicher stumbled up against obstacles which were created for him through the influence wielded by his predecessor, Papen, over President Hindenburg. From the moment of his own resignation Papen was working systematically for the overthrow of his opponent Schleicher.

Round Hindenburg there was a number of more or less definite groups fighting each other. But they were not fighting over personal antipathies or sympathies, but over partial interests of sections of the ruling class, the separate interests of politically influential groups.

General Kurt von Schleicher had risen from the Reichswehr to the position of Chancellor of the German Reich. The man who announced, in his wireless broadcast following his appointment as Chancellor, that he was a "social general," had for fourteen years had his hand in the political pie whenever it was necessary to push the political development of the Weimar Republic one step further in the direction of reaction. Schleicher first appeared in November 1918 as the connecting link between the General Staff of the army and the Social Democratic people's delegates in the beating down of the revolution. The name of the young captain attached to the General Staff appeared in those days linked with the names of Hindenburg, Groener and Ebert. He had considerable influence in the newly-created Reichswehr. In October 1923 he put through the "state of emergency," when Ebert handed over all executive power to the Reichswehr General von Seeckt in order to meet the revolutionary menace which resulted from the misery of inflation. Since his youth Schleicher had been in close communication with Hindenburg and his son, Colonel Oskar von Hindenburg, through his service in the Third Guards Regiment and on the General Staff. Schleicher succeeded in becoming a personal informant of Hindenburg. He had the strings in his hands when, in March 1930, Hindenburg threw the Social Democratic Chancellor, Hermann, and with him Social Democracy, out of the Government. Schleicher arranged Brüning's fall, when the controlling groups of German capitalism were tending more and more towards the summoning of the National Socialists to power. Schleicher himself took Groener's place as Minister of the Reichswehr.

Even when Papen was Chancellor, Schleicher had already begun to fill the most important posts in the government apparatus with his own reliable men. It was Schleicher who turned the scale when Papen's Government was rocking, and induced the majority of Ministers to deliver the ultimatum that Papen must go. Schleicher had to come more and more into the open. But it was easier to manœuvre on the smooth parquet floors of the government offices than to carry out a policy on the precipitous ground of the deepening economic crisis. His short term of office ran out without a programme, without a policy, with nothing but vague hints at all kinds of plans. His Government was only to serve the most powerful capitalist groups of Germany as a bridge to the Fascist attack on the growing revolutionary movement among the workers.

In the group closely associated with Hindenburg there was in the first place his son and personal adjutant, Colonel Oskar von Hindenburg. His Secretary of State was Dr. Meissner, who had filled the same position under Ebert. Von Papen too, after his term as Chancellor, was in Hindenburg's confidential circle. Papen had special support in the *Herrenklub*, a very influential association of politicians, bankers, big employers and big landowners, high civil servants and officers. Papen had connections with the National Socialists, with Hitler and Goering, with the Stahlhelm and with the German Nationalist Party under Hugenberg. A few weeks after his fall from office Papen met Hitler in Cologne, at the house of Schröder, the banker. Hitler, who on November 7th had issued a manifesto calling for a fight " to the last breath " against Papen, in the banker's drawing-room, agreed to the confidential proposals put forward by Papen. From Cologne Papen went to Dortmund, to conduct secret negotiations with Springorum and other representatives of Rhenish-Westphalian heavy industry on the question of the Government.

Schleicher, too, had close relations with the National Socialists, especially with their " socialist " wing led by Gregor Strasser. Schleicher attempted to exploit for his purposes the crisis in the National Socialist Party which was marked by the loss of two million voters in the elections of November 6th. He had links with the Social Democrat Leipart, president of the German Trade Union General Council, with the Christian Trade Unions and with the German Nationalist Commercial Employees Association. He tried to create some kind of trade union mass basis for himself through these " cross-threads " from the trade unions under Social Democratic leadership to the " socialist " wing of the National Socialists. At the same time, Schleicher presented the Junkers with millions and millions for " relief."

Confidential agents carried on negotiations between these groups. Every day new coalitions were being formed and dissolved. Every day the situation changed. Newspapers changed their owners, and their editors changed their political views. A struggle raged for the control of the Liberal papers of the Ullstein and Rudolf Mosse concerns. The *Tägliche Rundschau*, once Stresemann's organ, became Schleicher's mouthpiece. There was talk of money which had found its way to the paper from the well-filled chests of the Reichswehr. A new editor was appointed : Hans

Zehrer, leader of the so-called "Action Group" and editor of its journal *Action*, which carried on a special sort of Fascist propaganda with pseudo-revolutionary slogans. Papen tried to secure control of the *Berliner Tageblatt*. The export industries, the big shipping companies and the Reich Railways (Siemens) had as their organ the *Deutsche Allgemeine Zeitung*, which they had been subsidising for a considerable time.

During those weeks Schleicher also had the backing of Herr Krupp von Bohlen and Halbach and Privy Councillor Duisberg of the I.G. Farben-Industrie, the chemical combine ; these were the leading figures in the Reich Union of German industry. Papen had close connections with Springorum and Thyssen, Hugenberg and the big agrarian interests. All groups were agreed that the National Socialists would have to be drawn in as the political prop for a government of capitalist dictatorship. But there were differences of opinion as to the form and extent of their participation in the Government. The intrigues in Hindenburg's palace reflected these differences.

The East Prussian relief scandal.   Towards the end of January 1933, Schleicher felt that his Government was being more and more undermined by the intrigues of Papen and the big agrarian interests associated with him. He felt, too, that he was being pushed out of the circle of Hindenburg's confidential advisers. He therefore decided to have recourse to a defensive manœuvre which he had been contemplating for some time, and an immense mass of material appeared in the papers, exposing the *Osthilfe* corruption of the big agrarian Junkers. A commission of enquiry was set up by the Reichstag. The working masses were roused to fury. The scandal threatened to involve even Hindenburg himself.

As far back as the time when Hermann Müller was Chancellor the Junkers had received millions through the so-called *Osthilfe* to put their bankrupt estates on to a paying basis. The small peasants had got practically

nothing out of it ; the big landowners pocketed the lion's
share. In the Reichstag Committee of Enquiry it was now
revealed, at the end of January, 1933, that in addition the
rich landowners had received many hundreds of thousands
of marks " to which they were not entitled." An immensely
rich owner of six manorial estates and a personal friend
and neighbour of Hindenburg's, had secured 621,000 marks
by giving false particulars. Two Counts took 700,000 marks
in this way. A certain landowner who had ruined his property on gambling, wine and women, secured 281,000 marks.
Two controllers of offices through which the *Osthilfe* was
distributed, paid off their own debts and pocketed tens
of thousands in addition. A certain lord of the manor transferred his livestock to his wife, in order to secure 154,000
marks of the *Osthilfe*.

Day by day new names appeared in the list of those who
were involved in the *Osthilfe* scandal, including neighbours of Hindenburg's estate, people who had the run of
his house. There was a great uneasiness in the Hindenburg
family, for some of the Junkers involved in the scandal
were among those who had organised the presentation
of the Neudeck estate to Hindenburg on his eightieth
birthday. No gift-tax had been paid on this gift, and the
estate had been registered not in Hindenburg's name but
in that of his son, so that the State was also robbed of the
future succession duty. The Junkers and industrial magnates
had twice collected funds for repairs and equipment for the
Neudeck property, and a third time for the purpose of
putting it on a paying basis. The mud of the *Osthilfe*
scandal spattered the walls of the President's palace.

The Junkers decided : Schleicher must go !—as they had
decided before that Brüning must go.

Hitler becomes Chancellor.   On the morning of
January 28th the Schleicher Government resigned, when
Hindenburg refused to give authority for the dissolution of
the Reichstag. Papen was instructed by Hindenburg to
negotiate with Hitler for the formation of a Government

of " national concentration." Two days of unparalleled
tension followed. The Communist Party broadcast leaflets
calling for a general strike against the imminent Hitler
dictatorship. Schleicher negotiated with Leipart. The
struggle behind the scenes grew more acute. On the night
of January 29th–30th, Schleicher was toying with the idea
of the immediate proclamation of a military dictatorship
and the march of the Potsdam garrison on Berlin. It
seemed that a critical situation might develop at any
moment. Then Hindenburg decided to appoint Hitler
Chancellor, on conditions. And so it came about that the
Hitler-Papen-Hugenberg Government was formed on the
morning of January 30th, 1933.

In June 1932 the Papen-Schleicher Government had
depended on National Socialist toleration. Goebbels later
charged the representatives of the *Herrenklub* with having
" adroitly clambered to power over the broad backs
of the Nazis." In November 1932, the leader of the
National Socialist fraction in the Prussian Diet, Wilhelm
Kube, declared that the National Socialists would never
march with the battle-cry of " With Hugenberg for the
Stock Exchange and Capital ! " But during the following
months Papen had been preparing the National Socialists
to throw overboard their thundering declamations as
superfluous ballast when Hindenburg gave them the call.

The Chancellorship fell into Hitler's lap, but not as the
fruit of some heroic struggle. January 30th was not the
culmination of a " national revolution " which had conquered power by a bold attack. Adolf Hitler was given the
post of Chancellor when the leading sections of the ruling
class wanted not only to strengthen their power against the
working class but also to smother the smell of the
Osthilfe scandal.

On the evening of January 30th the storm troopers and
the Stahlhelm marched with flaming torches along the
Wilhelmstrasse, cheering Hindenburg and Hitler. The
storm troop men and the Stahlhelmers knew nothing of
what had been going on behind the scenes, and when they

acclaimed " the day of national awakening " they did not know that corruption and the lust for profit were its godparents.

The Wave of Resistance Rises.   On January 30th, 1933, the Communist Party made an official proposal to the Executive of the Social Democratic Party and to the General Council of the Trade Unions under Social Democratic leadership and also the Christian Trade Unions, that they should jointly organise a general strike for the overthrow of the Hitler Government. Social Democracy and the Trade Unions answered : " Hitler has come to power legally." It was necessary to wait, they said, until he violated legality. No fight should be put up now. The general attitude of the Social Democratic Press was that Hitler would soon be finished with.

Considerable sections of the German workers accepted these statements. The Communist Party was unable as yet to bring the majority of the working class into action. The hastily formed Hitler Government would have been unable to cope with the united assault of the working class in those first days of February. The Nazi storm troops had just been passing through a severe crisis, and in some places had lost half their membership. The police apparatus could not yet be relied upon by the new Government. It would also have had difficulties with Schleicher's Reichswehr. But the refusal of the general strike gave the Hitler Government the time it needed.

Nevertheless, the resistance of the workers was growing in Berlin, in Hamburg, in the Ruhr, in the Lower Rhine area, in Central Germany and in all parts of the Reich. The Hitler dictatorship was opposed by a working class whose fighting strength was as yet unbroken. On January 22nd they had refused to allow themselves to be provoked ; now a wide movement was developing for united action against the raging Fascist terror. Social Democratic, Christian and Communist workers united to defend newspaper and trade union buildings. Hitler could prohibit papers, refuse to allow demonstrations, and send his storm troops into the working-class quarters—but the working-class answer was the rise of a wide anti-Fascist movement in which all sections were united.

The Need for a Provocative Act.   Hitler had held power for some weeks, but the situation was far from favourable. The new Cabinet had dissolved the Reichstag and ordered new elections. Papen's terrorist decrees were again brought into force in sharpened form, and the *Osthilfe* scandal was buried in a secret commission. Hitler proclaimed on the wireless his non-existent " Four Years Plan." But the millions of his voters who were looking forward to " German socialism " could not be put off merely with a couple of emergency decrees and vague promises.

At the end of January Hitler had been compelled to enter the Government on the restricting conditions imposed by Hindenburg. There were many reasons why he was ready to compromise : the discontent among his members and supporters, crisis and numerous resignations from the National Socialist Party, besides the enormous debts of the Party. In bourgeois circles a number of former Nazi voters had already begun to show a tendency towards the German Nationalists. On November 6th, 1932, the Communists had won eleven seats in the Reichstag, while Hitler had lost thirty-five. In the new Government there were three National Socialist Ministers opposed by eight representatives of the German Nationalists and of the Stahlhelm. There could be no change in the Cabinet without Hindenburg's consent.

In view of the growing anti-Fascist feeling among the workers Hitler's election prospects were not good. Hugenberg and the German Nationalists held all the economic posts of vantage in the Cabinet, and masses of the people were beginning to realise that Hitler was carrying out the policy of the worst firebrands among the capitalists. The disillusionment of the masses would show itself in an increased Communist vote on March 5th. It had become

The Executioner of the "Third Empire,"
HERMANN GOERING, Premier of Prussia.

"I would rather shoot a few times too short and too
wide, but at any rate I would shoot."

(Goering at Essen, March 11th, 1933)

PLATE NO. 3.

an imperative necessity for the National Socialist leaders
to change the situation by an act of provocation planned
on a grandiose scale. Then the elections could be carried
out while the pogrom feeling against the Communists and
Social Democrats was at its height. At the same time the
position of the National Socialists within the Cabinet could
be strengthened.

Goebbels provided the plans for the most outrageous of
all the acts of provocation which a ruling class has ever
used against the insurgent working class. Goering, president
of the Reichstag and commander of the Prussian police,
was responsible for the exact fulfilment of the plan. The
original plans of the National Socialist leaders, to bring all
storm troopers to Berlin for the night of March 5th–6th,
had been shattered by the threat of their allies to bring out
the Reichswehr against them ; but the new plan of provocation provided the means to satisfy the National Socialist
demand for complete governmental power and also to
prepare the way for an unrestrained Nazi terror.

The National Socialist leaders moved into action. The
German Nationalist police president of Berlin, Dr. Melcher,
was transferred to Magdeburg, and his place in Berlin
was filled by the National Socialist retired Admiral von
Levetzow. On February 24th the Karl Liebknecht House,
the headquarters of the German Communist Party, was
once again searched by the police. Although the Karl
Liebknecht House had already been in the possession of
the police for some weeks, and was only left by the police
after a thorough search which produced no results, now
suddenly " seriously incriminating " material was found.
The day before the Reichstag fire gigantic headlines in the
whole bourgeois Press told readers of the " secrets " of Karl
Liebknecht House, of " subterranean passages," " treasonable material," and " plans for a Bolshevistic revolution."
The Press also reported an alleged Communist bomb
outrage on the railway in East Prussia (this outrage was
never mentioned again!) On January 25th there was a
small fire in the Berliner Schloss, which was announced

sensationally as a " Communist act." In this way public opinion was carefully prepared, from paper to paper, from day to day, for the " great *coup*."

The Communist Party received reliable reports that the Government had planned an act of provocation. The deputy Wilhelm Pieck spoke of it in the Sportpalast in Berlin. He mentioned a Nazi plan for a faked attempt to assassinate Hitler or some other act of provocation which was to take place some days before election day and lead to the prohibition of the Communist Party. The Communist fraction in the Reichstag made a similar statement at a conference of foreign Press representatives.

The Hitler Press, following instructions, raised the campaign against the revolutionary workers to boiling point. Everyone who was following the political situation realised that a crisis was imminent. Everyone felt that " there was something in the air." Then, on the night of February 27th–28th, all German wireless stations broadcast the message : " The Reichstag is in flames ! "

CHAPTER III : VAN DER LUBBE, THE TOOL

MARINUS VAN DER LUBBE was born in Leyden on January 13th, 1909. His father owned a small shop, and also traded his wares through the neighbouring villages. At the age of sixteen, after a short period as assistant in a shop, Marinus van der Lubbe became a worker in the building trade, which he had to leave after an accident which permanently injured his eyesight. Shortly before this he joined the Leyden branch of the Young Communist League. He was always ambitious and seeking prominence, and in January 1929 he resigned from the Young Communist League because he was not appointed leader of the Pioneers, organisation. He rejoined, but in December 1929 again resigned, owing to a conflict with the Young Communist League in connection with leaflets which he wrote and distributed over his own signature. He joined the League again in 1930, but was distrusted and did not take any active part. In April 1931 the question of his expulsion was raised, and van der Lubbe immediately resigned. From that date he had no connection whatever with the Young Communist League or Communist Party, but attacked the Communists whenever he had the opportunity.

Van der Lubbe's Life.   Marinus van der Lubbe was five months in the Leyden Hospital after his accident. He could not go back to his trade, and tried to earn his living in various ways. In the winter of 1927–28 he worked as a temporary waiter in the Station restaurant in Leyden, and in the summer of 1928 he was a porter in the " Van Holland " hotel at Nordweyk. After that, he did a little trading in potatoes on his own account, and then worked on a ferry transporting building materials between Nordweyk and Sassenheim.

In the summer of 1930 he went to Calais, and on his return stated that he had worked as an excavator and had also made some attempts to swim the channel. We have made detailed enquiries in Calais, but can find no evidence that he ever made such an attempt. But the fact that he boasted of this on his return to Leyden is characteristic of his outlook.

Enquiries into his life in Leyden have definitely established the fact that he was homosexual. This is of great importance for his later history.

His tour through Europe. Together with a friend of his, Holverda, he planned a "Workers' Sports and Study Tour" through Europe, and had cards printed with his and Holverda's photographs and the statement in four languages that they were undertaking a tour through Europe and the Soviet Union. Before they left there was a quarrel, and Holverda remained in Leyden. Actually, the postcards say that the tour was to begin on April 14th, 1931. We have in our possession one of these cards, *dated from Potsdam April 14th*, 1931. Not long after, van der Lubbe was back in Leyden.

He makes Dr. Bell's Acquaintance. When van der Lubbe returned from his first short visit to Germany he told his friends of a gentleman who had taken him on a long tour in his car. We do not know whether Lubbe's story was true, or whether he invented the gentleman from Leipzig. But we do know that on that first visit to Germany van der Lubbe made the acquaintance of a man who played a decisive part in Lubbe's future life.

In April or May 1931, Lubbe met Dr. Bell. We know this from a friend of Dr. Bell's ; he writes :

" If I remember rightly, it was in May 1931 that Bell told me he had made the acquaintance of a young Dutch worker who had made a very good impression on him. He must have met him when he was out in his car near Berlin or Potsdam. They met a hiker on the way, and gave him a lift in the car. He was a young Dutch workman. This young Dutchman later visited Bell in Munich. Bell called him Renus or Rinus. He had frequent meetings with him."

Marinus van der Lubbe visits Munich.   In September 1931 van der Lubbe again started out for Germany. He still had the postcards which he had had printed for his " Tour through Europe," and sold them on his way. At the frontier village of Gronau in Westphalia, in September 1931, he was arrested for selling cards in the street without a licence; the court in Münster imposed a small fine. At Bacharach on the Rhine van der Lubbe got into conversation with a motor cyclist ; he was also a Dutchman, Ploegk, a railway engine driver whose home was in the Hague, Bloemfonteenstr. 24. Ploegk gave Lubbe a lift in his side-car, and they put up overnight in Rothenburg, Ploegk at the hotel and Lubbe at a youth hostel. Ploegk told our investigator of the conversation he had had with van der Lubbe, who in reply to the question what was he doing in Germany, said that he was looking for work. Ploegk then asked van der Lubbe whether he would not be much more likely to find work in Holland than in Germany, to which Lubbe replied with great assurance that he would get work in Germany. Ploegk recalls that he was surprised at van der Lubbe's tone of assurance.

From Rothenburg the two went on to Munich, parting on the outskirts of the town. We know that van der Lubbe visited Dr. Bell in Munich. We do not know exactly how long he stayed there, but it must have been some days, as on his return to Leyden he gave his friends a detailed and accurate description of the town. He talked not only of the town, but also of the grand time he had had there, and of the many gentlemen whose acquaintance he had made there.

The most important acquaintance made by van der Lubbe in Munich was Captain Röhm. At that time Dr.

Bell was still adviser in foreign politics to Hitler's chief of
staff, Röhm. He was a close friend of Röhm's, so close, in
fact, that Röhm gave him the confidential task of establishing connections with the Reichsbanner commander, Major
Mayr. Röhm then felt that he was being persecuted by the
National Socialist murder gang, and he tried to get protection from Mayr through the intermediary Dr. Bell. All
these facts were established in court in October 1932, when
Captain Röhm brought an action against the Social Democratic journal *Münchener Post*.

Bell was not only adviser in foreign politics to Röhm; he
was also his confidant in personal matters. The *Münchener
Post* and other papers in 1932 published letters from Röhm
to young men, from which it is clear that Röhm was
homosexual. Dr. Bell knew many of Röhm's relations with
young men, for the reason that he himself procured many
of them for Röhm. Bell, who had intimate knowledge of the
situation within the National Socialist Party, kept a list of
these young men, intending to use it as a weapon against
Röhm if any conflict developed with him. Van der Lubbe's
name was on this list.

A Voyage of Adventure.   After leaving Munich, van der
Lubbe did actually carry out part of his "Tour through
Europe." We are in possession of a postcard written by him
from Cracow. Our investigator in Holland saw a letter
which he had written from Budapest and a card from
Belgrade.

When van der Lubbe returned to Leyden in January or
February 1932, he had a great deal to tell his friends about
his tour. One of these tales deserves to be told. Van der
Lubbe said that he had been in Poland and had reached
the frontier of the Soviet Union. A mighty river, he said,
divides Poland from the Soviet Union; he had tried to
swim this river, but was driven back by shots from the
Polish frontier guards; he was then arrested and kept a
few days in a prison from which he could see the Soviet
frontier across the river. Then he was sent about his business.

Van der Lubbe's friends were greatly astonished when our investigator informed them that there was no mighty river between Poland and the Soviet Union. This tale again is characteristic of van der Lubbe's boastfulness and desire for notoriety.

The cards and letters which van der Lubbe had written to his friends in Leyden are proof that at the end of 1931 and the beginning of 1932 he was in several towns in Hungary, Poland and Jugoslavia. It is probable that he was not alone, but in the company of some rich man. On his return to Leyden he said that a gentleman in Budapest had given him new shoes, that the Dutch consul in Jugoslavia had given him his fare back, and other improbable things which suggest that he actually travelled with some rich friend.

Dr. Bell introduced Lubbe not only to Captain Röhm, but to other National Socialists as well. From then on he was in regular communication with National Socialist circles. His friends in Leyden are unanimous in their statements that Lubbe received many letters from Germany, and that he always tried to conceal these letters from his friends.

A Guest of the Nazis.   Van der Lubbe's return to Leyden in January or February 1932 was unexpectedly prompt. He sent a postcard from Berlin, and arrived at Leyden at the same time as the card. He must therefore have travelled by train or by car. The question of where the money came from remains open.

After an interval of about two months van der Lubbe went on a third visit to Germany. But before that he achieved a little notoriety in Leyden, smashing some windows at the office of the relief organisation which had refused to increase his allowance. He was sentenced to three months imprisonment for this. Before going to prison, however, he managed to pay another visit to Germany. We know that he went to Berlin and Saxony. On June 1st and 2nd he stayed the night at Sörnewitz, where he was seen in company with the local councillor Sommer and also

Schumann, who owned a vegetable garden. Both are National Socialists. After the Reichstag fire Councillor Sommer reported van der Lubbe's visit in June 1932 to the Mayor of Brockwitz. This fact was recorded in a protocol, which was forwarded to the Saxon Ministry of the Interior, which notified Frick, Reich Minister of the Interior, of these facts. The facts became public as the result of an interpellation in the Saxon Diet by a Social Democratic deputy. They have not been denied by anyone.

The papers which reported this interpellation also reported that Councillor Sommer had disappeared a short time after he had made the report concerning van der Lubbe's stay at Sörnewitz. This statement too has not been contradicted.

After his stay in Sörnewitz van der Lubbe must have remained in Germany a few days longer. On his return to Holland he was arrested in Utrecht on June 21st, 1932. He was nine days in prison in Utrecht, and was then moved to the prison at S'Gravenhage (Hague) to carry out his three months sentence.

Van der Lubbe attacks the Communist Party.

Van der Lubbe was released from prison on October 2nd, 1932. He came from the Hague to Leyden, and did not go out of the country again before the end of the year. He paid a visit to his father at Dordrecht, and then went on to Amsterdam and the Hague. In these towns he spoke at a number of meetings, his speeches vigorously attacking the Communist Party. We have definite evidence of this. One document in our possession shows that van der Lubbe spoke at a Fascist meeting for the Fascists.

A second document describes van der Lubbe's attitude at a meeting of taxi-drivers who were on strike at the Hague. At this meeting van der Lubbe not only attacked the Communists but tried to incite the taxi-drivers to terrorist acts.

Van der Lubbe followed a consistent line since he finally left the Communist Party. From 1929 to 1931 he had been trying to find scope for his anarchist tendencies within the Communist movement ; and when his connections with it were finally broken in April 1931, he turned to attacking the movement. This attack became more and more vigorous at every meeting he addressed. The arguments which he was using during the last quarter of 1932 were clearly influenced by National Socialist propaganda. Lower middle class in origin, and only temporarily in the ranks of the workers, he had returned to the fold.

His Last Journey to Germany.   In January 1933, van der Lubbe was making preparations for another visit to Germany. Before he left he had to have treatment for his eyes again at the Leyden hospital, and he was four weeks in hospital. Shortly before his departure for Germany he visited Frau van Zijp, in whose house he had lodged. She told our investigator of her last talk with van der Lubbe, who told her that his passport had very nearly run out. She asked him whether it was really necessary for him to go to Germany, and whether he would not do better to stay in Leyden. Van der Lubbe replied that she need not worry, he had something important to do in Germany, he would only need his passport for this occasion, and then it would not matter if it ran out.

In the middle of February Marinus van der Lubbe left Leyden. Before his departure he had a new suit and new shoes. The *Vossische Zeitung* of March 2nd reported that he spent the night at Glindow, near Werder, on February 17th ; and that he went on to Berlin on February 18th. In Berlin he met the Nazi friends whose acquaintance he had made through Dr. Bell.

Van der Lubbe, the Tool.   On February 27th van der Lubbe was arrested in the burning Reichstag. The flames were the background of the hoax in which van der Lubbe for a few hours played the leading rôle. Then he passed from the stage. The searchlights of truth have pierced the fog of deception and mercilessly shown up Goering and

Van der Lubbe, after his arrest in the Reichstag, undergoing interrogation in the presence of journalists.

PLATE NO. 4.

Goebbels, who made use of van der Lubbe as their tool. Why did the murderer Heines and his associates, who had been entrusted by Goering and Goebbels with the technical carrying out of the incendiary act, choose van der Lubbe as the tool ?

Van der Lubbe had been in the Communist movement in Holland up to April 1931. The men who were carrying out the orders issued by Goering and Goebbels believed that this was enough to make it possible to put the guilt for the incendiary act in the Reichstag on to the shoulders of the Communists.

Van der Lubbe's homosexual connections with National Socialist leaders and his material dependence on them made him obedient and willing to carry out the incendiary's part.

Van der Lubbe's Dutch nationality was a further advantage. It enabled Goering and Goebbels to represent the burning of the Reichstag as an international plot.

For all these reasons van der Lubbe was chosen as the tool to carry out the incendiary act.

The leading figures in the plot were :

Dr. Goebbels : concocted the plot for setting fire to the Reichstag, also the fanatical lies and provocation.

Captain Goering : a drug fiend, directed operations.

Edmund Heines : a murderer, was entrusted with the leadership of the incendiary group.

Marinus van der Lubbe : the tool.

When the Chicago police in 1886 staged a bomb explosion carried out by paid provocators—an explosion which killed a large number of the police—it was seven years before the act of provocation was established. The tools had been well chosen. After the burning of the Reichstag it took only three days to make the whole world certain that the National Socialists had set fire to the Reichstag. The tool van der Lubbe was too ill-chosen.

CHAPTER IV: THE REAL INCEN-
DIARIES

The German Reichstag. The foundation stone of the German Reichstag was laid by Wilhelm I on June 9th, 1884 ; the building was completed in December 1894.

The German Reichstag building is in the Koenigsplatz, opposite the Bismarck memorial. The east front faces the Friedrich Ebertstrasse, the south front overlooks the Tiergarten, across the Simsonstrasse, while the north front overlooks the Spree.

The building consists of cellars, a ground floor, a main floor, an intermediate floor and two upper floors. The front of the building is 137 metres long. It is crowned by a large dome, round which are four smaller cupolas. The central feature of the main floor is the session hall in which the Reichstag met. The walls of the chamber are panelled in wood, except for the side behind the President's chair, which is stone. The dais, the tribunes and the deputies' seats are of wood. The seats are arranged in the form of an amphi-theatre in seven sections, divided by narrow, thickly carpeted gangways. There is a corridor running round the hall which leads into the lobby. The corridors and the hall are furnished with carpets, upholstered seats and heavy curtains.

In the main floor there are also numerous rooms and halls with windows looking out over the streets. The reading room, the archives and the library are partly on the main floor, and partly in the intermediate floor. The heating and ventilating apparatus is in the cellars. A small flight of stairs leads from the cellar to a subterranean passage, which leads out under the portico of the Reichstag and under the Friedrich Ebertstrasse. A door shuts off this subterranean passage from the stairs and also from the other rooms containing the ventilation apparatus. Hot pipes run along the walls of the passage. The main entrance to the Reichstag opens on the Koenigsplatz, but this entrance is only used on special occasions.

How does a visitor get access to the Reichstag?   In all its reports on the burning of the Reichstag, the Hitler Government gave no indication of how the incendiaries got into the Reichstag. They relied on the fact that practically no German or foreigner knows the formalities which have to be gone through in order to enter the Reichstag. The following shows what a visitor to the Reichstag has to do in order to get in.

1. Non-members and visitors can only enter the Reichstag through door 2 or door 5. Door 2 opens on to the Simsonstrasse, door 5 on to the Reichstagsufer.

2. Anyone entering the Reichstag through door 5 comes into a lobby across which there is a rope barrier. The officials stand behind this barrier.

3. Each visitor has to apply to one of the officials. It is impossible to get into the Reichstag without giving particulars to an official. Each visitor has to fill in a printed card with the name of the visitor, the name of the member whom he wishes to see, and the reason for the visit.

4. This card is then taken by a messenger to the member concerned. The member is asked whether he is willing to see the visitor.

5. While the messenger is looking for the member, the visitor has to wait in the waiting room. He is all the time under observation by the officials on duty.

6. If the member agrees to see the visitor, the latter is then brought to him by a messenger. The messenger conducts the visitor personally to the member and only leaves when the visitor is with the member.

7. All visitors are listed in a special register, which is made up from the cards already mentioned.

The Reichstag in Flames

PLATE NO. 5.

The Fire in the Reichstag.   Between 9 and 9.15 in the evening of February 27th, 1933, fire broke out in the Reichstag building. The first public announcement of the burning of the Reichstag was made that evening by wireless. The Berlin broadcasting station also announced that the incendiary was a Dutch Communist named Van der Lubbe. He was said to have made a full confession, and to have been caught in the building, dressed only in a pair of trousers, when the police officials came to the Reichstag. It was stated that he had a Dutch passport on him and also a membership book of the Dutch Communist Party. Early the following morning the official *Preussische Pressedienst* circulated the following account of the fire :

"On Monday evening fire broke out in the German Reichstag. The Reich Commissioner for the Prussian Ministry of the Interior, Minister Goering, immediately on his arrival took over the direction of all operations. As soon as the fire had become known, Chancellor Adolf Hitler and Vice-Chancellor von Papen also came to the Reichstag.

"This is undoubtedly the most serious act of incendiarism as yet experienced in Germany. The police investigation has shown that the fire was started at a number of points all over the Reichstag building from the cellar to the dome. Tar and torches were used, these being put in leather chairs and among the documents of the Reichstag, also near doors, curtains, wood-panelling and at other easily inflammable spots. A police official saw persons with burning torches in the dark building. He fired at once. One of the criminals was caught. This is the 24-year-old bricklayer Van der Lubbe of Leyden in Holland, who had on him a Dutch passport, which was in order, and stated that he was a member of the Dutch Communist Party.

"The central portion of the Reichstag has been completely burnt out, the sessions chamber with the tribunes and corridors have been destroyed. The damage runs into millions.

" This act of incendiarism is the most monstrous act of terrorism so far carried out by Bolshevism in Germany. Among the hundred centners of material which the police discovered in the search of the Karl Liebknecht house, there were instructions for the carrying through of the Communist terror on the Bolshevist model.

" According to these instructions, Government buildings, museums, mansions and essential plant were to be burnt down. The directions also state that in disturbances and conflicts with the police, women and children should be sent in front of the terrorist groups, where possible the wives and children of police officials. The systematic carrying through of the Bolshevist revolution has been checked by the discovery of this material. In spite of this the burning of the Reichstag was to be the signal for a bloody insurrection and civil war. Plans had been prepared for looting on a large scale in Berlin at 4 a.m. on Tuesday. It has been ascertained that to-day was to have seen throughout Germany terrorist acts against individual persons, against private property, and against the life and limb of the peaceful population, and also the beginning of general civil war.

" The Reich Commissioner of the Prussian Ministry of the Interior, Minister Goering, has taken the strongest measures to meet this terrible danger. He will maintain the authority of the State in all circumstances and with all the means at his disposal. It can be stated that the first attack of the criminal forces has been beaten back for the moment. Already on Monday evening, all public buildings and vital industries were placed under police protection to ensure public security. Special police cars are passing continuously through the parts of the town which are chiefly threatened. The whole of the police and criminal police in Prussia has immediately been put in a state of readiness. The auxiliary police have been called up. Orders have been issued for the arrest of two leading Communist members of the Reichstag on a charge of grave suspicion. The other Communist Party members of the Reichstag and officials have been put under protective arrest. Communist papers, periodicals, leaflets and posters have been prohibited throughout Prussia for four weeks. All Social Democratic newspapers have been prohibited for 14 days, as the Reichstag incendiary in his confession admitted that he had connections with the Social Democratic Party. Through this confession the united Communist-Social Democratic front has become a palpable fact. This situation demands of the authorities responsible for security in Prussia decisive action to fulfil their duty of maintaining the authority of the State in this moment of danger. The latest events have fully established the necessity of the special measures which had already been introduced (auxiliary police, authority to the police to shoot, etc.). These measures equip the State power to nip in the bud any further attack on the peace of Germany and thereby on the peace of Europe. Minister Goering appeals for the strictest discipline from the German nation in this grave hour. He expects the unwavering support of the population, for whose security and safety he answers with his own person."

The First Press Announcements.   On the morning of February 28th millions of people read the account of the burning of the Reichstag in their papers. The front pages shouted in great letters : " The German Reichstag in flames." This event overshadowed all other news. In London, Paris, New York, Amsterdam, Prague and Vienna the reader was furnished with long accounts of the burning of the Reichstag building. The reporters unanimously stated that the hall had been completely burnt out, including the dome above it, the glass roof being shattered, and the struts bent. The corridors round the Reichstag chamber and the lobby were also destroyed.

The Press of the world, however, contained a number of divergent statements with regard to the further details. The *Prager Tageblatt* of February 28th stated that the fire was noticed at about 10 o'clock in the evening. The *Temps* of March 1st stated that the fire had been discovered at 9.15 p.m. The London *Times* of February 28th reported that the fire had broken out at 9 p.m.

The reports in the papers also gave different accounts of how the fire had been discovered. The Hugenberg news agency *Telegrafen-Union* stated in an announcement which was printed by a section of the press in the morning edition of February 28th :

> " It has been established beyond question that the fire was developed into a conflagration with the aid of torches placed at various points. A police official noticed through one of the windows a man carrying torches moving stealthily, and immediately fired at him."

The *Temps* of March 1st states on the other hand that the first warning of the fire was given by an employee of the Engineering Institute opposite the Reichstag. The number of points at which the fire started is estimated differently by the various papers. The *Prager Tageblatt* of February 28th speaks of 20 points, while the Berlin correspondent of *The Times* states in the issue of February 28th that the police officer on duty told him that the fire had started in 4 or 5 places. The *Chicago Tribune* reports 10 points. The rapidity with which the fire spread shows conclusively that it was started at a number of points.

The Pogrom against the Left begins.   The fire in the Reichstag was still burning when police cars and motor-cyclists and the Nazi Storm Detachments were already on their way. The first arrest was made immediately after midnight. By the morning, police headquarters were filled with hundreds of arrested persons, who sat on long benches in the corridors. Communists, Socialists, pacifists, writers, doctors and lawyers had been torn from their beds in the night and taken to police headquarters. Many of them were already asleep when the wireless announcement of the fire was circulated.

The noon papers gave the first names of the arrested persons. Among them there were the writers Ludwig Renn, Egon Erwin Kisch, Erich Baron, Carl von Ossietzky and Otto Lehman-Russbildt ; the doctors Boenheim, Schminke and Hodann ; the lawyers Apfel, Litten, Barbach and Felix Halle ; the Communist members of the Reichstag Walter Stoecker, Ernst Schneider, Fritz Emmerich, Ottoman Geschke and Willi Caspar. The Reichstag member Torgler, who was accused of being jointly responsible for the burning of the Reichstag, on the morning of February 28th went to police headquarters to make a protest against the charge. He was arrested. The Communist and Social Democratic Press did not appear on the morning of February 28th. The printing works of the *Vorwaerts* and of the papers *Berlin am Morgen* and *Welt am Abend* were occupied during the night of the 27th, and the copies of the morning edition which had already been run off were confiscated. The printing works of the *Rote Fahne* which are in the Karl Liebknecht house had been occupied by the police some days previously, and the *Rote Fahne* had already been prohibited before the burning of the Reichstag.

Emergency Decrees.   The fire in the Reichstag was put out during the night. Within a few hours the President of the Reichstag signed a decree entitled " Emergency Decree for the protection of the Nation and the State." It contained the following clauses :

" In virtue of Article 48 of the constitution of the Reich and as measures of defence against Communist acts of violence which endanger the State, it is decreed :

" 1. Articles 114, 115, 117, 118, 123, 124 and 153 of the Constitution of the German Reich are suspended until further notice. Consequently restrictions on personal freedom and on the right of free expression of opinion, including the freedom of the Press, and of the right of association and assembly, are permissible beyond the limit laid down in these articles of the Constitution. In addition, the privacy of correspondence, of the post, telegraph and telephone is suspended, and house-searchings and the confiscation or restriction on the rights of property are permissible.

" 4. Any person who opposes any orders issued by the State authorities or officials authorised by them for the enforcement of this decree, or orders issued by the Reich Government in accordance with section 2, or who supports or incites to such opposition, is liable to imprisonment for not less than one month, or to a fine from 150 to 15,000 Reichsmarks, unless a heavier penalty is imposed under existing legislation.

" Any person whose opposition endangers life is liable to not less than six months hard labour, in extenuating circumstances, and if the opposition has fatal results, to the death penalty, or in extenuating circumstances to not less than two years penal servitude.

" Any person who incites to opposition to the public danger is liable to hard labour, or in extenuating circumstances to imprisonment, for not less than three months.

" 5. The death penalty is substituted for penal servitude for life where this is laid down under the Criminal Code, namely, under sections 81 (high treason) ; 229 (poisoning) ; 307 (arson) ; 311 (causing explosions) ; 312 (causing floods) ; 315 (2) (damage to railways) ; 324 (attempts to poison groups of persons).

" The following crimes are punishable with death, or, unless heavier penalties are imposed by previous legislation, with penal servitude for life or up to 15 years :

" (1) any attempt to murder the President or Ministers or Commissioners, whether of the Reich or of the States of the Reich, or instigation to such murder, or agreement or conspiracy with others aiming at such murder.

" In cases under section 115 (2) of the Criminal Code (serious rioting) or section 125 (2) (serious breaches of the peace), any act involving the use of arms or conscious and deliberate co-operation with armed persons.

" (3) any act to deprive any person of his or her liberty with a view to using him or her as a hostage in political conflicts."

The Campaign.   Special editions of the papers, ministerial speeches, wireless announcements and posters everywhere announced : " The Communists have set fire to the Reichstag ! Insurrection and civil war were to follow ! The Communists intended to violate your wives and murder your children ! The Communists intended to poison the water in the wells and the food in the restaurants and canteens ! " Every hour crimes of the Communists were hammered into the readers of the German papers and those who listened to the wireless. The campaign was developed on a systematic plan. The Press was crammed with atrocity stories of what the Communists had intended. The *Vossische Zeitung* of March 1st gave information which it had had from Government sources :

" The Government is of the opinion that the situation is such that a danger to the State and to the Nation existed and still exists. The material from the Karl Liebknecht house is now being examined by the Government's legal advisers. Official reports state that this material contains proof that terrorist acts had been systematically prepared by the Communists on a scale which would place the Nation and the State in the greatest danger. Among the confiscated Communist material definite plans have been found for the seizure of hostages, especially the wives and children of particular individuals, plans for incendiary acts on public buildings, directions for terrorist groups who were to be placed at certain points in the uniform of the police, Storm Detachments and Stahlhelm. There is, it is declared, well-founded suspicion that the Communist activities are to be continued and that the central leadership of their operations will if necessary be removed from Berlin. There is also good cause to believe that, as in Karl Lieb-knecht house, there are subterranean cellars and pass-ages at other points, through which the Communists escape at the moment of danger. In this connection, it is emphasised that the necessary steps have been taken at the German frontiers, to make the flight of suspected persons into foreign countries impossible. In connection with the act of incendiarism in the Reichstag, it is stated that irrefutable proof exists that the chairman of the Communist section in the Reichstag, Deputy Torgler, had been for some hours in the Reichstag building with the incendiary, and that he had also been with others who had been concerned in the crime. It is added that the other criminals may have been able to escape through the subterranean passages which, in connection with the heating arrangements of the Reichstag, link the Reichstag building itself with the building occupied by the President of the Reichstag. In this connection, refer-ence is made to the arrest of two persons who telephoned from the Reichstag building asserting that the President of the Reichstag, Goering, was the instigator of the incendiary act, and stress is laid on the fact that the people concerned were connected with the Social Democratic Party and press.

" The authorities state that the fight against Communism will now be conducted with extreme severity. Anyone who works with the Communists, or regarding whom there are sufficient grounds to suspect that he is working with them, will be as rigorously dealt with as the Com-munists themselves. The Government statements also make it clear that the elections will be held under all circumstances.

" It is to be noted that the decrees for the protection of the Nation and the State, and the decree which punishes high treason more severely than hitherto, are supplementary to each other. The authorities state that the clauses of the decree for the protection of the nation and the state which are particularly directed against Communism were necessary because of the documents found in Karl Liebknecht house. Thus, for example, the increased severity of the punishments laid down in the Criminal Code for the administering of poison and poisoning to the common danger has been due to the fact that the Communists intended to carry out acts of poisoning on a large scale, including the poisoning of food in restaurants frequented by politicians who were their enemies."

Minister Goering spoke on the wireless on March 1st, and this was relayed from all German stations. According to the unanimous reports published in the press Goering made the following statements in his speech :

" The Communists are using leaflets and handbills to rally workers capable of using arms for red mass self-defence. This pretext was to enable the masses of the revolutionary Communists to be mobilised and to bring them into battle against the Nation and the State. I should like to state openly that we are not carrying on a defensive fight but that we have passed to the offensive along the whole front. It will be my principal task to extirpate Communism from our people. For that reason we have also mobilised those forces of national Germany whose main task it must be to overcome Communism. . . .

" On February 15th it was ascertained that the Communist party was engaged in organising terrorist troops in units up to 200 men. These groups were to dress in Storm Detachment uniforms and then to carry out attacks on motor cars, stores, shops, etc. Similar attacks were to be carried out on allied associations such as the Stahlhelm and the national parties. By these means, it was hoped to break the unity of the national movement.

Terrorist troops in the uniform of the Stahlhelm were also to carry out similar activities. In cases of arrest, false particulars were to be given. In addition, numerous forged orders of the Storm Detachment and Stahlhelm leaders were found in which the Storm Detachments were directed secretly to hold themselves in readiness for the night of March 6th, in order to occupy Berlin, and they were to be prepared to use their arms and beat down all resistance, etc. These forged orders were then to be circulated to the authorities and among the citizens in order to create the fear of a National Socialist *putsch* and to throw the workers into the necessary state of confusion. There were also forged police orders instructing the police to hand over armoured cars. At a meeting of the Communist Party executive on February 18th, there was discussion of what was expressly called a pact of attack of the united proletariat against the bourgeoisie and against the Fascist State. On the same day, the leader of a group which was intended to blow up bridges, who had fallen under suspicion owing to a considerable quantity of explosives being missing, was arrested. A short time afterwards, an organisation of the Communist Party was discovered which was to work with poison. A poison plan was discovered in Cologne which made it clear that the poison was to be used in the food of the Storm Detachments and of the Stahlhelms. A further document proves that not only the wives and children of leading individuals were to be taken as hostages, but also the wives and children of police officials, who were to be put in front of demonstrations as a living wall of defence. The leadership of this murder organisation was in the hands of the Communist leader Muenzenberg.

" On February 22nd the central committee issued the slogan of the arming of the working class. The instructions state ' In the application of the terror, every means and every weapon must be employed.' Mass strikes were organised. Solidarity strikes were to be prepared. All persons able to use arms were to report, and all members were to prepare themselves for illegality."

Goering then spoke of an organisation plan for an armed insurrection entitled " The Art of Armed Insurrection." He stated that this armed insurrection was the first phase of civil war. Instructions were said to be given in it for the use of small terrorist groups, and for the starting of fires in thousands and thousands of places. The aim of these activities was said to be to entice the police and the Reichswehr into the country and then to start the insurrection in the unprotected towns. In making use of hostages, no humanitarian motives should be allowed to intervene. Goering's concluding words were :

" Let me tell the Communists : My nerves have never given way up to now, and I feel strong enough to repay their criminal activities in kind."

Who were the Incendiaries ?   From the moment when the news was spread of the burning of the Reichstag the question was raised throughout the press of the world : Who were the incendiaries ? Most of the German papers adopted the statement of the Hitler Government that the Communists had set fire to the Reichstag. The whole of the foreign Press, however, received the official information with considerable scepticism, which soon developed into open ridicule of the official account. The *Temps* of March 1st contains the following statement :

" The official communiqué is obviously intended to rouse the population to fury against the Left opposition. There is no way of testing the police statements. It can only be said that the burning of the Reichstag comes very opportunely for the Government election propaganda. It serves as prelude to action not only against the Communists, but also against the Social Democrats, and also serves the purpose of enabling the Nazi Storm

Detachments and the Stahlhelm to come out as an armed force."

In the same edition of the *Temps* it is said that the Democratic circles and circles of the Left in Berlin are sceptical regarding the origin of the Reichstag fire. In the issue of the following day, the *Temps* further states :

" The arrest of van der Lubbe and his accomplices is not sufficient to lift the veil which covers the Reichstag fire."

The London *News Chronicle* of March 1st declared :

" The suggestion that the German Communists had any official connection with the affair is just nonsense."

The London *Evening Standard* of March 1st, 1933, stated :

" It cannot be disputed that there are millions of people in Germany to-day who simply cannot and will not believe the extraordinary stories circulated officially about the ' Red ' revolution which has only just been averted. Nor is the official version of the setting alight of the Reichstag by a Dutch Communist implicitly believed by many people."

These few examples out of the many press-reports suffice to show that no credence was given outside Germany to the official declarations of the Hitler government. The whole world outside Germany was and is convinced that the National Socialists set fire to the Reichstag. We will give one more quotation which brings out the view of the outside world with particular clarity.

The leading article in the *Daily Telegraph* of March 2nd contains the following :

" Van der Lubbe's examination will perhaps explain how he smuggled in his supplies of benzine, and whether he worked alone or as one of the ' Ten ' who are reported by the Nazis to have had a hand in the job. As to this it may well be asked, first, 'where are the nine others?'; and second, 'where were the lynx-eyed Reichstag watchmen?'"

Within three days of the Reichstag fire the Hitler Government was confronted with the fact that no one abroad gave any credence to its reports.

Who Benefited from the Reichstag Fire? Every criminal investigator first puts the question : who derived any advantage from the crime ? And this question must be put in connection with the Reichstag fire.

The Hitler government asserted in its official report of February 28th that the Reichstag fire had been organised by Communists and that it was to have been the signal for a bloody insurrection and civil war. But is there, apart from the Government's assertion, a single shred of evidence that on the night of February 27th the Communist Party intended to resort to " bloody insurrection " ? The Communist Party's tactics are definitely at variance with such a suggestion.

On March 25th, 1933, the German Communist Party issued a statement on the burning of the Reichstag which contains the following :

" Anyone who has even the slightest knowledge of Communism, of the teachings of Marx and Lenin, of the decisions of the Communist International and of the German Communist Party, knows that the methods of individual terror, arson, acts of sabotage, and so forth, do not belong to the tactical methods of the Communist movement. The Communist Party has always stated that its aim was the carrying through of the proletarian revolution. In order to achieve this aim, the party uses the tactics of revolutionary mass struggle, the winning of the masses for the Communist movement through agitation and propaganda, and above all through the organisation of the daily struggle for the immediate interests of the workers. These are the tactics through which the Communist movement, on the basis of Marxist and Leninist principles, realises its aims in every country. It is obvious that the Reichstag fire could have no imaginable sense or purpose for the Communist movement."

Could setting fire to the Reichstag bring any advantages to the Communists ? The German Communist Party had been increasing its influence steadily during the preceding years. In the presidential elections of March 1932 it secured 4,960,000 votes for its candidate Ernst Thälmann. In the Reichstag elections of July 31st, 1932, it secured, in round figures, 5,300,000 votes. In the elections of November 6th, 1932, it reached 6,000,000 votes. The Communist Party entered the campaign for the election of March 5th, 1933, with exceedingly good prospects ; the whole foreign Press prophesied a great increase in the Communist vote.

The dissatisfaction in the Social Democratic ranks was growing. Repeated acts of provocation by the Nazis, the ejection of the Social Democratic ministers in Prussia by an officer and three men, the passivity of the trade union and party leaders, all contributed to driving wide sections of former Social Democratic voters into supporting the Communists.

There was equal dissatisfaction in the ranks of the National Socialists. In the November election of 1932 Hitler had lost over 2,000,000 votes. The process of disintegration was developing. When Hitler came to power, many of his adherents expected a decisive change for the better. It did not come. There was a danger of still further secession into the ranks of the Communists.

The Hitler Government included among the evidence of what the Communists had had in mind the pamphlet : *The Art of Insurrection*. The *Bayrische Kurier*, the organ of the Catholic Bavarian People's Party, in its issue of March 3rd, 1933, referred to the fact that this pamphlet dated from 1923. And the pamphlet contains the following quotation from Lenin :

" One must make sure, first, that all the class forces hostile to us have fallen into complete enough confusion, are sufficiently at loggerheads with each other, have sufficiently weakened themselves in a struggle beyond their capacities, to give us a chance of victory ; secondly, one must ensure that all the vacillating, wavering, unstable, intermediate elements—the petit-bourgeoisie and the petit-bourgeois democracy, in contradistinction to the bourgeoisie—have sufficiently exposed themselves in the eyes of the people, and have disgraced themselves through their material bankruptcy ; thirdly, one must have the feeling of the masses in favour of supporting the most determined, unselfishly resolute, revolutionary action against the bourgeoisie. Then, indeed, revolution is ripe ; then, indeed, if we have correctly gauged all the conditions briefly outlined above, and if we have chosen the moment rightly, our victory is assured. . . .

" With the vanguard alone, victory is impossible. It would be not only foolish, but criminal, to throw the vanguard into the final struggle so long as the whole class, the general mass, has not taken up a position either of direct support of the vanguard or at least of benevolent neutrality towards it. . . ."

Had Goering even glanced at the pamphlet, he would not have made the mistake of citing it as evidence against the Communist Party.

Hitler as Hugenberg's Prisoner.   On January 30th, 1933, the so-called Government of " national concentration " was formed, with Hitler as Chancellor. The terms on which Hindenburg appointed Hitler were extremely hard for the National Socialists. German Nationalist ministers had the absolute majority in the Cabinet. The Vice-Chancellor, von Papen, was appointed Commissioner for Prussia, although in previous Governments this post had been filled by the Reich Chancellor himself. The Ministry of the Reichswehr, which the National Socialists had claimed in the last stage of the struggle for power, was entrusted to General von Blomberg, a loyal supporter of Hindenburg. When the new Cabinet took the oath on January 30th, Hitler had to give an express undertaking, in the presence of all the members of the Cabinet, that he would not alter the composition of the Government, whatever the result of the election might be. The three National Socialist Ministers Hitler, Frick and Goering took their places in a Government of German Nationalists, who controlled all the economic ministries besides the Ministry of Foreign Affairs and the Ministry of the Reichswehr. According to the plans of the German Nationalists, Hitler was to be their prisoner. He was received by Hindenburg only in the presence of von Papen. There was no precedent for such treatment to a Chancellor.

No change could be made in this situation by legal methods. The German Nationalists were very pleased with themselves. The second leader in command of the Stahlhelm, Lieutenant-Colonel Düsterberg, in an election meeting on February 12th, made known to the public the fact of Hitler's undertaking not to make any change in the Cabinet.

The men round Hitler, especially Goebbels and Goering, did all they could to free Hitler from the embrace of the German Nationalists. Only a changed distribution of power within the Government could damp down the growing dissatisfaction of many National Socialist electors. An attempt at a *putsch* was too dangerous. The Reichswehr and the Stahlhelm were with Hindenburg. If it came to fighting it was likely that the Reichsbanner would side with the Reichswehr and the Stahlhelm against the Nazis.

Dr. Oberfohren's Memorandum. It was in this situation that the National Socialists entered the election campaign. Dr. Goebbels, the most ingenious of the National Socialist leaders, saw how things threatened to develop.

It was he who first thought of a grand *coup* which would at one blow change the political position of the National Socialists. Evidence of the origin and carrying through of this *coup* exists. On April 26th and 27th, 1933, the *Manchester Guardian* published articles on the Reichstag fire in which reference was made to a memorandum originating in German Nationalist circles. This memorandum was produced by the former chairman of the German Nationalist fraction in the Reichstag, Dr. Oberfohren. When it became known that Dr. Oberfohren was the author of the memorandum referred to in articles published in the *Manchester Guardian*, the attack on him began, and on May 7th he was found dead in his flat. The report issued by the Hitler Government stated that he had committed suicide. In reality he had been murdered by the Nazis.

After the March 5th elections Dr. Oberfohren had attempted to organise the fight of the German Nationalists and the Stahlhelm against the Nazis. As a confidant of Hugenberg's he was fully informed of all that went on in the Cabinet. He set down in a memorandum what he knew of the preparations for the burning of the Reichstag, and sent this memorandum to his friends.

We quote from this memorandum only the most important passages which indicate what was taking place behind the scenes during February. After stating that the repeated searches of Karl Liebknecht House had produced no results, Dr. Oberfohren gives an account of how the plan for the burning of the Reichstag was developed by the National Socialists.

Dr. Goebbels' Plan.   " Herr Doctor Goebbels, untroubled by any scruples, had soon prepared a plan which, if carried out, would not only overcome the opposition of the German Nationalists to the Nazi demands for the suppression of Social Democratic and Communist agitation, but in certain circumstances, if completely successful, would also secure the prohibition of the Communist Party.

" Goebbels considered it necessary that material should be found in Karl Liebknecht House which would prove the criminal intentions of the Communists and establish that a Communist insurrection was imminent and that therefore there was immediate danger in delay. As Melcher's police (Melcher was police president of Berlin) had still found nothing in the Karl Liebknecht House, a new police president for Berlin must be appointed from the National Socialist ranks. It was only with great reluctance that Herr von Papen allowed his nominee, Melcher, to be displaced. The National Socialist's nomination of Count Helldorf, head of the Berlin storm troops, was not accepted. Finally agreement was reached on Admiral von Levetzow, who, although he belonged to the National Socialist Party, also still had connections with the German Nationalists. It was a simple matter to smuggle material into the Karl Liebknecht House, which was then empty. The police had the plans of the office section and the cellars. The necessary documents could therefore be easily put there.

" From the first Goebbels was clear as to the necessity of underlining the seriousness and the credibility of the forged documents, on their discovery, by some incident, even if this was only hinted at. Provision was in fact made for this.

" On February 24th the police forced their way into the Karl Liebknecht House, which had been standing empty for some weeks, searched it thoroughly and sealed it up. That same day the official announcement was made that a quantity of extremely treasonable material had been found.

" On February 26th the Conti Bureau, the Government's news bureau, issued a very detailed account of what the result of the search had been. It is not worth while to repeat this statement, the penny-dreadful style of which struck even the most unprejudiced reader. A detailed account was given of secret passages, secret springs, secret tunnels, catacombs, subterranean vaults and other contrivances of similar character. The whole contents of the report produced a ridiculous effect, as for example the description of the cellars of an office building in the fantastic terms ' subterranean vaults ' and ' catacombs.' It was remarkable that in what were described as well-concealed rooms in the cellar the police should find several hundredweight of precise directions for the carrying through of an imminent revolution. The statement that what had been found in these secret vaults was proof ' that the Communist Party and its auxiliary organisations lived a second illegal existence below the surface ' was particularly nonsensical.

" Admiral von Levetzow, police president of Berlin, on the afternoon of Sunday, February 26th, made a report to the Minister of the Interior, Herr Goering, on what had been found in the Karl Liebknecht House.

" The discoveries in the Karl Liebknecht House gave rise to considerable dissension within the Coalition Government. Papen, Hugenberg and Seldte vigorously reproached Herr Goering for making use of such a swindle. They pointed out that the documents alleged to have been discovered were such clumsy forgeries that they could in no circumstances be produced in public. They pointed out that it should have been managed more skilfully, along lines similar to those used by the English Conservatives some time previously in connection with the forged Zinoviev letter. The crudeness of the description of the Karl Liebknecht House given by the Conti Bureau was emphasised. German Nationalists and Stahlhelmers pointed out that no one would believe that the Communists would have deliberately established their illegal headquarters in Karl Liebknecht House. The forgeries should have been carried out less clumsily, and the illegal rooms should have been discovered in some other quarter of Berlin.

" Nevertheless, as the whole affair had already been made

public, the German Nationalists could do nothing but agree to the further strengthening of the decrees against the Communists, on the basis of the material that had been discovered. Of course they were in no way concerned to protect the Communists, but merely objected to the crudeness of the methods used. At the same time, they also wanted to allow the Communists in any event to take part in the elections, as they wanted to prevent the National Socialists from securing the absolute majority in the Reichstag through the elimination of the Communist Party."

Goebbels' Plan is carried out. Dr. Oberfohren shows in his memorandum that Goebbels thought it necessary to heighten the effect of the material alleged to have been discovered in Karl Liebknecht House, by an incident of some kind. He thought that he would achieve the greatest success—we continue to give Dr. Oberfohren's account—by a series of acts of arson which were to culminate in a fire in the German Reichstag on February 27th. It was agreed that the most important Nazi leaders—Hitler, Goering and Goebbels—were not to make any engagements to speak at election meetings on that date, but were to be in Berlin. We give below an announcement published in the *Völkischer Beobachter* of the election speeches which would be made by Hitler. It is specially noticeable that Hitler kept free the dates from the 25th to the 27th of February :

February 23	.	.	.	Frankfurt-am-Main
,, 24	.	.	.	Munich
,, 28	.	.	.	Leipzig
March 1	.	.	.	Breslau
,, 2	.	.	.	Berlin
,, 3	.	.	.	Hamburg
,, 4	.	.	.	Königsberg

The *Völkischer Beobachter* adds : " It is possible that election meetings will also be arranged for February 25th and 26th.

The time of the meetings will be between 8 and 9 p.m."
So in order to be prepared for emergencies Hitler had kept
free the dates from February 25th to 27th. But in any event
it was announced beforehand that Hitler could in no circumstances speak in any election meetings on February
27th.

Contradictions in the Official Reports.   The first official
report stated that a police officer noticed people carrying
lighted torches in the dark building, and that he succeeded
in capturing the criminal ; it further stated that the criminal
was found in one of the cellars and allowed himself to be
arrested without showing any resistance. On March 4th,
however, a further statement describes the arrest of van
der Lubbe as follows :

" Police on the Brandenburg Tor side of the Reichstag
noticed the fire in the building. One of the police saw
torches quite clearly and immediately fired. At first
there was some doubt about this incident. Since then,
however, the marks of the bullets have actually been
found. The police then rushed into the Reichstag. They
found in the lobby, not, as was originally reported, in
the cellars, the man Marinus van der Lubbe, who was
there overpowered by one of the officers after considerable resistance."

This is the first contradiction in the official reports.

Charges against Torgler and Koenen.   On the evening
of March 1st, the official *Preussische Pressedienst* issued the
following statement :

" The official investigation of the grave act of incendiarism
in the building of the German Reichstag has up to the
present shown that at least seven persons must have
been required for the bringing in of the inflammable
material alone, while the placing of it and simultaneous
setting fire to the various points in the huge building
must have required at least ten persons. There can be

ERNST TORGLER, Chairman of the Communist fraction in
the Reichstag.

Accused by the Nazis of being concerned in the burning of
the Reichstag, and arrested when he presented himself at
police headquarters to rebut the charge.

PLATE NO. 6.

no doubt whatever that the incendiaries were so completely familiar with all details of the vast building that only unrestricted access over a number of years could have given this definite knowledge of all the rooms. Grave suspicion therefore rests on the Communist party deputies, who particularly in recent weeks have been noticeably often meeting in the Reichstag building under the most divers pretexts. This familiarity with the Reichstag building and with the duty arrangements of the officials also explains the fact that for the time being only the Dutch Communist who was caught in the act was arrested, as after he had carried out his criminal deed he was unable to escape owing to his ignorance of the building. The arrested man, who is also known in Holland as extremely radical, has been continuously present at the meetings of the Communist Action Committee and was drawn in to carry out the act of incendiarism.

" The investigation has further established that three witnesses, some hours before the outbreak of the fire, saw the arrested Dutch criminal in the company of the Communist deputies Torgler and Koenen, in the corridors of the Reichstag, at about 8 o'clock in the evening. A mistake on the part of these witnesses is out of the question in view of the criminal's appearance. As moreover the deputies' entrance to the Reichstag is closed at 8 p.m., and the Communist deputies Torgler and Koenen at about 8.30 p.m. asked for their coats and hats to be brought to their rooms, and only left the building through another door at about 10 p.m., extremely grave suspicion rests on these two Communists. For it was between these times that the fire was arranged.

" The rumour that deputy Torgler voluntarily presented himself at police headquarters is not correct. It is true that, through his legal adviser, he asked for a safe-conduct when he realised that escape was impossible. But this was refused, and the deputy was arrested."

On March 4th the chief of the political police issued a report stating that :

" In so far as the investigation has up to now produced results giving rise to well-founded suspicion of the complicity of third persons, in the interests of the pending prosecution and of the security of the State no statement can be made."

So that on March 1st grave suspicion rests on Torgler and Koenen, and the security of the State does not prevent the announcement of the grounds for this suspicion. On March 4th any information bearing on the grounds for suspicion would endanger the security of the State. This is the second contradiction.

In the *Pressedienst* message of March 1st, which has already been quoted, it is stated that Torgler and Koenen left the Reichstag building at about 10 p.m. According to the messages issued by the *Wolff Bureau*, the *Telegrafen-Union* and the foreign correspondents, the fire was discovered in the time between 9 and 9.15 p.m. At 9.15 the fire brigade started operations. At about the same time, the police surrounded the Reichstag and prevented any access to it. A few minutes after the fire had been discovered Goering arrived on the spot, and shortly after his arrival Hitler, Goebbels, Papen and Prince August Wilhelm also arrived. But in spite of this the deputies Torgler and Koenen quietly left the burning Reichstag, which was cordoned off by the police and surrounded by a crowd of thousands of people. And it did not occur to anyone to ask them a single question.

This is the third contradiction.

A Complete Alibi. Two waiters in the Aschinger restaurant near the Friedrichstrasse Station have deposed on oath that the Reichstag deputy Torgler took his evening meal in the restaurant not later than 8.30. Torgler must therefore have left the Reichstag at the very latest soon after

8 o'clock, and not at 10 o'clock as the official statement asserts.

A sworn deposition made by the Reichstag deputy Wilhelm Koenen is printed below. This shows that Torgler and Koenen left the Reichstag that evening between 8.10 and 8.15 p.m. We give the deposition in full, because Koenen arrived at the Reichstag at about 6.30 p.m. on February 27th, and was with Torgler until 1.30 a.m. the following morning. These two deputies have a complete alibi which shows that there is not a word of truth in the charge against them made by the Hitler Government. Koenen's deposition is as follows :

" In the afternoon of February 27th I went, as I had done almost every day the previous week, to the police headquarters in the Alexanderplatz to see Detective Commissioner Dr. Braschwitz, in order to discuss with him further the question of releasing election material from Karl Liebknecht House. Shortly after 3 p.m. we went round to Karl Liebknecht House, with some detective officers, and there a few small lots of posters, streamers and other election material were released by the police and packed and sent out. When this had been completed, at 5.40 p.m., I took leave of the Detective Commissioner, arranged to meet some of our helpers next day in a neighbouring restaurant to organise the despatch of further material, and then telephoned to our Fraction secretariat in the Reichstag, as I had to discuss some points in connection with the distribution of speakers for the last week of the election campaign.

" Following on this telephone conversation I went direct to the Reichstag for the purpose stated, reaching there shortly before half-past six. There I met my colleague Ernst Torgler, who as chairman of the official election committee of our Party was concerned in the allocation of Party members of the Reichstag to the meetings which had been arranged. At about 7.15 p.m. I had settled the business I had come for, and Torgler asked me to wait a few minutes for him, as he was only waiting for a telephone call which would soon be through. Then we could go and have a meal together. I then told him of the constant difficulties which were being made over the release of election material from Karl Liebknecht House. We agreed that Torgler, as head of the Party's central election committee, should telephone to Dr. Diehls, head of the political section of the Berlin police, to lodge a further protest against the withholding of election posters and other election material.

"This conversation with Dr. Diehls took place at about 7.30 p.m. Following on this I got myself put through to the assessor, who as Dr. Diehls' right hand man was responsible for handing over the material, and put my point-of-view as to the difficulties which were being created, also discussing what had to be done the following day, in connection with which I had already made a further appointment to meet the Detective Commissioner at Karl Liebknecht House.

"After this telephone conversation with police headquarters Torgler had another telephone conversation, at about a quarter to eight, with the lawyer Dr. Rosenfeld. Then, as the call from a Party friend which he had been expecting since seven o'clock still did not come through, he telephoned down to the porter at door 5 and asked him, in the event of a call coming through to him after eight (when the exchange in the Reichstag closed), to call him down on the internal telephone from the Fraction secretariat room.

"Meanwhile the cloak-room attendant at the south door telephoned to ask whether Herr Torgler was now leaving, or whether his hat and coat should be brought up as usual to the Secretariat room. Torgler asked for his things to be brought up to him, and this was done at about eight o'clock. At eight o'clock the cloak-room and door 2 are closed.

"Then at last, at a couple of minutes past eight, the call which we had been waiting for came through, and had to be dealt with by the porter at door 5, the only door still open. Torgler was called down on the house telephone, and naturally, having to come down from the third floor and not wanting to keep his friend waiting unnecessarily, he lost no time over getting down. A few minutes later Torgler returned from the porter's office direct to the Fraction room, and soon after that we put on our things and, together with the woman secretary of the Fraction, left the Reichstag through door 5 at perhaps a quarter past eight.

" So far from leaving the building in flight, as is alleged, it so happened that we left the Reichstag building that evening at a much slower pace than we had ever done before. The secretary of the Fraction, who went out with us that night, was suffering from an inflamed vein which made it difficult for her to walk, so that we went at a snail's pace.

" It was at this very slow pace that we walked to the Friedrichstrasse Station, where the secretary left us and went down to the Underground. We went straight, that is, therefore, at about half-past eight, to the Aschinger Restaurant at the Friedrichstrasse Station, where we had supper. There we met three other Party friends, and stayed for some time talking to them. Two of these friends left us after they had had a meal, somewhere between half-past nine and a quarter to ten. At ten o'clock there was a change of shift for the waiters, so we paid our bills shortly before ten.

" It was already past ten o'clock when the new waiter came up to our table and, addressing me by name, said : ' Herr Koenen, have you heard, the Reichstag is on fire.' I was astounded, and replied : ' Man, are you mad ? It's quite impossible ! ' He answered excitedly : ' No, it's true, all the taxi-drivers say so. You can ask them at the counter by the door. Thousands of people are already collected there.'

" Thus it was that we came to learn of one of the most monstrous crimes in the history of the world.

" (*Signed*) WILHELM KOENEN."

This affidavit exposes the fourth contradiction in the official reports.

The message issued by the *Preussische Pressedienst* of March 1st, 1933, states that Torgler did not present himself at police headquarters, but that he was arrested. The deposition printed below, which was given on oath by the barrister Dr. Kurt Rosenfeld, who accompanied Torgler to police headquarters, shows that this statement is untrue.

" On the morning after the burning of the Reichstag, Herr Ernst Torgler rang me up on the telephone and asked me whether I was willing to go with him to police headquarters, where he intended to go in order to rebut the charges which had been made against him in connection with the Reichstag fire. I expressed my willingness to go with him, and at once telephoned to police headquarters to inform them that I should be coming at once with Torgler. If I remember rightly, I spoke to an official of the name of Heller. I then drove to police headquarters in a car with Torgler and asked to see Herr Heller, to whom I said : ' Here is Herr Torgler, and I must ask you to question him in connection with the charge that he is supposed to have had some sort of connection with the Reichstag fire.' The news that Torgler had presented himself voluntarily to be interrogated brought several police officers into the room where I was, asking : ' Is it true that Torgler has come of his own accord ? '

" Herr Heller then went with Herr Torgler into another room, while I waited in the ante-room. After a long time Herr Torgler came out of the room again, and we waited together until Herr Heller called us both into another room and in my presence declared that Torgler was under arrest.

"(Signed) KURT ROSENFELD."

This is the fifth contradiction.

The *Preussische Pressedienst* of March 1st reported that deputy Torgler had been several hours in company with the incendiary in the Reichstag building, and that he had also been in the company of other persons implicated in the fire. If Torgler had really been an accomplice, the most elementary common sense would have prevented him from showing himself in public with van der Lubbe.

This is the sixth contradiction.

The statement issued by the official *Preussische Pressedienst* on March 1st asserts that the Communist deputies of the Reichstag were familiar with the Reichstag building and with the duty arrangements of the staff. In fact, the Communist deputies of the Reichstag were not familiar with the duty arrangements of the staff, as they had no seat on the presidium of the Reichstag and were moreover excluded from all Committees which dealt with the administration of the Reichstag building. And moreover, as we shall show, on the day of the burning of the Reichstag the duty arrangements of the staff had been altered by the National Socialist House inspector, so that although Goering, president of the Reichstag, was in a position to know about this alteration, the Communist deputies could not have known of it.

This is the seventh contradiction.

Van der Lubbe not a Communist.   The official *Pressedienst* messages of February 28th state that van der Lubbe " stated that he was a member of the Dutch Communist Party." (The version broadcast on the wireless, that van der Lubbe had had on him a membership card of the Dutch Communist Party, was dropped even on the night of the Reichstag fire, because it was too incredible.) The first journalist who interviewed van der Lubbe after the burning of the Reichstag was the reporter of the Amsterdam paper *De Telegraaf*, whose message was published in his paper on March 2nd :

"Marinus tells me that for some years now he has not been a member of any party. He is not a convinced Communist."

In fact, Marinus van der Lubbe resigned from the Young Communist League of Leyden in April 1931, in order to forestall his expulsion.

This is the eighth contradiction.

The *Wolff Telegraph Bureau* reported from Amsterdam on March 2nd :

" The attempt made by the Dutch Communists to repudiate van der Lubbe cannot succeed, for police headquarters in the Hague have information that Lubbe was not expelled but merely removed from the front line and given the cold shoulder because his radical ideas did not suit the cautious party leadership in Holland."

The German authorities wanted to create the impression that a Communist who had been " given the cold shoulder " by the Dutch Communist Party (in reality van der Lubbe had not been a member of the Young Communist League since April 1931) was used by the German Communist Party for terroristic acts. Was it not the National Socialists who had been for years asserting that the closest links existed between the Communist Parties, which are all only sections of the Communist International ? How then can it be imagined that a Dutch Communist who had been given the cold shoulder would be received by the German Communist leaders with open arms and entrusted with the most confidential work ?

That is the ninth contradiction.

The same report issued by the *Wolff Telegraph Bureau* goes on to say :

" As recently as December 22nd, 1932, Lubbe took part in a meeting of taxi-drivers in the Hague who were on strike, and made a long Communist speech. This information given by the Dutch police is extremely important in its bearing on the Reichstag fire as an organised Communist terroristic act."

This information given by the Dutch police is indeed extremely important in its bearing on the Reichstag fire. In the meeting of taxi-drivers van der Lubbe did not make a Communist speech, but, as he had frequently done before, attacked the Dutch Communist Party.

We have definite evidence of this in a signed statement made by A. Terol, a member of the staff of the *Tribune*, and countersigned by a number of other persons present at the meeting.

This is the tenth contradiction.

The statement made by the chief of the political police on March 4th asserted that van der Lubbe knew German. Statements by everyone who knew him, and also the statements made by the journalists who visited him in prison and spoke to him, are all unanimous that van der Lubbe only speaks broken German. The *Lokalanzeiger* of February 28th states that van der Lubbe was interrogated with the aid of an interpreter.

This is the eleventh contradiction.

The same statement made by the chief of the political police says :

" Van der Lubbe is also known to the police as a Communist agitator. . . . On April 28th, 1931, he was arrested by the police in Gronau in Westphalia for selling post-cards of Communist tendency."

In actual fact, van der Lubbe did sell post-cards at Gronau in Westphalia ; they were post-cards of himself and his friend Holverda. The post-cards bear the following text in four languages : " Workers' Sports and Study Tour of Marinus van der Lubbe and H. Holverda through Europe and the Soviet Union. Start of the tour from Leyden, April 14th, 1931." There is not another word on the card, not the slightest indication of Communist agitation. Van der Lubbe was arrested merely because he had no licence to sell cards on the street.

This is the twelfth contradiction.

The chief of the Berlin political police further stated :

" He (van der Lubbe) in his examination only admitted the true facts of the case in so far as he was confronted with witnesses."

A few lines lower down the same report says :

" He (van der Lubbe) confessed every detail."

No names of eye-witnesses of the act of incendiarism have been given by the Hitler Government. Even the official *Preussische Pressedienst* did not assert that van der Lubbe had been seen setting fire to the Reichstag by the police or by anyone else. And if this is so, then, according to the statement issued by the chief of the political police, he did not make any confession. On the other hand, the same police official states that van der Lubbe confessed every detail.

This is the thirteenth contradiction.

The so-called national Press, which is inspired by the police, announced the day after the Reichstag fire that van der Lubbe had been in Moscow and had been trained there ; in reality van der Lubbe had never been in the Soviet Union. He went direct from Leyden to Germany.

This is the fourteenth contradiction.

Van der Lubbe left Leyden between the 13th and the 15th of February. According to a statement published in the *Vossische Zeitung* of March 2nd, 1933, he spent the night of the 17th–18th February in a hostel at Glindow near Werden. On February 18th he went on foot to Berlin. In an interview which the Criminal Commissioner Heisy gave to the Dutch Press on March 13th, he stated that van der Lubbe had made the acquaintance of Communists at labour exchanges and through them was brought into the Communist " Action Committee." Van der Lubbe did not arrive in Berlin until the evening of Saturday, February 18th, at the earliest. On the Sunday following, February

Dt

19th, the labour exchanges were closed. If the statement made by the police is correct, therefore, he could not have made the acquaintance of Communists at a labour exchange before Monday, February 20th, at the earliest. The reader must imagine for himself : a Dutchman, speaking broken German, without any transfer papers from the Dutch Communist Party, on February 20th makes the acquaintance of Communists at a labour exchange in Berlin, is brought by them into contact with the leaders of the party, and commissioned by them to set fire to the Reichstag on February 27th !

This is the fifteenth contradiction.

A statement issued by the official *Preussische Pressedienst* of March 1st says :

> " The arrested man has been continuously present at the meetings of the Communist Action Committee and was drawn in to carry out the act of incendiarism."

On March 3rd the Central Committee of the German Communist Party made the following statement in reply :

> " Of course no meetings of any Communist Action Committee have been held in the Reichstag or elsewhere at which the man arrested in the Reichstag, van der Lubbe, was present. In the first place no Communist Action Committee exists, but only the Central Committee of the German Communist Party and its Political Bureau. In the second place no individuals take part in meetings of the Communist Party or of any of its units who are not members either of the German Communist Party or of some other section of the Comintern."

This reply to Goering's assertions reveals the sixteenth contradiction.

Catacombs in Karl Liebknecht House.   A statement issued by the official *Preussische Pressedienst* on February 28th, 1933, says :

" Among the hundred centners of material which the police discovered in their search of the Karl Liebknecht House were instructions for the carrying out of the Communist terror on the Bolshevik model. According to these instructions government buildings, museums, mansions and essential plant were to be burnt down. The further direction is given that in riots and conflicts women and children are to be put in front of the terrorist troops, if possible the wives and children of police officials. The discovery of this material has checked the systematic carrying through of the Bolshevik revolution."

The Reichstag deputy Wilhelm Koenen, who was constantly working in the Karl Liebknecht House during the last few days of February as a leading official of the Communist Party, describes the searches in Karl Liebknecht House as follows :

" In the forenoon of February 17th a gigantic crowd of detective officers, accompanied by several companies of ordinary police, rushed into the building and occupied every room. Once again, for perhaps the hundredth time, every room, every corner, every cupboard was thoroughly searched. They had taken the precaution of bringing skilled workers with them to take to pieces the desks for which there were no keys. All the cellars too were carefully searched. In the cellars, as usual, there was only the material which had been left over from various campaigns or had been returned to the office in the course of years. In the basement rooms there were also supplies of paper and bookshop stocks. On that occasion the police inspector still considered it necessary, at my request, to show me any papers confiscated as suspicious and to state that they were confiscated or to give me a receipt for them. Among the papers seized in the course of this exhaustive search, which lasted many hours, there was neither the book *The Art of Armed Insurrection* nor any other so-called seditious publication. Nor was there any mention of these in the police reports issued immediately after the raid. It was only a week later, on February 24th, although I had been almost every day with police inspectors in the Karl Liebknecht House in connection with getting out election material, that police headquarters suddenly asserted that in the course of a new search in the so-called catacombs seditious material had been found, including the book *The Art of Armed Insurrection*. This alleged new search, if it took place at all, must have been carried out without any civilian witnesses and without any representative of the people concerned being present. This is all the more significant as I had been practically every day in the Karl Liebknecht House negotiating with the police inspectors to recover election material, paper, books and so forth and getting them despatched. Although I was therefore available every day, I was neither summoned nor even informed when the alleged discovery was made. It would have been particularly easy to inform me of it as I was there on the 24th, on Saturday the 25th, and again on Monday the 27th, and was talking to detectives and inspectors in connection with the delivery of the material recovered from the police.

" On February 25th, after the report of the passages, vaults and catacombs had already appeared in heavy type in the ' great ' Press, when I had finished with the inspector in charge in connection with the release of election material, I asked him where the ' catacombs ' were. A number of comrades who were helping with the despatch of the election material were also present. He then to our surprise pointed to a trap-door about a yard wide in a room on the ground floor which was used as a porter's office ; the trap-door was raised, so that we could see a ladder leading down into the basement. A comrade who had worked in the building for many years and knew it well said : ' Man, that's the trap-door to our old beer-cellar ! ' We all laughed, and asked the same question : ' Is that supposed to be the " catacombs " ? ' The inspector answered only with a rather embarrassed nod.

" That part of the building used to be an inn. The explanation of the passages through which people were supposed to be able to get away to other streets is equally simple. Karl Liebknecht House is a corner house, which as an office building for commercial undertakings had store-rooms and working-rooms in the basement, and these were described by Goering's police as vaults, passages and catacombs."

These two statements expose the seventeenth contradiction in the official reports.

" Signal for Civil War."   The *Preussische Pressedienst* announced on February 28th :

" The burning of the Reichstag was to be the signal for a bloody insurrection and civil war. Looting on a large scale had been organised for Tuesday in Berlin. It has been ascertained that to-day was to have seen throughout Germany terrorist acts against individual persons, against private property and against the life and limb of the peaceful population, and also the beginning of general civil war."

The *Vossische Zeitung* of March 4th, 1933, reported :

" The work of the police has up to the present prevented the material being put into the hands of every Communist. It has only got into the hands of a few functionaries in secret communications."

The last search of Karl Liebknecht House took place on February 24th. It was on this occasion that the terrorist material is alleged to have been found. The political police state that the instructions for the terror did not reach all Communists, but were only known to a few functionaries.

So that the German Communist Party would have had to circulate through every area in Germany, in the three days between February 24th and 27th, the material stored in the Karl Liebknecht House ; secondly, within the same three days, it would have had to get together the special groups who were to carry out the terrorist acts ; thirdly, it would have had to instruct and train these groups to carry out the terrorist acts ; and fourthly, it would have had to prepare and organise the rest of the members for the civil war which was to be unleashed through these terrorist acts.

In February 1933 the German Communist Party had over three hundred thousand members, distributed all over Germany. The party would have had to work miracles to organise within three days for the carrying through of all the plans attributed to it by the official statements.

This is the eighteenth contradiction.

The " Incriminating Material " has not been pro-duced.   During the evening of March 1st the official *Preussische Pressedienst* issued the following announcement :

" The Prussian Ministry of the Interior states, in connec-tion with the decree issued by the Reich Government against the Communist danger, dated February 28th, that particularly heavy penalties have been imposed for a number of crimes, because of the grave and acute danger which has been fully established, and of the inhuman and carefully prepared system of unrestricted Communist terror. Germany was to have been thrown into the chaos of Bolshevism. The assassination of individual leaders of the Nation and of the State, out-rages against essential services and public persons, the seizure as hostages of the wives and children of prominent men, were to produce fear and dismay among the nation and cripple any attempt at resistance on the part of the citizens.

" The Reich Commissioner for the Prussian Ministry of the Interior, Minister Goering, will in the very near

future make public the documents which prove the
necessity of all the measures which have been taken.
The enormous amount of material is being sifted once
again and a final examination of it is being made with
a view to ensuring that the security of the State cannot
be further endangered by its publication."

Up to the present time the documents have not been
published. This is the nineteenth contradiction.

Goering denies his own Statement.   On March 2nd,
1933, the *Deutsche Allgemeine Zeitung* and the *Tägliche Rundschau*
published the following message from the official *Preussische
Pressedienst* :

" In certain foreign newspapers the slanderous assertion,
emanating from German Marxist circles, is being circulated that the fire in the Reichstag building was
organised not by Communists but from the National
Socialist side. The originators of this slander have
already been arrested, and will be brought to due
punishment as soon as the investigation has been completed. Among other things it is asserted that the Dutch
Communist who was arrested is in reality an *agent
provocateur*, and was induced to carry out the act of
incendiarism by leading National Socialists. This is
supposed to be proved by the fact that the criminal had
used his coat and shirt as inflammable material, but had
not even removed the Communist documents and his
passport which were found on him. Significance is
further attached to the fact that the police authorities
have not published the photograph of the incendiary
and the documents found on him, and have also offered
no reward for persons who could give further information about the criminal and establish his connections
with Communist and Social Democratic politicians.
This unusual procedure in an important criminal case
is supposed to be evidence that the authorities are

hindering the elucidation of the crime, in order to be able to use a National Socialist act of provocation as a pretext for anti-Marxist measures.

" In reply to this it is stated from official sources that these slanderous arguments are of course devoid of any basis. The photographs of the criminal and of the documents found on him have not yet been published purely in the interests of the investigation. Publication will take place in the course of to-day. Moreover, the Berlin correspondents of foreign newspapers can obtain the photographic reproductions in the course of to-day from the IA Department at police headquarters. The photograph of the criminal will also be handed to-day to the Dutch police in order to confirm the criminal's identity. This will remove the possibility of further slanders. A specific warning is issued against the dissemination of such slanders."

But before the other German papers could publish this announcement, its publication was forbidden. Goering instructed the Wolf Bureau to circulate a statement that the *Deutsche Allgemeine Zeitung* and the *Tägliche Rundschau* had been taken in by a Communist forgery.

Apparently Goering wanted to make people believe that anyone can simply ring up a newspaper and say : " *Preussische Pressedienst* speaking," and then secure publicity for any kind of story. In reality telephone messages from press agencies to newspapers are very strictly controlled. Before accepting any message, the editorial stenographer first asks for confirmation from the control. Goering's *démenti* cannot cause any doubt as to the fact that at first he intended, through the *Preussische Pressedienst*, to bluff the world, and then later—too late—realised the danger of the message, and tried to hold it back.

This is the twentieth contradiction.

The Hunt for Accomplices.   The Conti-Service of the official Wolff Telegraph Bureau announced on March 4th, 1933 :

" that the Communist Reichstag deputy Schumann, at a Communist election meeting at Gehren (Thuringia) on February 24th, foretold the burning of the Reichstag building. Schumann's actual words are reported to have been : " This evening the Reichstag will be in flames. But that makes no difference. If this dance hall is burnt down, then we will get a swung floor."

The *Vossische Zeitung* of March 5th, 1933, states :

" A report was sent out from Thuringia and further broadcast by wireless, to the effect that the district authorities in Arnstadt in Thuringia were in possession of a report relating to a Communist election meeting held at Gehren on the evening of the wicked act of arson in the building of the German Reichstag ; that the local police official who was present at the meeting recorded in his report a statement made by the speaker, the Communist Reichstag deputy Schumann, in which the fire in the Reichstag was foretold in advance. Investigations since made have, however, as the *Thüringer Allgemeine Zeitung* now states, shown that there is a wireless apparatus in the restaurant where the meeting was held, and that the landlord, on the basis of the radio announcement, had sent to tell the speaker in the course of his speech that the Reichstag was on fire. It has been established that the police officer concerned made an error of one hour in his report, and that Schumann only began his speech at about 10.15 p.m. It can therefore be taken for granted that he had already heard of the radio announcement that the Reichstag was on fire."

This is the tweny-first contradiction.

On March 7th, 1933, the *Vossiche Zeitung* stated, on the basis of information received from the police :

" Duren, 6.3.—In the German frontier village of Lammer-dorf, near the Belgian frontier, a Russian emigrant was arrested yesterday evening on suspicion of having been concerned in the burning of the Reichstag. Shortly before his arrest he had despatched a telegram from a Belgian post office to Paris, the contents of which cannot as yet be disclosed. On being sent back across the frontier by Belgian frontier guards, he was arrested on this side of the frontier. He admitted during his interrogation that he came originally from Russia and had been living for some time in Berlin. He had severe burns on his arms and legs. The mysterious foreigner was to-day handed over to the criminal authorities.

" He obstinately refuses to say anything more regarding his activities in the capital of the Reich, and up to the present has not even given his name."

On March 8th, 1933, the *Vossiche Zeitung* printed a statement received from the authorities at Aix-la-Chapelle :

" *Not an accomplice of the Reichstag incendiary.* The authorities at Aix-la-Chapelle state that the Russian citizen who was arrested near Fringshaus as an incendiary, as investigations have shown, cannot be implicated. The man concerned has been active as a journalist in the Communist Party. For this reason he was expelled from the country a year ago. But there is no further evidence against him. His expulsion has been carried out."

This is the twenty-second contradiction.

Did van der Lubbe alone start the fire ?   Early in March the Hitler Government sent Heisig, a detective commissioner, to Leyden, to make investigations regarding van der Lubbe's antecedents. Heisig gave an interview to representatives of the Dutch Press, which was published in a number of papers on March 14th. This contains the following :

" As for the important question whether Lubbe had assistants or accomplices, it is probable that he alone started the fire, but that the preparatory measures had been carried out by accomplices."

This statement absolutely contradicts the official statement made on March 1st, that the simultaneous lighting of the fire at so many points in the gigantic building must have required at least ten persons. The judge in charge of the investigation, Vogt, therefore hastened to deny, on March 15th, the statement made by Heisig :

" A report has been published in a number of papers that van der Lubbe started the fire in the Reichstag by himself. This is not correct. The investigation conducted by the court has given good reason to believe that van der Lubbe did not commit the crime on his own initiative. In the interests of the investigation details cannot at present be given."

This is the twenty-third contradiction.

Lubbe's " Connections" with the Social Democrats. The official *Preussische Pressedienst* of February 28th, gave the information that in his confession, van der Lubbe had admitted to connections with the Social Democratic Party. On February 28th the Executive of the Social Democratic Party issued a statement in the following terms :

" During the night of the 27th–28th February, the whole Social Democratic Press of Prussia was prohibited for fourteen days. The prohibition is based on the statement that an arrested man has confessed that he started the fire in the Reichstag building and had previously had a certain connection with the Social Democratic Party. The suggestion that the Social Democratic Party would have anything to do with people who set fire to the Reichstag is repudiated by the party."

This statement issued by the Executive of the Social Democratic Party was confirmed by a statement made by the examining magistrate, Judge Vogt, which was published on March 22nd, 1933 :

" The investigation has so far shown that the Dutch Communist van der Lubbe, who was arrested as the person who set fire to the Reichstag building, was in communication immediately before the fire not only with German Communists but also with foreign Communists, including some who had been condemned to death or to long terms of penal servitude in connection with the explosion in the Sofia cathedral in 1925. The persons concerned are now under arrest. The investigation has not produced the slightest grounds for believing that non-Communist circles had any connection with the burning of the Reichstag."

On February 27th van der Lubbe is said to have admitted connections with the Social Democrats ; on March 22nd there were not the slightest grounds for believing this assertion.

This is the twenty-fourth contradiction.

Van der Lubbe and the Bulgarians. In the statement referred to above, Judge Vogt declares that van der Lubbe had connections with the people responsible for the Sofia cathedral explosion. Van der Lubbe had therefore not only performed the miracle of establishing, within 7 days, connections with the leaders of the German Communist Party, through Communists whom he got to know by accident at a labour exchange. He also succeeded, within these 7 days, in getting into touch with Bulgarians who are said to have been responsible for the Sofia cathedral explosion.

This is the twenty-fifth contradiction.

The Bulgarians who were arrested and charged with complicity in the burning of the Reichstag are : Dimitrov, Popoff and Taneff.

Georg Dimitrov was one of the theoretical leaders of the Bulgarian Communist Party. In 1923 he took part in the rising of the Bulgarian workers, and in 1924 he was sentenced *in contumaciam* to 15 years' hard labour. He has not been in Bulgaria since 1923. He had no part whatever in the Sofia cathedral explosion.

Blogoi Popoff emigrated to Jugoslavia in 1924, and only returned to Bulgaria at the end of 1930. He also was not concerned in the Sofia cathedral explosion of 1925.

The third arrested Bulgarian, Taneff, is merely a worker who was not in any way concerned in the Sofia cathedral explosion.

The aim of the assertion—that the arrested Bulgarians had blown up the Sofia cathedral—is quite clear. The Hitler government hoped to produce the impression that the burning of the Reichstag was an international Communist plot.

This is the twenty-sixth contradiction.

The judge in charge of the investigation asserted that Dimitrov had been seen with van der Lubbe at 3 p.m. on February 26th in a restaurant in the Düsseldorferstrasse. The judge also produced a witness, who swore that he had seen van der Lubbe with Dimitrov on that date. But the witness disappeared into oblivion shortly afterwards : for Dimitrov was able to prove that on February 26th he had not been in Berlin at all, but in Munich.

This is the twenty-seventh contradiction.

No Material for a Great Communist Trial.

On March 27th Judge Vogt stated that a criminal warrant had so far been issued only against van der Lubbe. But on April 3rd he caused a statement to be circulated that, in all, five warrants had been issued in connection with the burning of the Reichstag—for van der Lubbe, three Bulgarian Communists and the Communist Reichstag deputy Torgler. Torgler was arrested on February 28th, the Bulgarians on March 3rd. Up to March 27th, that is to say during the period when the main enquiries were being made, no warrants had been issued for Torgler and the Bulgarians. The warrants were issued only when the announcement that the only criminal warrant issued was for van der Lubbe had created a sensation in the Press of the world.

This is the twenty-eighth contradiction.

Judge Vogt's statement of April 3rd says that, " for the time being, only warrants for protective arrest have been issued in respect of a few other suspected persons." On June 2nd it was officially announced that :

" the preliminary investigation conducted by Judge Vogt against the accused van der Lubbe, Torgler, Dimitrov, Popoff and Taneff, on charges of setting fire to the Reichstag and high treason, was concluded on June 1st. All the documents have now been sent to the Reich Public Prosecutor at Leipzig."

On April 3rd there were still " a few other suspected persons." On June 1st they are no longer there.

This is the twenty-ninth contradiction.

On April 22nd Judge Vogt authorised the following official statement with regard to the progress of the investigation :

" The Supreme Court proposes to combine the investigation in the many pending cases of high treason against members of the Communist Party into one single enquiry on a large scale. It is expected that the investigations will be concluded in 8 to 10 weeks, so that then all the cases of high treason can be dealt with together by the Supreme Court. The cases concerned are all those arising in connection with the change of government in Germany, that is to say, all crimes during the course of January and February. This will also include the proceedings connected with the act of incendiarism in the Reichstag. This case has so far not made very rapid progress owing to the fact that the accused, and

particularly the Bulgarians, refuse to make any statement. The grounds for suspicion of complicity against
the Reichstag deputy Torgler have been more securely
established."

A month later, on May 25th, there was no longer any talk
of a great Communist trial. The Hitler Government was
forced to issue, through a parliamentary news bureau, the
news :

" That the trial in connection with the act of incendiarism
    in the Reichstag will be associated with other cases
    against Communist leaders in a great Communist trial,
    as has been suggested, is not to be expected. The trial
    of van der Lubbe and his accomplices will come before
    the Supreme Court as soon as the necessary preliminary
    labours have been concluded."

This is the thirtieth contradiction.

The *Völkischer Beobachter*, Hitler's official organ, published
the following statement on March 3rd, as coming from an
official source :

" The chief of the press section of the National Socialist
    fraction in the Reichstag discovered a missing pane in
    the glass roof over the room of the Communist deputy
    Torgler, and after further search discovered a long
    ladder above it, lying against the window of a Com-
    munist deputy's room in the second upper story.
" Detective inspectors immediately instituted a thorough
    search. For it was here that the incendiaries must have
    come down before the crime or got up again after the
    crime."

On March 1st Goering had declared that the incendiaries
had got away through the underground passage which
connects the Reichstag building with Goering's house. This

declaration of his confirmed what many people thought : that the Reichstag incendiaries had made their way into the Reichstag through his house and had escaped through his house. In order to weaken the overwhelming impression caused by Goering's declaration, the chief of the press section of the Nazi fraction in the Reichstag was sent to discover a missing pane and a ladder. The detective force, after three days thorough search, had failed to see what the sharp eyes of the leader of the press section discovered in a moment.

This is the thirty-first contradiction.

Van der Lubbe Confesses what is Required.   Dr. Oberfohren stated in his memorandum that Goebbels' plan was to start a series of incendiary acts which were to culminate in the burning of the Reichstag. For incendiary acts incendiaries are necessary. Van der Lubbe confesses that he set fire to the Reichstag. Van der Lubbe confesses that on February 25th he tried to set fire to the Berliner Schloss. In connection with this the Press of February 27th reported :

" It has only now become known that a small fire broke out on Saturday in an office room on the fifth floor of the Berliner Schloss, which was quickly put out by a fireman stationed on the premises. The origin of the fire is not yet fully explained. But it is thought to have been an act of incendiarism.

" An hour before the fire started the caretaker had started his round through the Schloss and had even passed through that room. At the time there was nothing suspicious to be seen. Soon afterwards the room was in flames. Investigation showed that there was a burning fire-lighter on the window-sill, and another under the window and also on the steam pipes. The police investigation has not yet been concluded."

Van der Lubbe confesses that on February 25th he tried to start a fire in the Welfare Office in Neukölln. Van der

Lubbe confesses that on February 25th he made an attempt to start a fire in the Berlin Town Hall.

This van der Lubbe is a real child of the devil. To start fires on one day in three different places in Berlin ! And he is a man who only speaks German brokenly. He had only arrived in Berlin on February 18th, 1933. Seven days later he had sufficient knowledge of the place to start fires in the Schloss, in the Town Hall and in the Welfare Office. He only required nine days to learn enough about the Reichstag to enable him to walk in and out as if it were his own house.

Van der Lubbe had to appear as a dyed-in-the-blood Communist. Such a Communist, as conceived by Dr. Goebbels, must have a forged passport. Consequently van der Lubbe must make some alteration in his name on the passport. The passport was " forged " by putting two dots over the " u," changing it into " ü."

Van der Lubbe was only too willing to take " Communist leaflets " into the Reichstag with him. Certainly no criminal has ever met the police so completely equipped with " credentials."

A Talk with Torgler the Day Before the Reichstag Fire.

As chairman of the Communist fraction in the Reichstag, Ernst Torgler was often called upon to answer enquiries from the Press and from journalists. At a Press conference on February 24th he told the journalists present that the Communists had information of an act of provocation planned by the Nazis. He stated that among other plans there was talk of staging an attempt to assassinate Hitler. The whole of the foreign Press and a section of the German Press published Torgler's statement. Shortly after this conference the parliamentary correspondent of the *Vossische Zeitung*, Adolf Philippsborn, arranged an interview with Torgler, and an account of this interview, written by Philippsborn, was published in the *Gegen-Angriff* of July 1st, 1933. It runs as follows :

" As a parliamentary journalist I have for many years been in contact with deputies belonging to all parties

in the Reichstag. It so chanced that I had arranged an
interview with Torgler on February 26th, 24 hours
before the Reichstag fire. Torgler came with his
daughter, who is 11 years of age. As the head of his
party fraction, I showed him some material on the
secret plans of the National Socialists. We then talked
for about two hours about the whole political situation.
I have never been a sympathiser with the Communist
Party, and I referred to a number of weaknesses of the
party. Torgler admitted some of the points, but energeti-
cally defended the general standpoint of his political
friends. Finally I put the following questions to him :

" ' There is a rumour going about that the Communists
propose to take some action against the Nazi Government before the Reichstag elections (March 5th). Is
this true ? '

" TORGLER : ' That is nonsense. The Government is only
waiting for such an opportunity to prohibit the Communist Party.'

" ' Will the Communist leaders call a strike ? '

" TORGLER : ' Of course we are calling for a political
mass strike as a means of struggle against Fascist acts
of violence. But we know that this can only be successful
if the trade unions withdraw their opposition and line
up with us in a fighting front.'

" ' Can this interview then be summed up by saying
that the Communist Party does not intend to take any
action which could give the Nazi Government the occasion for an offensive against the Marxist working
class ? '

" TORGLER (emphatically and with conviction) : ' Yes,
that is the position. We Communists know that by ourselves we are too weak for the fight. We know that Hitler,
Goering and his colleagues are only waiting for some
pretext which will give them the opportunity to prohibit the Communist Party and cancel the mandates
of party deputies elected to the Reichstag. We know
that we are shadowed by spies, and that our telephone

conversations are listened to. We are not going to run into the trap these gentlemen have prepared for us.'

" On the evening following this conversation the Reichstag was in flames, and a few hours later Torgler had been arrested as the 'criminal.' I then had the conviction, and still have it, that Torgler told me the absolute truth. And for that reason, although I am an opponent of Communism, I am prepared to say it to anyone, including Herr Goering, who knows it better than I do, and to the judges at the trial.

" Hands off Ernst Torgler, he is not guilty !"

The proof of the Nazis' guilt.   The contradictions in which the Hitler Government became entangled in its accounts of the Reichstag fire are by themselves enough to show who were the real incendiaries. But apart from these contradictions there is direct evidence that the National Socialists were guilty of this act of incendiarism. We do not propose to print here all the evidence which we have at our disposal, but only the most important and striking parts of it.

The fire in the German Reichstag was discovered at 9.15. The mass arrests in Berlin began soon after midnight. Almost all the warrants were accompanied with photographs of the accused, and the date of issue was inserted in ink. On February 28th approximately 1,500 persons were arrested in Berlin alone.

Is it possible to fill out 1,500 warrants, sign them, and in the majority of cases attach photographs to them, in three hours ? Information which we have received from dismissed police officials provides the explanation of this promptness. The warrants were got ready during the days immediately preceding the burning of the Reichstag. Only the date was not filled in. By the morning of February 27th all the warrants were ready. They were signed before the date was filled in.

On February 22nd the Prussian Government decided to strengthen the police with auxiliary police. Only members of the so-called national associations, that is, of the National Socialist storm troops and of the Stahlhelm, were allowed to join the auxiliary police. While the control of the auxiliary police was left in the hands of the local authorities, the Minister of the Interior, Goering, reserved to himself the right to control them in Berlin itself. The decision was made public on February 27th, the date of the Reichstag fire.

In the first official announcement of the Reichstag fire, Goering triumphantly stated that the organisation of the auxiliary police, for which he was responsible, had proved to be justified and necessary.

The National Socialist leaders and Ministers were not content with setting up the auxiliary police. On February 27th the whole of the storm troop forces in Berlin were confined to their quarters and barracks. A member of the storm troops, who left Germany at the end of March, gave the following information to the Paris *Intransigeant* :

" At noon on February 27th we received the order to remain in our quarters until further notice. We were strictly forbidden to show ourselves in groups in the streets. Only our collectors were allowed out with their collecting boxes, and a few others were sent on special errands. We did not know what was in the wind, and we waited, until suddenly at ten o'clock in the evening the order came : All at the double to the Brandenburger Tor ! Leave your weapons ! You are wanted for cordon duty : the Reichstag is on fire.

" The Berlin group leader Ernst collected a few of us in the tavern at the corner of the Wilhelmstrasse and the Dorotheenstrasse. He instructed us to go to various parts of the town and to spread in the beerhouses and at the street corners the story that the Communists had set fire to the Reichstag, that definite evidence had been found—in short, the whole story as it appeared in the Press the following day.

" At that time it was not yet known that van der Lubbe was a Dutchman and that deputy Torgler had been the

last to leave the Reichstag. This was all told us as an
absolute fact, and indeed with such definiteness that we
all felt violently angry with the incendiaries. We rushed
out, and carried out our tasks with the greatest zeal.
The more often I told the story, the more detailed it
became, and soon I felt as if I had been an eye-witness
of the arson."

Group-leader Ernst has a high position in the Hitler
hierarchy. But it requires more than a group-leader's
intellectual powers to know, by a few minutes after 10
p.m., that Torgler had been the last to leave the Reichstag.
Group-leader Ernst was privy to the plan of Goebbels and
Goering ; he was allocated the special task of transforming
the storm troop men into heralds to spread the story of
the " Communist " incendiaries.

Hitler Betrays Himself. On February 27th, 1933, fire
broke out in the German Reichstag. On February 27th,
1933, although the election campaign was at its height, the
most important National Socialist leaders were in Berlin.
On February 27th Hitler did not speak at any meeting.
On February 27th Goebbels did not speak at any meeting.
They were in Berlin with Goering. None of the three had
any meeting or any work to do that night.

A few minutes after it became known that the Reichstag
was on fire, Goering made his appearance on the scene, and
Hitler and Goebbels were there a few minutes later. Sefton
Delmer, the Berlin correspondent of the *Daily Express*, one
of the few English papers to back Hitler, was in their company. And the report he sent to the *Daily Express* is more
damaging than any published by papers hostile to Hitler.

Sefton Delmer describes the scene at the Reichstag,
perhaps twenty to thirty minutes after the fire had been
discovered. Hitler is reported as having turned to von
Papen and said :

" This is a God-given signal ! If this fire, as I believe,
turns out to be the handiwork of Communists, then

there is nothing that shall stop us now crushing out this murder pest with an iron fist."

Then turning to Sefton Delmer, he said :

"You are witnessing the beginning of a great new epoch in German history. This fire is the beginning."

The Chancellor of the Third Reich spoke these words at a time when the " guilt " of the Communists could not have been established, when van der Lubbe was only just being interrogated with the help of an interpreter. According to unanimous Press reports, the interrogation of van der Lubbe, which began immediately after his arrest, continued into the early hours of the morning. Van der Lubbe was arrested at about 9.20 p.m. At the time when Hitler spoke the words quoted above, van der Lubbe could not have made his " comprehensive confession " which might have served Hitler as the ground for his accusations against the Communists. Hitler's lack of self-control made him put the blame on the Communists a little too early ; he did not wait for his cue.

An Ally Charges the Nazis with the Act of Arson.

The *Deutsche Allgemeine Zeitung*, the organ of heavy industry, had been demanding since 1930 that Hitler should be entrusted with the government. Heavy industry was then trying to make the German Nationalists believe that Hitler would be content to share power with them.

The first weeks of the National Government's existence brought out the sharp contradictions within the Coalition government. Oberfohren's memorandum shows these contradictions clearly. The *Deutsche Allgemeine Zeitung* tried to strengthen the position of the German Nationalists. In the early stages it spared no criticism of the National Government. And soon after the Reichstag fire, when the National Socialists became preponderant in the Coalition Government, it even went so far as to assert that Goering's statements were untrue and to express doubts of the guilt of the Communists. On March 2nd the following appeared in the paper :

" From a political standpoint there is only one quite uncomprehensible point about the Reichstag fire : that a Communist could have been found who was so foolish as to commit the crime. Apart from a few speeches, newspaper articles and proposals put forward, up to now we have seen very little of any united front between the Communists and the Social Democrats. It is extremely improbable that such a united front could have been widened out to achieve an act of incendiarism in the German Reichstag. We fear that closer examination of the presuppositions for the well-known statement made by the Minister of the Interior will show that the charge he made cannot be maintained. If that is the case, it would have been better not to have raised it."

This is not from a Marxist journal, but from the journal of heavy industry. A few months after the Reichstag fire, the *Deutsche Allgemeine Zeitung* was " brought into conformity." Its chief editor was removed ; not before Hugenberg also sank into the background. But though the article failed to prevent the break-up of the German Nationalist Party, it is nevertheless significant that an ally of Hitler should expose Goering's lie and cast doubt on the guilt of the Communists.

Why did Goering leave the Reichstag unprotected ? The messages issued by the official *Preussische Pressedienst* on February 28th stated that among the material found in Karl Liebknecht House there were instructions for setting fire to the Reichstag. The search of Karl Liebknecht House took place on February 24th. Already on February 24th and 25th the whole of the bourgeois Press was in an uproar over the alleged murderous plans of the Communists. The police president of Berlin made a report to Goering on

February 26th on the material alleged to have been found in the catacombs of Karl Liebknecht House. As Minister of the Interior, Goering was in control of the Prussian police. As president of the Reichstag, Goering was in control of the Reichstag building. There was no one else in such a position as he was in to protect the Reichstag against any plot. There was no one whose duty to do this was greater than his.

Goering neither called on the police to protect the Reichstag, nor did he take any protective measures within the Reichstag itself. If the material alleged to have been found was real, then at the very least Herr Goering is guilty of abetting the crime. The only conclusion that can be drawn from the fact that the documents alleged to have been found in the Karl Liebknecht House have not yet been published, as also from the fact that Goering took no steps to protect the Reichstag, is : that the material from the Karl Liebknecht House existed only in the reports of the official *Preussische Pressedienst*. The Communists neither intended, nor did they make any preparations, to set fire to the Reichstag. The incendiaries were National Socialists.

Goering sends home the Reichstag officials.   Goering not only took no steps to protect the Reichstag building; he also saw to it that the Reichstag officials left the Reichstag before the normal time for finishing duty. On February 27th the National Socialist inspector of the building released the officials on duty at one o'clock in the afternoon. The staff told him that it was contrary to the terms of their employment to leave before the end of their spell of duty. The National Socialist inspector told them to go off duty, as there was nothing to do.

Early in March the foreign Press published the information that the staff of the Reichstag had been released from their duties at an early hour on February 27th. The Hitler Government has not dared to deny this.

Fire-Brigade Director puts the blame on Goering.   On March 24th the surprising announcement was made that the chief fire-brigade director of Berlin, Gempp, had been provisionally granted leave of absence, as he had tolerated Communist intrigues in the service. The Communist intrigues which Gempp was supposed to have tolerated consisted in the fact that in a conference with the inspectors and men of the fire-brigade he had made statements in connection with the Reichstag fire which threw a curious light on Goering's attitude at the scene of the fire. Gempp's statements concerned the three following essential points :

" In a conference with his inspectors and officers shortly before his dismissal, Herr Gempp complained that the fire-brigade had been summoned too late. This was the only explanation of why a storm troop detachment some twenty men strong was already on the scene of the fire by the time that the fire-brigade at last appeared.

" Herr Gempp complained further that the Minister of the Interior, Goering, had expressly forbidden him to circulate a general call and thereby to summon stronger forces to fight the fire.

" Finally, Herr Gempp had noticed that in the parts of the Reichstag building which were not destroyed there were great masses of unused incendiary material lying about ; in fact, in various rooms and under and in cupboards, etc., there was material which would have completely filled a lorry."

The above report was published in the *Saarbrückener Volksstimme* of April 25th, 1933, and thence found its way into the Press of the world. Goering did not reply to the report published by the *Saarbrückener Volksstimme*—not even by denying that the report was true. He used it as an opportunity of accusing Gempp of disloyalty. The *Deutsche Allgemeine Zeitung* of April 29th, 1933, reports how Goering reacted to the disclosure made by the *Volksstimme* :

" DISCIPLINARY ACTION AGAINST DIRECTOR GEMPP. We have received the following from Commissioner Dr.

Lippert : Fire-brigade director Gempp, chief of the Berlin fire-brigade, who was provisionally granted leave of absence by Dr. Lippert, State Commissioner, was accused of having tolerated Communist intrigues in the service under his control. Gempp then requested that disciplinary proceedings should be started against him. This request was not granted at the time, in view of the fact that Gempp was suspected of other offences. Disciplinary proceedings have now been opened against him, as he is charged with dereliction of duty under section 266 of the Criminal Code in connection with the purchase of a motor car through one of the functionaries at that time, the Social Democrat councillor Ahrens."

It is not only in the Gempp case that the National Socialists have used the tactics of getting rid of dangerous opponents by means of criminal charges.

From the charges brought by Gempp against Goering it is clear that Goering was interested in the spreading of the fire, and not in putting it out. The National Socialists intended to use the incendiary act to deal a deadly blow against Marxism. With this in view, it was necessary that the damage done by the fire should be as great and impressive as possible, and therefore it was not to be put out too soon. Three days after the fire the building was opened for the public to see the effect. The same National Socialist inspector of the building who had sent the staff away early on February 27th was now the official guide through the ruined building. Tens of thousands of people crowded in to see the sight. The guide explained " in an expert way " how the fire had been started by the Communists, and he did not omit to amplify his description with atrocity stories of what the Communists had intended to do.

Goering, who had not the courage himself to deny what the *Saarbrückener Volksstimme* reported, compelled Gempp to issue a *démenti*. Gempp seems to have refused to do so for some time. It was only on June 18th, 1933, that a statement by him appeared in the German Press, in which he declared that the report published in the *Volksstimme* was false. There are some *démentis* which establish the truth of the report that is denied, and Gempp's delayed *démenti* is one of this kind. Under the pressure of the charges made against him, and from fear of the sentence of imprisonment with which he was threatened, Gempp gave way to Goering's threats.

Where are the instigators of the fire? In the second March number of the conservative weekly journal *Der Ring*, which is edited by Heinrich von Gleichen, we find :

" The fire in the Reichstag led to extremely severe counter-measures by the Government of the Reich. The authorities are maintaining a state of preparedness for all eventualities. The public and the leading articles in the Press are asking : How was it possible ? Are we then really a nation of blind hens ? Where are the instigators of this fire, whose results show how sure they were of their aims ? To give a single answer to all questions, we must say in all seriousness and to the point : We have no secret service such as the English and other nations have. . . .

" If we had such an institution, then we should by now know exactly where the instigators of the Reichstag fire were to be found, in fact, we should already know the actual persons. They are *perhaps members of the best German international society.*" (Our emphasis. Editors.)

Heinrich von Gleichen is one of the most influential members of the *Herrenklub*. Since Papen was Chancellor, von Gleichen has been one of the wire-pullers of the Government's policy. His connections with the President's palace are more than excellent. In the extract quoted by us from the *Ring*, von Gleichen openly charges the Hitler Government with not having done anything to clear up the Reichstag fire. He asks : Where are the instigators of this fire, whose results show how sure they were of their aims ? Can anything else be meant by this than that the National

Socialists organised the fire, in order confidently to win one position of power after the other ?

After this issue, the *Ring* was prohibited.

Dr. Bell tells tales out of school. Elsewhere in this book an exact account is given of Dr. Bell's death at the hands of the Nazis. Here we deal only with his rôle in connection with the Reichstag fire. We do not propose to rely on the reports which state that before the Reichstag fire, between 8 and 9 on February 27th, Dr. Bell told English and American journalists that the Reichstag was on fire. This statement was deliberately circulated by the Hitler Government. The Nazis wanted a favorable opportunity for a *démenti* and for thus discrediting what Dr. Bell had really stated.

Dr. Bell knew van der Lubbe very well, and he was also kept closely informed by van der Lubbe of the connections he had formed with Nazi circles in Munich and Berlin. Although for about a year Dr. Bell had been hostile to the National Socialist Party, he still had a number of men within the party who kept him informed. He knew exactly what had taken place in connection with the Reichstag fire. In the National Club in the Friedrich-Ebertstrasse, on March 3rd or 4th, Bell betrayed what he knew about the Reichstag fire to a politician belonging to the People's Party. This politician wrote to some of his friends telling them the information, which Bell had given him, as to who were the real incendiaries. One of these letters fell into the hands of Dalueges, the chief of the secret police.

The letter cost Bell his life. On April 3rd he was murdered in the village of Kufstein in Austria, by Nazis who went there from Munich.

The Murder of Hanussen. The clairvoyant Erik Hanussen gave a house-warming party, on the day before the Reichstag fire, at his new flat in Berlin, Lietzenburgstrasse 16, which he called the Palace of Occultism. Some of the Nazi leaders were present on this occasion, including Count Helldorf, leader of the Berlin Nazis, as well as artists, actors and journalists. Among them there was also a reporter of the *Berliner 12-Uhr-Blatt*. In the séance which Hanussen staged, he said, among other things : " I see a great house burning."

In the first March number of his weekly paper, *Hanussens Bunte Wochenschau*, Hanussen printed an article on the political situation. He wrote in this article that he had known in advance of the Reichstag fire, but that he was not able to speak openly of it.

It is clear that some leading Nazi must have given Hanussen information before the Reichstag fire, which enabled Hanussen to " foresee " it. Hanussen must have known a great deal. This is clear from a sworn deposition given us by Dr. Franz Höllering, formerly editor of the *Berliner 12-Uhr-Blatt*.

" The undersigned, Dr. Franz Höllering, hereby declares on oath : In my capacity as editor-in-chief of the *Berliner 12-Uhr-Blatt* and of the *Montag Morgen*, I was brought into touch, between February 1st and March 4th, 1933, with Erik Hanussen, as the publisher of his National Socialist clairvoyant journal, which was set up and printed in the same printing works as the papers named above. I did not get to know Hanussen personally, but I had a telephone conversation with him on one occasion when he was trying to get into touch with the business manager of the printing works and the editor Roli Nürnberg, who were not there at the time. That was in the night of February 27th, the night of the burning of the Reichstag. The first report of the discovery of the fire had hardly reached the office when Hanussen rang up on the telephone. He wanted to know from me how far the fire had spread and whether the incendiaries had been caught. I replied that an unconfirmed report had reached me about a Communist troop which was alleged to have set fire to the Reichstag with the help of torches. At the same time I pointed

out that this report was incredible. I said in so many
words that the Communists, particularly in the existing
political situation, would never have committed such a
suicidal act of folly. Hanussen replied in an excited
voice that he was of quite the opposite opinion, that
he knew it was a Communist plot, and that I would very
soon see the consequences. This call came through
between 9.30 and 9.45. I made enquiries of my staff,
which knew of Hanussen's close connections with Count
Helldorf, particularly through his frequent telephone
calls to the printing works. Hanussen was generally
regarded as exceptionally well informed on National
Socialist plans.

" *(Signed)* DR. FRANZ HÖLLERING."

Thus at a time when the first vague reports of the fire
in the Reichstag had only just reached the editorial offices
of the newspapers, Hanussen was already saying that the
fire had been started by the Communists and that it would
have serious consequences. This statement of Hanussen's
shows more clearly than anything else that his informant is
to be found in high Nazi circles.

The Jew Hanussen did not long enjoy the rule of Hitler
which he had so earnestly desired. On April 7th, 1933, his
body was found in a little wood by the side of the Baruth-
Neuhof road. He had died at the hands of the Nazis.

The Third Man who Knew the Secret.   After Bell,
Hanussen. After Hanussen, Dr. Oberfohren. Of these
three persons who knew the secret of the burning of the
Reichstag, Dr. Oberfohren was the most dangerous. Bell
could be got rid of as a political adventurer, Hanussen as a
charlatan. Dr. Oberfohren was an influential politician,
leader of the German Nationalist fraction in the Reichstag.
In February 1933 he had declared in an election speech
that the Hitler Government would continue to exist in its
then composition, whatever the results of the election.
Events after February 27th shook his belief that the National

Socialists would stand by the undertaking sworn by Hitler on January 30th. Dr. Oberfohren put forward within the German Nationalist Party the proposal that it should begin the fight against Hitler's policy of concentrating power in his own hands. In order to win his friends for this fight he recorded what he knew of the Reichstag fire and of the struggle within the Cabinet, in the memorandum which has already been quoted. The following description by Dr. Oberfohren deals with what happened after the Reichstag fire.

The German Nationalists and the Fire.

"However much the German Nationalist Party is in agreement with the sharpest measures against the Communists, it cannot approve of the act of incendiarism carried out by its coalition friends. It is true that the Cabinet meeting on Tuesday agreed to the sharpest measures against the Communists, and partly also against the Social Democrats. However, no doubt was left that the act of incendiarism would most seriously damage the reputation of the national front abroad. In this meeting of the Cabinet the sharpest expressions of condemnation were not spared. The National Socialist Ministers did not succeed in pressing through the prohibition of the Communist Party. As already said above, the German Nationalists needed the Communist deputies in order to prevent the National Socialists from having an absolute majority in Parliament. At this Cabinet meeting Herr Goering was strictly forbidden to produce in public his forged material from Karl Liebknecht House. It was pointed out that the publication of these crude forgeries would only make things still worse for the Government. It was particularly inconvenient for the Government that the Communist deputy Torgler, leader of the Communist fraction in the Reichstag, had put himself at the disposal of the police on Tuesday morning. His flight would have been preferable. The fact that, after thousands of Communist functionaries had been arrested and in spite of the threat of a court-martial, he had presented himself to the police was extremely inconvenient for the Government. Herr Goering was commissioned to deny that Torgler had given himself up voluntarily. The echo in the world Press, however, which followed the Reichstag fire, was so unexpectedly unanimous in attributing the act of incendiarism to leading members of the government that the prestige of the National Government was most seriously shaken.

" However convenient it was for Goering and Goebbels that the Communist and Social Democratic election propaganda had been silenced, however well they knew that the broad mass of lower middle-class persons, clerks and peasants would believe the story of the Reichstag fire and would consequently give their votes to the National Socialist Party as the leader of the fight against Bolshevism, they were seriously disturbed at the attitude of the German Nationalist Ministers in the Cabinet. Once again they did not get the prohibition of the Communist Party. In spite of their boundless pretensions, they felt that they were held in an iron embrace by the German Nationalists, the Stahlhelm and the Reichswehr. It was clear to them that they must get out of this embrace as soon as possible. They discussed all kinds of proposals.

" Finally the groups decided to make a bid for power by a *coup* in the night of March 5th–6th. The plan was to occupy the Government quarter and demand from Hindenburg a change in the composition of the Cabinet. In this event, Hindenburg was to appoint Adolf Hitler to take over the functions of President of the Reich, and at the same time Hitler was to appoint Goering Chancellor. The discussions led up to the decision to carry through the plan in connection with a great propaganda march of Nazi storm troops and protective corps through Berlin, at which Hitler would take the salute, on Friday, March 3rd. This great propaganda march was then organised. Numbers of provincial storm troop sections arrived in Berlin ; the streets were cleared by the police for the triumphal march ; traffic was diverted, and thousands of people crowded to the Wilhelmstrasse to see the march past the leader Adolf Hitler. As rumours had been gaining ground that the Government quarter was to be occupied in the course of this march, at the last moment the German Nationalist Ministers in the Cabinet insisted that Adolf Hitler should abandon the march past in the Wilhelmstrasse. The thousands waiting in the Wilhelmstrasse were suddenly told, to their astonishment, that the Nazi march would follow another route and would not touch the Wilhelmstrasse, but would go through the Prinz-Albrechtstrasse into the west of the town. However, the German Nationalists were obliged to agree, for their part, to abandon a Stahlhelm march through the Government quarter, which had been announced for the day of the elections as an act of homage to Hindenburg. The Stahlhelm leaders agreed to the change.

" The position was extremely serious for the German Nationalist Ministers. The election results in Lippe-Detmold had shown how great the danger was that German National electors would pass over to the National Socialists in a body. German Nationalist propaganda could not compete with the unrestrained propaganda carried on by the National Socialists. The *Herrenklub*, the groups connected with the Stahlhelm, and the German Nationalist leaders discussed the position. After the occupation of the Government quarter on March 3rd had been averted, it was necessary to prepare for the threatened *coup* on the night of March 5th–6th with more than the Reichswehr and the Stahlhelm. It was clear that the masses were now no longer behind the old Field Marshal, but behind their idol Adolf Hitler. It would be futile to oppose these masses and the sentiment of the masses merely by the use of arms. It was therefore necessary to act as

E†

unscrupulously as Goering and Goebbels had done in connection with the Reichstag fire. The following plan was made. An official statement was to be made public dealing with the results so far arrived at in the enquiry in connection with the Reichstag incendiaries. This statement was so worded that if necessary it would be possible to refer to it to show that they were already then on the tracks of the National Socialist criminals. This official statement could then be used for the Press on the night of March 5th–6th as a weapon against the National Socialist Ministers, if these really attempted to carry out their plan of occupying the Government quarter. It was hoped by these means to throw the National Socialist masses into confusion and if possible to win them for the national front under the leadership of the German Nationalists and for Hindenburg ; to disclose the plans for the forcible seizure of power ; to accuse Goering, Hitler and Goebbels of the act of incendiarism in the Reichstag, on the basis of the official *communiqué* already issued ; and to call on the millions of National Socialists to stand united behind Field Marshal Hindenburg to save the national front against Marxism. It was hoped by these means to make the national masses prepared to accept a military dictatorship under Hindenburg. Hindenburg himself was not to be present at the Stahlhelm demonstration, but was to spend the night of March 5th–6th outside of Berlin under the protection of the Reichswehr, and the Reichswehr itself was to be mobilised for action."

Murderer and Incendiary.   Dr. Oberfohren wrote in his memorandum :

" In the meantime, the men charged by Herr Goering, under the leadership of Heines, Silesian storm troop leader and Reichstag deputy, passed along the heating passages from the palace of the President of the Reichstag and through the underground passage into the

Reichstag. The point at which each of the selected storm troop and protective corps leaders was to start a fire was arranged in detail. A general rehearsal had been held the previous day. Van der Lubbe went with them as the fifth or sixth man. When the observation posts in the Reichstag sent word that the air was clear, the incendiaries set to work. The starting of the fire was completed within a few minutes. Then, their work accomplished, they made their way back by the same route as they had come. Van der Lubbe alone remained behind in the Reichstag building."

Dr. Oberfohren's statement that Heines was in charge of the incendiary column is confirmed from other sources, including Dr. Bell. Heines was specially suitable for this " work " : he murders when he is told to, he shoots when he is told to, and he sets fire when he is told to.

The Incendiaries' Base. Even if Goering's tools had prepared the act of provocation more carefully, and had not made the whole series of contradictions which in themselves are overwhelming evidence of the Nazis' guilt, the case against the Nazis would still be clear to all eyes to see.

The *Vossische Zeitung* of March 1st, 1933, contains the following statement, emanating from Government sources :

" It is stated that there is irrefutable evidence that deputy Torgler, chairman of the Communist fraction in the Reichstag, was in the Reichstag building for several hours with the incendiary, and that he had also been in company with other persons who participated in the incendiary act. It is added that the other criminals may have been able to escape through the underground passage used in connection with the heating equipment of the Reichstag, which connects the Reichstag building itself with the building of the President of the Reichstag."

As we have already said, there is in fact an underground passage leading from the Reichstag building to the house of the President of the Reichstag. At the time of the Reichstag fire the occupant of this house to which the underground passage leads was Hermann Goering. He occupies the house through which, according to his own version, the criminals escaped.

Hermann Goering is not only Prime Minister of Prussia, Minister of Police and President of the Reichstag. Hermann Goering is also one of the chiefs of the storm troop organisation. Hermann Goering has at his disposal a special storm detachment, storm detachment G. His house is constantly guarded by a staff guard consisting of at least thirty men.

The official *Preussische Pressedienst* announced that at least seven men must have been concerned in bringing the incendiary material into the Reichstag, and the actual operation of starting the fire must have taken ten men. If we accept this statement, at least ten men must have been concerned in the fire.

It can be safely assumed that the fire was started at a number of different points in different parts of the building. Otherwise it would be impossible to explain the rapidity with which the fire spread in the huge building. To start the fire at several points required a considerable quantity of inflammable material, weighing several hundredweight. In his report to fire-brigade inspectors and men, Director Gempp stated that after the fire he observed a considerable quantity of incendiary material which had not been used, and that a lorry would have been required to carry it. This statement by Director Gempp confirms the assumption that the incendiaries must have taken a large quantity of incendiary material into the Reichstag.

How was the Incendiary Material Taken into the Reichstag?   We have given a description of the obstacles a visitor has to overcome in order to get into the Reichstag. Visitors are only admitted through door 5. They have to

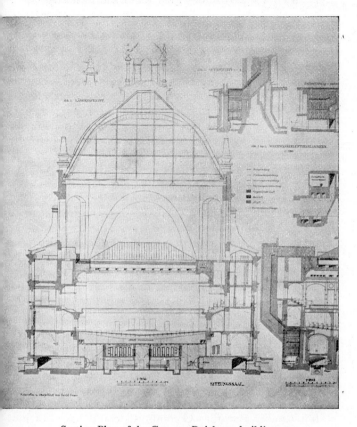

Section Plan of the German Reichstag building.
The entrance to the underground passage leading to Goering's house
is just above the word " Sitzungssaal."

PLATE NO. 7.

pass through a series of officials. Can it be imagined that between seven and ten men carrying several hundred-weight of incendiary material can have slipped into the Reichstag without being noticed by a single one of the Reichstag officials? Even the most prejudiced observer must admit that no incendiary and no group of incendiaries could have dared to bring in the material through door 5.

The case is just the same with the so-called deputies' entrance, door 2. Only deputies are allowed to enter by this door. The idea that deputies could have brought hundredweights of incendiary material past the officials at door 2 is no less absurd than the idea that the material could have been brought in by door 5.

The incendiaries would therefore have been obliged to choose some other way, a *secret* way, which would allow them to bring the material into the Reichstag and distribute it at the points required. There is such a secret way into the Reichstag, namely, the underground passage which connects the house of the President of the Reichstag with the Reichstag building itself. This underground passage was the strategic route for the incendiaries.

But anyone who wants to use the underground passage to the Reichstag was obliged first to pass through Goering's house, the house of the President of the Reichstag. He was therefore obliged to get past the guards who were constantly watching Goering's house. He would also have had to run the risk of being seen by someone in Goering's house.

Is it conceivable that Communists could have got into Goering's house and through it and through the underground passage, without being stopped and arrested by the guard of 30 men? Is it conceivable that Communists could have taken hundredweights of incendiary material through Goering's house without having been stopped and arrested by the guard? Is it conceivable that Communists could have escaped through Goering's house?

It is out of the question. Any Communist who in those days of February had tried to enter Goering's house would without doubt have been arrested. It was impossible for

Communists to reach the Reichstag by way of Goering's house and the underground passage. But for whom then was it possible ?

Only leading National Socialists could have entered Goering's house without attracting attention and without arousing even the slightest suspicion. Many meetings took place in this house between Goering and the leading officials of the National Socialist Party. No storm troop man would have thought of stopping men who held high positions in his party and whom he often saw visiting Goering's house. There was no danger for such people ; they could go in and out as they liked. This is true of all the higher officials. They could have brought the incendiary material required in small quantities without any difficulty and without attracting any attention. The guards would not have noticed anything if a number of chests described as " documents " or even as " arms " had been delivered to the basement of the house. (The transport of arms was taking place in those days wherever there was a Nazi headquarters.)

Goering's house was the key position for the attack on the Reichstag. Whoever controlled Goering's house could do what he liked to the Reichstag building. Goering's house was the bridge head from which the incendiary column advanced to the assault. Goering's house was the depot where the incendiary material was stored. Goering's house was the safe port into which the criminals could flee when they had perpetrated their crime.

The Incendiary Column. We said above that only leading National Socialists could have entered Goering's house without arousing suspicion. Dr. Oberfohren also speaks of selected leaders of the storm troops and protective corps. It is clear that the National Socialist leadership which devised and organised the plan of the Reichstag fire were very much interested in seeing that the carrying out of the plan was entrusted to their most reliable prætorians. Goebbels and Goering could not put themselves into the hands of any storm troop members ; they could not run the risk that some discontented storm troop man might expose the real incendiaries. Therefore they had to seek their accomplices in the ranks of the highest officials of the party. Men had to be found who on the one hand would not shrink from any crime, and on the other were so closely linked with the National Socialist leadership and with their fate that they could not be suspected of any treachery. And the ranks of the leaders of the National Socialist Party leadership are full of persons who satisfy these conditions. We know from Dr. Oberfohren's memorandum that the murderer Heines was put in charge of the incendiary column.

How Was the Incendiary Act Carried Out ?   The incendiary column assembled in Goering's house. Heines, Schulz, Helldorf and the others could get past the guards without interference, as they were known as storm troop leaders. Van der Lubbe probably went in with Count Helldorf.

The first task which had to be carried out was the transport of the incendiary material, for which purpose the incendiaries used the underground passage to the Reichstag from Goering's house. It is probable that several journeys had to be made. They began their operations at an agreed signal which told them that the last deputy had left the Reichstag. There was no danger of discovery by the Reichstag officials on duty, for these had been sent home by the Nazi inspector before the end of their spell of duty. The distribution of the incendiary material at the various points, and pouring petrol, benzine, etc., over it, must have taken some little time, at least twenty minutes. Then the fire was started at the different points.

The first reports issued by the police and the fire brigade spoke of seven to ten incendiaries and of the fire having started at many points. No one in Germany believed that the incendiaries had got into the Reichstag in the usual way and had left by the usual way. The question was raised : How did the incendiaries escape ? Any careless talk by a policeman, any careless talk from the fire brigade, any newspaper report might create an alarming position. Goering was in an extremely difficult situation. He resorted to an old trick. Before anyone else suggested that the incendiaries must have escaped through the underground passage, Goering wanted to say it himself. He hoped thereby to meet the imminent danger, to present something that was highly suspicious as quite harmless. Goering himself stated that the incendiaries had escaped through the underground passage. But later he bitterly regretted that he had said this. The trick had not come off. And so this underground passage to Goering's house was never again mentioned in any Minister's speech or in any official report. Goering's statement was to be forgotten.

We have not forgotten it. It is a fact that the incendiaries escaped through the underground passage, but they could only use this passage because they knew it led to Goering's house. Goering's house meant safety. The official *Preussische Pressedienst* of February 28th stated that the incendiaries had full knowledge of the building. Who other than Goering's friends were in the best position to gain full knowledge, to examine and test the underground passage ? Goering was master in the Reichstag. He could give his friends information about every corner of it. He was master in the palace of the President of the Reichstag. He could receive his friends there. He could arrange a store and hiding place for the incendiary material. He was Prussian Minister of the Interior. He controlled the police throughout Prussia. All the possibilities of organising the burning of the Reichstag were in the hands of Goering.

Van der Lubbe in the Burning Reichstag.   The *Preussische Pressedienst* tried to persuade the public that van der Lubbe had been unable to escape because he did not know the building. According to Goering and the *Preussische Pressedienst* all of van der Lubbe's accomplices were quite familiar with the building ; it would have been easy for them to take van der Lubbe with them and to " save " him. *But van der Lubbe could not be "saved."* He had to be left behind in the burning Reichstag, and was left behind, because *he was the evidence against the Communists.*

Van der Lubbe played his part to the best of his ability. He let himself be arrested in the burning building. He had discarded his shirt and coat so as to present a " true picture " of a " Communist incendiary." He confessed to having set fire to the Reichstag. He confessed to any act of incendiarism required : in the Welfare Office in Neukölln, in the Berlin Town Hall, in the Berliner Schloss. And van der Lubbe will confess to everything which his employers ask him to confess. He will say against Torgler whatever his employers tell him to say. He will say against Dimitrov everything that is wanted. He will inculpate everyone whom his National Socialist friends wish to destroy. He will exculpate everyone whom his National Socialist friends wish to protect.

Hermann Goering.   But all of van der Lubbe's confessions could not prevent the failure of the second task which had been entrusted to him : by giving himself up and confessing, to shelter the real incendiaries. The figure of van der Lubbe was too small for this ; his rôle was too obvious. Everyone saw through the trick ; they realised that behind van der Lubbe was Captain Hermann Goering, one of the storm troop chiefs, Minister of the German Reich, Premier and Minister of the Interior of Prussia, President of the German Reichstag. Captain Goering was born in Rosenheim, Bavaria, on January 12th, 1893. His biographers tell us of his heroic deeds as an airman during the war. They forget to add that his flights were carried out when he was under the influence of morphia. Goering's biographers tell us that in 1925–26 he was in Stockholm working for an aeroplane company. They forget to add that Hermann Goering, according to the official reports of the Stockholm police, was put into the asylum at Langbro, because a doctor had certified him to be of unsound mind. He was subsequently taken to the Konradsberg Hospital

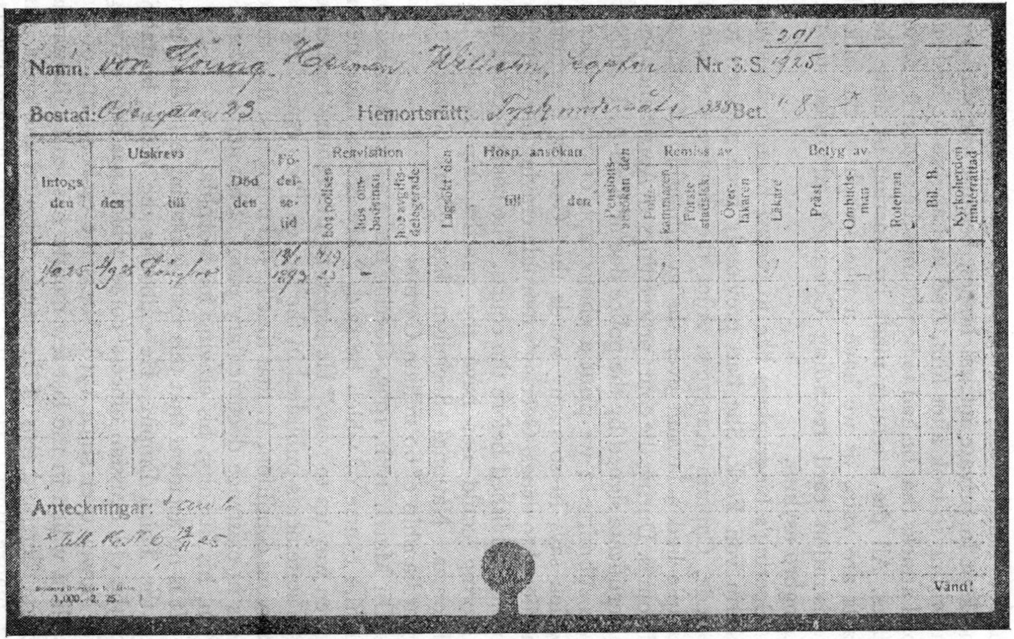

Registration Card, Langbro Asylum, of Captain Hermann Wilhelm Goering, who was admitted on September 1st, 1925.

PLATE NO. 8.

near Stockholm, but as a result of his conduct he was taken back to Langbro and there kept shut up. He could no longer be kept in private mental homes, because the staff were unwilling to look after him. And in Langbro he had such bad attacks that he had to be put into the section for serious cases. All the attempts made by Goering to deny these facts are vain, as we have a photograph of the official registration card recording Goering's admission to the Langbro asylum.

Goering's biographers like to record his marriage with Karin von Fock. She had previously been married to a Swede, Captain Kantzow. After the divorce the former couple had a lawsuit over the guardianship of their son Thomas. During the court proceedings on April 22nd, 1926, a certificate signed by the police doctor Karl A. Lundberg was submitted ; we print a photograph of this certificate, which says in so many words that Goering is seriously addicted to drugs. Goering's morphia craving has therefore been established before the courts. The court decided that Goering could not have the guardianship of the boy Thomas. National Socialism has given Goering the guardianship of 60 million Germans.

On March 10th, 1933, Goering made a speech in Essen, in the course of which he said, " My nerves have never given way up to now." He hoped by this remark to silence the statements published in the foreign Press regarding his nervous condition. At that time he did not realise that there was in existence documentary proof of his nervous condition, his insanity, his craving for morphia.

It is no accident that this man is playing a leading part in the Third Empire. He embodies the whole brutality of the old Prussian officers' corps, which has been striving for power ever since 1918. He is the embodiment of the sadism which in the last few months has led to thousands of murders and tens of thousands of brutal and cruel acts of maltreatment. He is the embodiment of that officers' clique which murdered Rosa Luxemburg and Karl Liebknecht, which shed streams of blood in Hungary,

Att Kaptenen Göring lider af morfinism och att hans hustru Carin Göring, född Fichenrinn Fock, lider af epilepsi och att desför deras hem måste anses olämpligt för hennes son Thomas Kantzow, intygar

Stockholm 16 April 1926

Karl A. R. Lundberg
leg. läk.

Certificate of the Stockholm Police Doctor that "Captain Goering is a morphia addict, and his wife, Frau Karin Goering, *née* Baroness Fock, suffers from epilepsy, and that their home must therefore be regarded as unfitted for her son Thomas Kantzow. Karl A. R. Lundberg, Doctor. Stockholm, April 16th, 1926."

which set up white gallows in Finland and is now making the whole of Hitler's Germany into a brown hell.

Goering represents the content of the policy of the National Socialists. National Socialism does not represent the workers or the employees or the middle class, but it represents the interests of the ruling class, of the *noble caste*. Power was put into the hands of the National Socialists in order that they should maintain the existing economic system and protect it against the menacing forces of social revolution. To protect these interests, National Socialism has taken its highest officials from the ranks of the former officers' corps, of the nobility and the high State officials. This Captain Goering, brutal in the extreme, lying and cowardly in the extreme, shows the true face of National Socialism.

This Captain Goering was the organiser of the Reichstag fire. His party comrade Goebbels invented the plan. Goering carried it through. All the opportunities for doing so were in his hands. All the necessary power was in his hands ; he held all the threads. It was the morphia-fiend Goering who set fire to the Reichstag.

Chapter V: DESTRUCTION OF THE WORKERS' ORGANISATIONS

" Now the hour of reckoning has come, when we draw
  conclusions. Let them be under no illusion that this
  reckoning may come to some unexpected end. The end
  of the revolution is the end of the November criminals,
  the end of that system, the end of that period ! We will
  hunt out these men from their last hiding-places and we
  will not rest until the body of our nation has been rid
  of the last traces of that poison."

(Hitler on May 7th, 1933, at Kiel.)

Hitler Expropriates !   Hitler has not nationalised a
single trust, nor has he expropriated a single financial
magnate. But in the first few months of his rule he has
carried through the expropriation of the political and trade
union working-class organisations of Germany.

All Communist and Social Democratic newspapers were
prohibited from the night of the burning of the Reichstag.
During that week the Karl Liebknecht House in Berlin, the
former headquarters of the Communist Party, was expropriated under the Hitler Government's emergency decree of
February 5th, 1933. Then all the printing establishments
and buildings owned by the Communist Party throughout
Germany were expropriated ; and the same procedure was
applied to the Berlin evening paper *Welt am Abend*.

The Attack on Trade Union Property.   Even before
the burning of the Reichstag systematic attacks on trade
union buildings and People's Houses all over Germany had
been made by storm troop detachments. On March 9th, in
Chemnitz, the business manager of the Social Democratic
printing works, Landgraf, was shot by storm troopers when
they occupied the works. On the same date workers armed

with rifles and hand grenades defended the Trade Union House at Wurzen against a storm troop attack. In Braunschweig, Hans Saile, the circulation manager of the Social Democratic paper *Volksfreund*, was shot by storm troopers who occupied the offices of the paper. On the same date there was a partial strike of the Dresden workers against the looting by Nazis of the People's House in that town. On the same date the Trade Union House in Berlin was looted.

The following account of the attack on the trade union headquarters and the Otto Braun House in Königsberg has been given us by an eyewitness :

" The Health Section of the Trade Union Association was having its usual monthly meeting and social gathering. Nazi storm troopers came into the building, and suddenly the doors of the room were torn open and about sixty men, armed with revolvers, forced their way into the hall and fired a number of shots at the ceiling and the wall. Five people were wounded, one seriously, by bullets glancing off the walls. Then the bandits drove men and women out into the street without their hats and coats, which were confiscated. After that, the Nazis went through the Trade Union offices, destroying everything.

" In the case of the Otto Braun House, two uniformed police officers came to the building at 11.20 p.m. and took away the revolver which was in the possession of the night watchman. They then told him that they would hold him as a hostage, and that they would have to shoot him if any armed person was found in the house. Ten minutes later a strong storm troop detachment made its appearance and entered the building. The caretaker of the building with his wife and two daughters lived there in a flat ; three Nazis went to the flat and, threatening the caretaker with their revolvers, ordered him at once to open all the rooms in the building. Then the storm troopers began to smash up everything. They first made for the office of the Reichsbanner organisation, and chopped up every piece of furniture into tiny fragments, using axes which they had brought with them. Valuable pictures were destroyed ; the cash-box was broken open, and every desk smashed. The office was left simply a heap of rubbish. The district office of the Social Democratic Party was dealt with in the same way, and also the office of the Freethinkers organisation. Then the business manager of the *Königsberger Volkszeitung* was fetched by three storm troopers, and forced to take them through the offices at the point of the revolver. He was then made to open the garages, which were let to private individuals and firms, and to put the motors there out of action. With three revolvers pointing at him, he was forced to burn a black-red-gold banner in the street."

The Saarbrück *Volksstimme* of March 13th contains the following report of the occupation by Nazis of the offices of the Mineworkers' Union in Bochum :

" The central offices for the Reich, which are also the headquarters of the Bochum mineworkers union, were attacked by Hitler's bandits belonging to the storm troops and protective corps, and destroyed from top to bottom. All documents were set alight, the fire spreading to parts of the building, and the whole of the Central Executive, or those members who were there, including the president, Husemann, a member of the Reichstag, were carried off by the storm troopers and protective corps men."

These few examples are only a small sample of what went on at that time in every part of Germany. The swastika flag was hoisted over every trade union building, every People's House, every newspaper office belonging either to the Social Democratic Party or to the Communist Party.

Moral Provocation. The burning of the Reichstag was not enough in the way of acts of provocation for the

National Socialists, who also resorted to moral provocation. They called the Karl Liebknecht House " Horst-Wessel House " and made it the headquarters of the political police.

Karl Liebknecht's name is known to the workers of the whole world. In defiance of martial law, Karl Liebknecht raised his voice against the slaughter of the war.

Who was the National Socialist " hero " Horst-Wessel ? He was a student, the son of a Berlin clergyman. Even the Nazis cannot deny that this " hero," who used to hunt " Marxists " at night with his storm troops, lived on the earnings of a prostitute. He was killed in this prostitute's flat by one of her former lovers. The legend-writers of National Socialism say that Horst-Wessel only wanted to " save " this woman's " soul." The National Socialist Press asserted—and this became the official legend—that Horst-Wessel had fallen at the hands of the Communists.

Organisations Dissolved.   There has not been and there is not now any formal prohibition of the Communist Party in Germany. But the campaign of terror has in fact put all Communist leaders and functionaries outside the law. All organisations which were believed to stand on the basis of the class struggle were outlawed.

The trade union organisations of the revolutionary workers among the miners and the metal-workers of Berlin, and the whole of the revolutionary trade union opposition, were driven underground. Revolutionary workers' organisations uniting all parties, such as the anti-Fascist League, the Red Sports organisations, the revolutionary associations of writers and artists and photographers, etc., were treated in the same way as the Communist Party from the moment of the Reichstag fire.

The German Red Aid, a working-class organisation for the support of political prisoners and their families, which helped all workers irrespective of their political affiliation, was driven underground. Even aid for the victims of Fascist barbarity has to be organised secretly.

The International Workers' Relief, which organised help for strikers during industrial disputes, was also outlawed ; its property was confiscated and its officials and members were persecuted.

All the social and cultural organisations of the working class were suppressed : the children's organisations, the League for the Protection of Motherhood, the Association of Social and Political Organisations. All pacifist organisations met the same fate : the League for Human Rights, the German Peace Society, and many others.

The elections of works councils which took place at the end of March were overshadowed by the campaign of repression of the workers' organisations, and could not give a true reflection of the feeling among the workers. A report from the " Union " engineering factory in Dortmund is typical of how these elections were carried out in almost all German factories :

"At the ' Union ' works in Dortmund the foreman, Dickmann, whose duty it was to superintend the ballot, was arrested on the day before the election. The Nazis took charge of the ballot papers and called on the workers to vote. Any worker who refused to vote was told that he would be regarded as an enemy of the National Government. The table at which the ballot papers were filled in was surrounded by armed Nazis. Each worker who came up to vote was listed, and a note was kept of which ballot paper he placed in the envelope and handed in. At the end of the ballot the leader of the Nazis took charge of the ballot box and with his friends counted up the votes. Not a single worker of any other organisation was allowed to check the result."

Yet in spite of such methods the elections did not give the Nazis a majority in most factories throughout Germany. What the Nazis could not get by intimidation and falsification was therefore secured by them through the open use of force during the month of April : the " cleansing " of the works councils by the removal of all elected trade union and revolutionary representatives. Even representatives of the Christian Unions who were known as anti-Fascists were removed from office. Storm troopers marched into the room where the works council was meeting, maltreated and imprisoned some and forced them to resign under threat of their lives. Appointed Nazi " works councillors " were put in to correct the election results in every factory.

Destruction of the Trade Unions.   The " National Labour Day " of May 1st, when hundreds of thousands of workers were driven to participate in the official demonstrations by the threat of instant dismissal, served as a preparatory step to the occupation of all trade union offices by the Nazis on May 2nd. The dissolution of the trade unions in the form in which they had hitherto existed was proclaimed in the name of a " Committee for the Protection of German Labour " which no one had heard of until that moment.

It did not help the German General Trade Union Federation that it had called on the workers to participate in the Hitler demonstration of May 1st. The trade union offices were occupied, and the trade union leaders maltreated. The " German Labour Front " took over the whole trade union apparatus. We give below a few documents showing the methods that were used in these attacks on the trade unions :

" The National Socialists take over the trade unions : the leaders arrested : action throughout the Reich."
(Headlines in the *Deutsche Allgemeine Zeitung*, May 2nd, 1933.)

. . . .

" Yes, we have power, but we have not yet won the whole nation. We have not yet won you workers a hundred per cent. . . ."
(From the manifesto issued by Dr. Ley, May 2nd, 1933.)

. . . .

" Cleansing of the free trade unions and creation of
a Labour organisation ; storm troops occupy all trade
union buildings : 50 trade union leaders arrested : the
second stage of the National Socialist revolution."

> (Headlines in the *Völkischer Beobachter*,
> May 3rd, 1933.)

.   .   .   .

" After *Germany*, in the most comprehensive meaning of
the word, had acknowledged on May 1st the National
Socialist conception of the idea of ' Labour,' on May 2nd
the implications of this acknowledgment were applied
throughout the movement. The so-called free trade
unions have been disloyal to their own real nature and
have degenerated themselves and the trade union *idea*
to the level of international Marxism."

> (From Alfred Rosenberg's leading article in the
> *Völkischer Beobachter*, May 3rd, 1933.)

.   .   .   .

" The National Socialist Factory Organisation journal,
the *Arbeitertum*, which deals with the theory and practice of the National Socialist Factory Organisation,
becomes from to-day the official organ of the German
General Trade Union Federation and of the AFA
Federation."

> (From the Ley Committee manifesto issued on
> May 2nd, 1933.)

.   .   .   .

" The chapter of Marxist incitement of the workers is
closed. After the action taken against the Marxist trade
unions met with such tremendous response throughout
the nation and particularly in the working class, the
General Association of Christian Trade Unions, the Trade
Union Association of German Employees', Workers' and
Officials' Associations (Hirsch-Duncker), the Federation of Employees' Trade Unions, and other smaller
associations, under the influence of this mighty national movement found themselves compelled to declare

in writing that they put themselves unconditionally
at the disposal of the leader of the National Socialist
German Labour Party, and would carry out without
reserve the instructions of the Action Committee for the
Protection of German Labour which he has appointed."

(From the manifesto issued by Dr. Ley on
May 4th, 1933.)

.   .   .   .

"Innumerable cases of corruption among the leaders of
the Marxist trade unions : balance sheet mysteries and
dark financial transactions : eight million organised
workers brought under the leadership of Adolf Hitler."

(Headlines in the *Völkischer Beobachter* of
May 5th, 1933.)

The first manifesto issued by Dr. Ley, the head of the
" Action Committee for the Protection of German Labour,"
was written in a very " friendly " tone :

" We have never destroyed anything which had any kind
of value for our nation, nor shall we in the future.
This is a fundamental principle of National Socialism.
This holds good particularly of the trade unions, which
have been built up out of the pennies which the workers
have earned with such bitter toil and starved themselves to give. No, workers, your institutions are sacred
and inviolable to us National Socialists. I myself am
the son of a poor peasant, and I know poverty : I
myself was for seven years in one of the largest factories
in Germany."

It may be remarked in passing that Dr. Ley was never a
worker, but in his seven years of employment with the
I. G. Farbenindustrie, A.G. (the chemical trust), was a
highly paid official of the company, and received a large
sum when he left.

At the moment when they took over the trade unions
by force the National Socialist leaders used the tactics of

making a solemn promise to the organised workers that their institutions would be maintained. At the same time, the National Socialist Press started a great campaign on the " corruption in trade union offices " ; and the Nazi storm troopers stood ready with their revolvers and rubber truncheons to persuade everyone of the friendship felt by the Nazis to the working class.

A few weeks later, on June 10th, Dr. Ley issued his " Fundamental Ideas on Corporate Organisation and the German Labour Front," which he himself described as the " foundation on which generations will be able to build anew for centuries." The essential paragraph in this so completely new " foundation " reads as follows :

" LEADERSHIP IN THE FACTORY. Corporate organisation will as its first work restore absolute leadership to the natural leader of a factory, that is, the employer (!), and will at the same time place full responsibility on him. . . . Only the employer can decide."

This passage, which proclaims the absolute dictatorship of the employer in the factory, contains not a trace of the " sacredness " and " inviolability " of the trade union organisation. Henceforward the trade unions are to be merely auxiliary instruments used by the State of Fascist dictatorship.

" It is better that we should give it (Marxism) a last shot to finish it off than that we should ever allow it to rise again. The Leiparts and the Grassmanns may hypocritically declare their devotion to Hitler as much as they like—but it is better that they should be in prison. Thereby we deprive the Marxist ruffians of their chief weapon and of the last possibility of strengthening themselves afresh. The diabolical doctrine of Marxism must perish miserably on the battlefield of the National Socialist revolution."

(From Dr. Ley's manifesto of May 2nd, 1933.)

"Corruption on Corruption."   One of the National
Socialist methods of fighting is to "settle" their opponents
by bringing charges of corruption against them.   It was
this method that they used to silence Gempp, the Berlin
fire-brigade director, who knew too much about the burning of the Reichstag. And this was the method they used
to settle accounts with large numbers of the officials of the
Weimar Republic and many leaders of bourgeois organisations which had not yet been "brought into conformity."
And it was the method they used to revenge themselves on
Gerecke, who in 1932 had been head of the Hindenburg
election committee and therefore one of the chief opponents
of Hitler's candidature for the presidency.

When, under Dr. Ley's guidance, the Free Trade Unions
had been "brought into conformity," the National
Socialist leaders started their great campaign of exposing
the "corruption in the trade unions" by way of rounding
off their soon-forgotten promises of raising trade union
benefits and lowering contributions. Long accounts were
published in the Fascist Press of how luxuriously the central
offices of the various trade unions were furnished. Columns
in the Press recounted the high salaries drawn by the trade
union leaders. The National Socialist leaders, who had
placed the trade union apparatus under the bureaucratic
political control of Fascist Commissioners, tried to rouse the
militant members of the trade unions against the bureaucracy of their former leaders and against their policy of
industrial peace, and to exploit this to get support for the
"cleansing" carried out by the Fascists. The poverty of
the workers, and the refusal of strike pay to them in former
economic struggles, was contrasted in the Fascist Press
with the comfortable lives led by the trade union leaders.
The *Völkischer Beobachter* screamed in heavy type that the
president of the A.F.A. Federation, Aufhäuser, had arranged "compensation" for himself when he retired
amounting to eighteen months' salary at 940 marks—a
total of 16,920 marks.

In addition to facts which savoured of corruption the

National Socialist " unmaskers " produced cases of corruption which they simply invented. Any use of money which did not suit the policy of the Nazis was labelled as " dishonest." It was " unmasked " that in the presidential election campaign 300,000 marks of trade union money had been handed over by the General Trade Union Federation to the Social Democratic Party in aid of their campaign for Hindenburg. The Central Union of Employees had given 50,000 marks to the Reichsbanner organisation in the spring of 1932, and two amounts of 15,000 marks to the Social Democratic Party funds in July and November 1932. The revolutionary trade union opposition always opposed the use of trade union money for supporting the capitalist policy of the Social Democrats ; but it is merely political trickery for the National Socialist leaders, who have themselves destroyed the workers' militant organisations, to oppose the use of trade union money for purposes which have nothing to do with the class struggle.

Confiscation of the Social Democratic Party's Property.

The next step was the confiscation of all property belonging to the Social Democratic Party and the Reichsbanner :

" Berlin, May 10th, 1933. An order has been issued for the confiscation of all the property of the Social Democratic Party and of its newspapers, as well as of the Reichsbanner and its Press. The ground for confiscation is the great number of cases of dishonesty which have been discovered as a result of the taking over of the Trade Unions and the Labour Banks by the National Socialist Factory Organisation. In addition to the confiscation of the property of the Social Democratic Party, it must be stated that the property of all organisations connected with the party is also confiscated."

(*Angriff*, May 10th, 1933.)

On the same date all money belonging to the Social Democratic Party in Post Office accounts, party publishing concerns and in the Labour Bank was confiscated. The offices of the Social Democratic organisations, of the Reichsbanner and of the party Press were closed. The official *Preussische Pressedienst* announced that Leipart, the trade union leader and Social Democratic member of the Reichstag, was to be prosecuted for " breach of trust and fraud " on the ground that " specific contributions of trade union money had been used for purposes other than those for which they had been provided."

The same steps were taken against all organisations connected with the Social Democrats : the Workers' Gymnastic and Sports Federation, the German Freethinkers' League, the Workers' Welfare Association, etc. On May 11th the Consumers' Co-operative Society was put " into safe hands " :

" In order to safeguard the immensely valuable property of the Co-operative Societies, which is undoubtedly in danger, in the view of the leader, the Reich Minister for Economics and other authorities concerned, it is necessary to put the Consumers' Co-operative Societies into safe hands with a view to their liquidation.

" It is desirable that the societies in the first instance should not be impeded in their operations. But it is expressly emphasised that on the other hand there should be no further extension of the societies. . . . Dr. Ley, leader of the German Labour Front, has entrusted the director of the Labour Bank, Karl Müller, with the carrying through of the necessary measures."
(*Völkischer Beobachter*, May 12th, 1933.)

Under the slogan of the " fight against corruption " the property of the trade unions was then confiscated :

" Following on the confiscation of the property of the Social Democratic Party and of the Reichsbanner organisation, the Corruption Department of the Prussian Ministry of Justice has now confiscated the entire property of the trade unions. Dr. Ley, the leader of the German Labour Front, has assumed responsibility for carrying this step into effect."

(*Völkischer Beobachter*, May 13th, 1933.)

On June 23rd, 1933, the Hitler Government dissolved the Social Democratic Party in the form which has now become usual : the party was forbidden to undertake any political activity, and its representatives were turned out of all parliaments. Even the support given by the Social Democratic Party to Hitler's declaration on foreign policy, on May 17th in the Reichstag, and the efforts made by Löbe, the new Party leader, to secure toleration from the Hitler Government by repudiating the section of the Social Democratic Party Executive which had emigrated, proved to have been in vain.

Expropriation of Communist Property. On May 27th, 1933, after every piece of property of the Communist Party and of the Press and organisations associated with the party had been confiscated for some months, the following Act on the Confiscation of Communist Property was published :

" I. (1). The Supreme Authorities of the Federal States or officials authorised by them may confiscate for the benefit of the State any property and rights of the Communist Party of Germany and of its auxiliary and substitute organisations as well as property and rights which are used or destined to be used for the furtherance of Communist aims. (2) The Minister of the Interior of the Reich may requisition the Supreme Authorities of the Federal States to take measures for the enforcement of sub-section (1).

" II. The provisions of Section I do not apply to property leased or put at the disposal of the Communist Party without transfer of ownership, except when the lessor or supplier had in view the furtherance of Communist aims.

" III. All existing rights relating to the property which is confiscated are cancelled. The confiscation of real estate does not however affect existing rights affecting the property. The Authorities enforcing the confiscation may declare such rights cancelled where the value given in exchange for the rights was intended for the further-ance of Communist aims.

" IV. In cases of hardship creditors having claims on the confiscated property may receive compensation from the proceeds of this property.

" VII. Provides that no compensation shall be given, and :

" VIII. Empowers Dr. Frick, Reich Minister of the In-terior, to issue regulations for the enforcement of the Act."

The *Welt am Abend*, a militant working-class paper with a big circulation in Berlin, was confiscated among the other property of the Communist Party, or of what were alleged to be Communist organisations. When it became clear that the official National Socialist newspapers were not pene-trating working-class circles, the Goebbels Ministry of Propaganda bethought itself of a new way of deceiving the workers. At the end of May a new National Socialist journal began to appear, with the same title and the same general make-up as the *Welt am Abend*. Its first few issues also followed the nature of the contents of the old paper ; a so-called objective report on the Soviet Union was pub-lished, and in other ways an attempt was made to appeal to working-class readers. But within a very short time the new paper found itself obliged to defend itself publicly against the exposure of its aims which had been made in illegal leaflets circulating among the workers of Berlin.

The " Corporate " Aims of the National Socialists. The clearer it became that the National Socialist Government could do nothing to overcome the economic difficulties facing Germany, but was in fact driving Germany forward to catastrophe, the more brutally the Nazis applied their dictatorial powers. They necessarily pushed forward towards the absorption of all power, towards the monopoly of all power in the hands of their own party and of its pseudo-workers' organisations. The Catholic convention in Munich, at which the Vice-Chancellor von Papen was one of the official speakers, was dissolved by the police. Christian organisations were forbidden to undertake any activity other than religious. The growing rival force of the German Nationalist factory and defence organisations was forcibly destroyed by the police. The few representatives of the Christian trade unions in the newly formed " Great Convention of Labour " which formed the central organisation of all the trade unions which had been " brought into conformity," were thrown out of the Convention under a regulation issued by Dr. Ley on June 23rd, on the ground that they were " enemies of the National Government."

In his " Fundamental Ideas on the Corporate Organisation and the German Labour Front," which were published in the *Völkischer Beobachter* of June 8th–10th, 1933, Dr. Ley sets forth in programmatic form the " Corporate " aims of the National Socialists after the workers' organisations have been destroyed :

A. The workers are forbidden to fight for higher wages, because such a fight is only the expression of " greed for money " ; Ley's actual words are :

" We know how the greed for profit can get control of men, we know how the greed for money dominates everyone. One man strives to get more wages, another strives for higher dividends. But just because we know this we recognise with equal clarity that this ' beast ' within individual men should not be allowed to be nurtured by artificial organisations, but that it must be the task of a higher State leadership to set bounds to this human weakness, to restrain it, if necessary to put brutal (!) limits and barriers in its way . . ."

B. The " leadership " of the employer in the factory is to be restored without any limitation. Dr. Ley says :

" For this reason Corporate organisation will as its first work restore absolute leadership to the natural leader of a factory, that is, the employer, and will at the same time place full responsibility on him. The works council of a factory is composed of workers, employees and employers. Nevertheless, it will have only a consultative voice. Only the employer can decide. Many employers have for years had to call for the ' master in the house.' Now they are once again to be the ' master in the house.' "

C. The " inflexible " wages agreements of the past are to be smashed to pieces. Wages agreements must be " as living and flexible as possible."

D. The last illusion of independence is stripped from the former Labour Courts. Their place is taken by so-called " Corporate Courts," composed of representatives of employers and selected Fascists masquerading as representatives of workers and employees.

The programme put forward by Dr. Ley is not a private suggestion of his own, but a programme worked out at Hitler's instructions, on behalf of the party and the Government. Its hostility to the workers and friendliness towards the employers is obvious. The " Corporate organisation " which is supposed to be going to overcome the division of society into classes and the class struggle is based at all points on the sharpening of the employers' class dictatorship.

The appointment of twelve " Labour Trustees " with power to dictate working conditions in all areas of Germany is to serve the same purpose : the complete abolition of any rights possessed by the workers to a voice in determining their own conditions of life. The occupation by Nazis of all trade union posts and of all positions in the State and every form of organisation paves the way for the establishment of a universal National Socialist bureaucracy. In the conditions existing under capitalism, with the forcible abolition of all control from below, this monopoly must necessarily be the source of the worst forms of corruption.

But each day that passes shows that all the mania for destruction, the arbitrary measures and murder-lust of the National Socialist leaders, is powerless to destroy the militant movement of the German working class.

CHAPTER VI: THE CAMPAIGN AGAINST CULTURE

At the same time as their main attack against the German working class and its organisations, Hitler and Goebbels are also waging war against the best sections of the German intelligentsia. Nazi boots trample on the life work of the most prominent scientists and artists. In the literal sense they trample on the brutally treated bodies of many intellectuals, who are hated by the Nazis on account of their independence, their progressive and liberal outlook, although in many cases they have had no connection whatever with the militant workers. Under Hitler even a liberal outlook is a crime which must be mercilessly avenged.

Goebbels commands the Brown inquisitors, who think that they can turn back the wheel of history to long before the French Revolution. Everything Jewish or supposedly Marxist, everything that embodies the progress and enlightenment of the last hundred and fifty years, is to be rooted out. In Hitler's Germany there is no room for conceptions of any " spiritual freedom," for any moderate goodwill felt by bourgeois professors to scientific impartiality, for even the most distant expression of the social struggle for the freedom of the masses in works of art. These are driven from professional chairs, from the stage, from the desks of lecturers and conductors ; they are driven from the hospitals, from the research institutes and the academies. The pyres of advanced literature in German city squares blazon far into the distance the message that the Brown barbarians intend not only to extirpate physically the most courageous and self-sacrificing anti-Fascists, but also to destroy everything of any vitality and worth and even anything that was at all progressive even from a bourgeois standpoint.

The last standard-bearers of intellectual " liberalism " are now being physically and intellectually murdered by that Brown force which the ruling powers have unchained in order to postpone the collapse of the capitalist system. The most recent events in Germany have shown more clearly than ever that in our epoch the future of culture is inseparably connected with the working class struggle for freedom.

Persecution of Scientists.   Fascism's deadly hatred is naturally directed against those intellectuals who have sided with the working class struggle for freedom or are connected with pacifist organisations. The attack on them followed immediately after the burning of the Reichstag. The first series of arrests which began after the incendiary act of the Brown *provocateurs* affected particularly the German group of the League of Doctors against Imperialist War which had been formed at Amsterdam. Since the end of February the leader of this group, Dr. Felix Boenheim, has been in one of Hitler's prisons. Dr. Boenheim is an extremely respected specialist for internal diseases, and his many scientific works have made him famous. He belongs to no party. The scientific importance of his works secured for him a responsible post in the Hufeland Hospital, one of the largest in Berlin. The mere fact that Dr. Felix Boenheim put himself at the head of the doctors' movement against war has been enough to expose him to the undying hate of the Hitler Fascists. His work on behalf of the international doctors' league has been arbitrarily denounced as " high treason." He has not been allowed any legal aid. In spite of his imprisonment for several months he has been refused any contact with his family.

Max Hodann, known for his activities in the sphere of advice to working men and women in sexual matters, and author of a number of popular scientific works, has for some months been in the hands of Hitler's myrmidons.

The well-known Marxist scientist Hermann Duncker, a name which ranks high in the workers' movement throughout the world, was imprisoned in spite of his age and the fact that he was seriously ill. His life is in serious danger.

F†

The man who was regarded by a whole generation of social democratic workers as one of their most esteemed teachers is now being physically and mentally destroyed in Hitler's prisons.

The writer Karl August Wittfogel, author of an extremely well-informed book on China, the writers Ludwig Renn, Karl von Ossietzky, Kurt Hiller, Egon Erwin Kisch, Erich Mühsam, Klaus Neukrantz, Erich Baron and many others, and the doctors Professor Scheller of Breslau, Dr. Asch of Berlin, and Dr. Wohlgemuth of Hamburg have been arrested. The scientific institutes, universities and schools are to be turned into drill-halls for " Storm troop culture." The persecution of scientists of high standing who are suspected of Marxist, pacifist or liberal ideas, touches even the ranks of the German Nationalist Party. The lecturing staffs of the most important German universities are being wiped out with a relentlessness worthy of the Vandals. Denunciation and the grabbing of posts by incompetent but at least ambitious "near-scientists" are now the order of the day.

The Flower of German Science Driven Out. We select only a few examples from the list of dismissals, persecutions and of persons " granted leave of absence." The best known case is that of Albert Einstein, whose reputation as a physicist is world-wide. Albert Einstein, a Swiss subject, member of the Prussian Academy of Sciences, has incurred the hatred of the Nazis for his left-democratic political views, his active interest in the Jewish question and his world-renowned scientific achievements. Einstein's scientific works were burnt in the bonfire at the University of Berlin, amid the delighted howls of the Nazis. This act alone is enough to make Hitler's Germany a laughing-stock in the world of modern science.

No branch of modern industry can thrive without the exact sciences. But Hitler's régime has driven from their posts the most outstanding representatives of the exact sciences and mathematics. The University of Göttingen has a long tradition behind it, and in the last fifty years has trained a whole generation of brilliant research workers. The most prominent professors of this University have been driven out.

James Franck, an experimental physicist with a world-wide reputation and a Nobel prize winner, was forced to take " voluntary " leave of absence because he is a Jew.

Professor Born, also a well-known physicist, is no longer allowed to carry on his " un-German " researches in Germany.

Courandt is a mathematician, an authority on the theory of functions. Bernstein is one of the most important European experts in actuarial mathematics. Emmy Noether has a reputation in the field of mathematics and higher algebra. All of these were driven out.

The Berlin Faculty of Mathematics was also deprived of its most outstanding teachers, and the Berlin Technical University has also to record heavy losses. Among those who have been driven out is Professor Arthur Korn, a physicist who invented the first practical method of achieving television. The Berlin mathematicians who were sacrificed in the " cleansing " of the university include Schur, the algebraist, and Professors Misses and Bieberbach. This outburst of fury directed against the representatives of the exact sciences is suicidal even from the standpoint of the modern capitalist development of industry, and stands in sharp contrast with the opportunities which the Soviet Union has offered to all genuine scientists.

Among the victims of the Nazi cleansing there is a Nobel prize winner of the name of Fritz Haber. Haber, the leader of an important school of chemists, was a scientific figure of the first rank even before the war. He invented the first practical method of obtaining nitrogen from the air. He is anything but a pacifist. During the war his inventions were of the greatest service to Imperial Germany. His name represents the highest development of modern German chemistry. *The Times* of May 4th, 1933, justly remarked that it is an irony of fate that the Nazis should " compel " this man to resign his post, when the fact that Germany was able to hold out for four years was in all probability due to him more than to any other man. Professor Polanyi, who was also driven out, was one of Haber's principal colleagues.

Among others who had to make room for the cultural barbarism of the Nazis we must also mention Professor Bück of Berlin, who has worked on the Planckian quantum theory ; the Königsberg mathematician Hensel, known for his original work on the theory of number ; the Kiel professor Adolf Frankel, author of an important work on the theory of quantity ; and the Berlin physicist Pringsheim, whose works deal with important problems of radiation.

All the scientists mentioned are well-known research workers and lecturers of high standing in scientific circles. Even this very incomplete list is enough to show that these expulsions amount to the virtual destruction of German science, that German Fascism is fighting every scientific advance with its inquisitions and incendiarism.

No Passports for Scientists.   The appointment of Albert Einstein to the Institute of France, and the lectures given in Stockholm by Professor Bernhard Zondek, a dismissed gynæcologist, led to the demand being seriously put forward that the passports of expelled University professors should be taken from them—that the " un-German " spirit of these scientists should not be allowed to benefit foreign universities. In connection with Einstein's appointment at the Institute of France, the *Tägliche Rundschau*, a journal of the Right, on April 17th, 1933, demanded that the Government should at once deprive the sixteen dismissed university professors of their passports, as otherwise there could be no guarantee that one or other of them might not shortly occupy a chair in Paris, Oxford or London, and use that post to carry on his anti-German politics ; that in this connection it was necessary to remember that some of these professors, such as Kelsen, Lederer and Bonn, had extremely good connections abroad.

Germany's Greatest Doctors may not Work in Germany.
Bernhard Zondek has been described by Euler, the
Swedish Nobel Prize winner for medicine, as " the one
outstanding genius." Zondek invented a method of chemical
analysis of the urine which makes it possible to ascertain
pregnancy in the earliest stages. This method is of extreme
importance for social hygiene as well as from the purely
medical standpoint. Zondek has done brilliant work in
the investigation of hormones. He has been attempting to
produce the sex hormones, substances which are different
in men and women ; their existence was only recently
discovered. He is one of the pioneers in this method of
research, and quite recently achieved astounding success
in the " artificial " reproduction of sex hormones. But the
Hitler Government deprives him of his professorial chair !

Friedmann, who has been carrying on research into
tuberculosis, has been removed from his post in Berlin.
He is the inventor of a very valuable anti-tuberculosis
serum, tuberculin.

Moritz Borchardt, director of the surgical department in
the Moabit Hospital in Berlin, was in his youth an assistant
of the famous German surgeon von Bergmann, and subsequently doctor in charge of the Virchow Hospital in Berlin ;
he has applied surgery in the fight against tuberculosis.
He has now been removed from his post by a National
Socialist " Commissioner of Health."

**The Destruction of the Hirschfeld Sexual Science In-
stitute.**   A reliable witness who, although not himself
attached to the Institute, was able to see and hear exactly
what occurred, has made the following deposition as to
the destruction of this scientific institute, which is known
throughout the world :

" On the morning of May 6th, the *Berliner Lokalanzeiger*
reported that the cleansing of Berlin libraries of books
of un-German spirit would be begun that morning, and
that the students of the Gymnastic Academy would make

a start with the Sexual Science Institute. This institute was founded by Dr. Magnus Hirschfeld in 1918, in the house formerly occupied by Prince Hatzfeld, and was shortly afterwards taken over by the Prussian Government as an institution of public importance. Its unique collection of exhibits, its research work, its archives and its library won for it an international reputation and international connections. Many foreign scientists, doctors and writers came to Berlin for the purpose of working at the institute."

" On the publication of the press notice referred to, an attempt was made to remove for safe-keeping some of the most valuable private books and manuscripts ; but this proved to be impossible, as the person removing the books was arrested by a guard which had evidently been placed round the institute during the night. At 9.30 a.m. some lorries drew up in front of the institute with about one hundred students and a brass band. They drew up in military formation in front of the institute, and then marched into the building with their band playing. As the office was not yet open, there was no responsible person there ; there were only a few women and one man. The students demanded admittance to every room, and broke in the doors of those which were closed, including the office of the World League for Sexual Reform. When they found that there was not much to be had in the lower rooms, they made their way up to the first floor, where they emptied the ink bottles over manuscripts and carpets and then made for the book-cases. They took away whatever they thought not completely unobjectionable, working for the most part on the basis of the so-called ' black list.' But they went beyond this, and took other books also, including for example a large work on Tutankhamen and a number of art journals which they found among the secretary's private books. They then removed from the archives the large charts dealing with intersexual cases, which had been prepared for the

International Medical Congress held at the Kensington Museum in London in 1913. They threw most of these charts through the windows to their comrades who were standing outside.

" They removed from the walls other drawings and photographs of special types and kicked them round the room, leaving it strewn with torn drawings and broken glass. When one of the students pointed out that this was medical material, another replied that this was of no importance, that they were not concerned with the confiscation of a few books and pictures, but that they were there to destroy the Institute. A long speech was then made, and a life-sized model showing the internal secretion process was thrown out of the window and smashed to pieces. In one of the consulting rooms they used a mop to smash a pantostat used in the treatment of patients. They also took away a bronze bust of Dr. Hirschfeld, and a number of other statues. On the first occasion they only seized a few hundred books out of the library of the Institute.

" The staff was kept under observation during the whole of the proceedings, and the band played throughout, so that a large crowd of inquisitive people gathered outside. At 12 o'clock the leader made a long speech, and then the gang left, singing a particularly vulgar song and also the *Horst-Wessel* song.

" The people in the Institute assumed that this concluded the robbery proceedings, but at three o'clock in the afternoon a number of lorries filled with storm troopers appeared and explained that they would have to continue the work of confiscation, as the men who had been there in the morning had not had time to make a proper clearance. This second troop then proceeded to make a careful search through every room, taking down to the lorries basket after basket of valuable books and manuscripts—two lorry-loads in all. It was clear from the oaths used that the names of the authors whose books were in the special library were well known to the students. Siegmund Freud, whose photograph they took from the staircase and carried off, was called ' that Jewish sow Freud ' ; and Havelock Ellis was called ' that swine.' Other English authors wanted by them were Oscar Wilde, Edward Carpenter, and Norman Haire ; and also the works of Judge Lindsay, the American juvenile judge, Margaret Sanger, and George Silvester Viereck ; and of French writers, the works of André Gide, Marcel Proust, Pierre Loti, Zola, etc. The sight of the works of the Danish doctor Leunbach also made them break out into oaths. Many bound volumes of periodicals were also removed. They also wanted to take away several thousand questionnaires which were among the records, but desisted when they were assured that these were simply medical histories. On the other hand, it did not prove possible to dissuade them from removing the material belonging to the World League for Sexual Reform, the whole edition of the journal *Sexus* and the card index. In addition, a great many manuscripts, including many unpublished ones, fell into their hands.

" They repeatedly enquired when Dr. Hirschfeld would be returning ; they wanted, as they expressed it, to be given the tip as to when he would be there. Even before this raid on the Institute storm troopers had visited it on several occasions and asked for Dr. Hirschfeld. When they were told that he was abroad, owing to an attack of malaria, they replied : ' Then let's hope he'll die without our aid : then we shan't have to hang him or beat him to death.'

" On May 7th, the Berlin and foreign press reported the attack on the Sexual Science Institute, and the Executive Committee of the World League for Sexual Reform sent a telegraphic protest, pointing out that a considerable portion of the material was foreign property, and asking that it should at least not be burnt. No attention was paid to this telegram, which was addressed to the Minister of Education, and three days later all the books and photographs, together with a large number of other works, were burnt on the Opera square. More than ten thousand volumes from the special library of the Institute were destroyed. The students carried Dr. Hirschfeld's bust in their torchlight procession and threw it on the fire."

The Nazi report described this "deed of culture" in the following terms :

ENERGETIC ACTION AGAINST A POISON SHOP
GERMAN STUDENTS FUMIGATE THE "SEXUAL SCIENCE INSTITUTE"

"Detachment X of the German student organisation yesterday occupied the 'Sexual Science Institute,' which was controlled by the Jew Magnus Hirschfeld. This institute, which tried to shelter behind a scientific cloak and was always protected during the fourteen years of Marxist rule by the authorities of that period, was an unparalleled breeding-ground of dirt and filth, as the results of the search have proved beyond question. A whole lorry-load of pornographic pictures and writings as well as documents and registers have been confiscated. . . . The criminal police will have to deal with a part of the material found ; another part of it will be publicly burnt."—(*Angriff*, May 6th, 1933.)

"Un-German" Sociologists and Jurists.   In turning out well-known sociologists and jurists the National Socialists have also got rid of many good conservative elements. The best known of these dismissed professors is the Heidelberg sociologist, Alfred Weber, who in conjunction with his brother Max Weber, now dead, published many profound studies of the forms of development of the primitive economy of a number of peoples and cultures in countries outside Europe. Weber is by no means a Marxist, but a bourgeois professor ; but he committed the mortal sin of not describing other peoples and cultures as half-apish and " sub-human " as laid down by National Socialism. The Berlin Commercial Academy loses its rector, the prominent liberal economist Professor Bonn. The Professor of Constitutional Law, Anschütz, was compelled to leave Heidelberg University. He had been for many years a professor at Berlin University ; even in Imperial Germany he was an authority of the first rank in his sphere, and subsequently he was an authoritative commentator on the Weimar Constitution.

Many of his colleagues were also sent into the wilderness : Professor Kelsen of Cologne ; Harms, his colleague at Kiel ; Feiler, former editor of the *Frankfurter Zeitung* ; the Right Social Democrat Emil Radbruch, the Social Democrats Sinzheimer in Frankfurt, Lederer in Heidelberg and Heller in Frankfurt—all of them jurists. The greatest German authority on civil law, Professor Martin Wolff, was forcibly driven out of his lecture-room by swastika students. The liberal Lewin Schücking, of Kiel, an authority on international law, who represented Germany at the Hague International Tribunal, was driven from his post.

Prominent psychologists, too, were driven from their lecture-rooms. William Stern, of Hamburg, who has published important works on child psychology, and Max Wertheimer, of Frankfurt, are no longer allowed to lecture at German Universities. In Hamburg, in addition to a half-dozen of less well-known professors, the philosopher Ernst Cassirer was dismissed ; he was a man of great learning and reputation, of the so-called Marburg school.

Books by Weight.   " In Berlin the political police have confiscated approximately 10,000 hundredweight of books and periodicals and removed them to the stables of the former mounted police, where they are being carefully examined. The seizure of the books was not carried out everywhere without friction. As soon as it became known that the operation was in progress, many libraries put their books into hiding places to prevent their seizure by the police. Most of the hiding places were however discovered. Many of the books were found scattered in coach-houses, cellars, sheds, under floors and in private houses."— (*Völkischer Beobachter*, May 21st, 1933.)

On the bonfires.

"We are not and do not want to be the land of Goethe and Einstein. Not on any account." (*Berliner Lokal-Anzeiger*, May 7th, 1933.)

When the caliph wanted to burn the famous library of Alexandria, some people begged him to preserve this valuable collection.

"Why?" asked the caliph. "If these books contain what is in the Koran, then they are superfluous. And if anything else is in them, then they are pernicious."

And so the library of Alexandria was burnt.

On May 10th the square in front of the Berlin opera house, opposite the university, was aglow with the flames of a great bonfire. The whole square was cordoned off with brown and black detachments of the storm troops and protective corps. Lorries brought in gigantic heaps of books. Bands played, orders rang out, the Minister of Propaganda, Goebbels, rushed up in a car. In the year 1933 this extraordinary spectacle of the burning of books took place, to the sound of the *Horst-Wessel* and *Deutschland* songs.

On to the bonfire were thrown the works of Karl Marx, Friedrich Engels, Lenin and Stalin, Rosa Luxemburg, Karl Liebknecht and August Bebel. "Deutschland, Deutschland über alles!"

On to the bonfire were thrown the works of pacifist writers, bourgeois poets and social reformers, whose names ranked high in bourgeois Germany. The flames consumed the works of Thomas Mann and Heinrich Mann, Leonhard Frank, Magnus Hirschfeld, Siegmund Freud, Jacob Wassermann, Stefan Zweig, Bert Brecht, Alfred Döblin and Theodor Plivier. "Deutschland, Deutschland über alles!"

This destruction of all advanced creations of the intellect took place not far away from the pedestal of Alexander and Wilhelm von Humboldt in the Berlin University. Wilhelm von Humboldt, who founded this university and became one of the standard-bearers of the spirit of the Enlightenment, aimed at raising Junker Prussia to the level of the bourgeois world of the West. Now German students in Nazi uniform carried out this pogrom against advanced literature, in front of his statue. " Deustchland, Deutschland über alles ! "

The crackling flames in front of Berlin University, the pall of smoke over the heads of a chauvinistic mob, a speech from Goebbels, Reich Minister of Propaganda—this made a spectacle which the *Berliner 12 Uhr-Mittagsblatt*, a loyal Hitler journal, with unconscious irony described as " spectral." It has forgotten the fires lighted by the oppressors of every age, and what came of them. The flames in front of Berlin University were to consume not only Marxist works, but the highest achievements of bourgeois culture and science of the last hundred and fifty years.

The mania for the destruction of all advanced literature raged through every province of Germany. Tens of thousands of private libraries were confiscated in the course of raids on houses, and often destroyed on the spot. The library in the Leipzig Volkshaus, one of the largest and most valuable libraries in Germany, with rare and irreplaceable publications of the working-class movement, fell victim to the Brown " culture-bearers' " hatred of Marxism.

Here are some instances of the public burning of books, reported by the German National *Telegrafen-Union* of May 10th :

" Berlin, May 10th. In Munich a ceremony was carried out in the inner court of the University, which was presided over by the rector. The official speech was made by the Bavarian Minister of Education, who spoke of the national revolution and the tasks of the universities. At the end of the proceedings there was a torchlight procession to the Königsplatz, where the burning of un-German books was carried out.

" In Dresden the poet Wilhelm Vesper spoke at the students' demonstration ; here too there was a long torchlight procession to the Bismarck colonnade, where after an address by the senior Dresden student all filthy and disgusting literature was burnt.

" In Breslau the students' demonstration took place at the castle square. After the official speech by Professor Bornhausen about forty hundredweight of filthy and shameful books were burnt.

" In Frankfurt-am-Main Professor Fricke opened the proceedings, which took place on the historic Römer-burg. A wagon filled with the books which were to be burnt as a symbol was drawn by two oxen to the place where the bonfire had been made. The burning of the books concluded with the singing of the *Horst-Wessel* song."

A few days earlier the works of the great German poet Heinrich Heine had been committed to the flames in Düsseldorf.

In his speech at Berlin, Herr Goebbels spoke of the burning of the books as " a very symbolical act." The burning was not symbolical. The German Fascist reactionaries are determined in actual fact, and quite unsymbolically, to burn anything printed which does not suit them, just as they are determined physically to exterminate all writers and distributors of anti-Fascist literature.

A Black List.   The Hugenberg organ, the *Nachtausgabe*, published on April 26th, 1933, the following black list of literature which deserved to be burnt :

BELLES LETTRES : Schalom Asch, Henri Barbusse, Bertholt Brecht, Max Brod (excepting his novel *Tycho Brahé*), Alfred Döblin (except for *Wallenstein*), Ilja Ehrenburg, Albert Ehrenstein, Arthur Floesser, Lion

Feuchtwanger, Iwan Goll, Jaroslav Hassek, Walter Hasenclever, Arthur Holitscher, Heinrich Eduard Jacob, Joseph Kalenikow, Gina Kaus, Egon Erwin Kisch, Heinz Liepmann, Heinrich Mann (except *Flöten und Dolche*), Klaus Mann, Robert Neumann, Ernst Ottwald, Kurt Pinthus, Theodor Plivier, Erich Maria Remarque, Ludwig Renn (only *Nachkrieg*), Alfred Schirokauer, Arthur Schnitzler, Richard Beer-Hoffmann, Ernst Toller, Kurt Tucholski, Arnold Zweig, Stefan Zweig, and *Katherine wird Soldat*, by Adrienne Thomas.

POLITICAL SCIENCE : Lenin, Karl Liebknecht, Karl Marx, Hugo Preuss, Walter Rathenau, Rudolf Hilferding, August Bebel, Max Adler, S. Aufhäusser, E. I. Gumbel, N. Bucharin, L. Bauer and Helen Keller. All of Lassalle, except his *Assizes Speeches* and *On the special connection of the present Historical Period with the idea of the Workers as a Class*.

HISTORY : In general, all pacifist and "defeatist" works, also all pro-Bolshevik literature on Russian history, must be destroyed ; this includes the works of Otto Bauer, Karl Tschuppik, Oskar Blum, Paul Hahn, Müller-Franken, Kurt Kersten's *Bismarck und seine Zeit*, Franz Mehring's *Zur deutschen Geschichte* and *Zur preussischen Geschichte*, and the works of Glasier and Upton Sinclair.

Gutjahr, head of the Berlin-Brandenburg section of the German students' organisation, directed the burning of the books on the square in front of Berlin University. In addition to the works of the authors enumerated above, he also ordered to be thrown on to the flames the works of Engels, Siegmund Freud, Emil Ludwig, Alfred Kerr, Ossietzky, Theodor Wolff, Georg Bernhard, Bertha von Suttner, Rosa Luxemburg, Theodor Heuss, Freiherr von Schöneich and Vandevelde.

The ideological weakness of the Brown rulers manifests itself in this war of destruction waged against science and literature for the purpose of destroying everything that is necessary to an understanding of the history of culture and science. But Hitler's burning of all the works of progressive German thought cannot wipe out the memory of what mankind has owed in the past to German thought. The flames of the fires on the Berlin Opera Square have not destroyed Germany's ability to help forward the development of human culture. Not Hitler, Goebbels, Goering and Rust are the representatives of the " real German mind," but the millions of men and women whom the Hitler régime is now persecuting as anti-Fascist workers, scientists, artists and intellectuals.

" Cleansing " of the Prussian Academy of Poets.   We are not here concerned with whether the Prussian Academy of Poets has produced any positive and really creative work during the existence of the Weimar Republic. Measured by their swastika successors, the poets who have been ejected from the Academy or forced to resign from it are indeed giants.

First among the " purged " members of the Academy is Thomas Mann, the Nobel Prize winner and perhaps the most representative writer of bourgeois Germany. His " crime " was that in recent years he had been drawing closer to a Social Democratic standpoint and had even on several occasions raised his voice against deliberate judicial murders, as in the cases of Sacco and Vanzetti and Rahosi. He once described the National Socialist Party as " the most noxious refuse of the age," and this crime will never be forgiven him.

His brother Heinrich Mann tried to maintain the position of " a free and independent mind." He caricatured the middle-class of Imperial Germany (" Der Untertan ") and also of the Republic (" Die grosse Sache "). He supported the Amsterdam international anti-war movement, and he has therefore, like his brother, had his books burnt and he himself has been hunted out by Hitler's "culture bearers."

Jacob Wassermann is another of the writers who has incurred the Nazis' hatred ; his books have been translated into many languages. His chief crime is that he is a Jew and that he has expressed liberal ideas in his novels.

Alfred Döblin, by profession a doctor in a working-class quarter of Berlin, also wrote a number of fantastic and, to some extent, exotic novels (*Die drei Sprünge des Wang Lun, Wallenstein, Berge, Meere und Giganten*). His last novel was *Berlin Alexanderplatz*. In public debates Döblin described himself as a " class-conscious bourgeois." He experimented a great deal in his style and treatment, somewhat like the Irishman James Joyce and the American Dos Passos.

Franz Werfel, who never went outside the range of bourgeois ideas, was the pioneer of expressionism twenty years ago. His novel *Verdi* won him great popularity. The Nazis could not leave him alone.

Others ejected were René Schickelé, the German poet of Alsatian origin ; and Leonhard Frank, author of the anti-war book *Der Mensch ist gut*, and the novels *Die Räuberbande* and *Die Ursache*. Although he had been moving to the Right during recent years, his past was enough to win for him the Nazis' hate.

Dramatists turned out of the Academy included Georg Kaiser, whose talent was unique though extremely anarchist in tendency ; and Fritz von Unruh, the dramatist of the Weimar Republic. Bernhard Kellermann, a gifted story-writer of liberal tendencies, the poets Mombert and Rudolf Panwitz, and Ludwig Fulda, a writer of comedies, were all ejected. One of the few German women writers of any literary ability, Ricarda Huch, resigned from the Academy early in April. Among the politically colourless members of the Academy, such as Oskar Loerke and Jakob Schaffner, Gerhardt Hauptmann must also be mentioned : these were allowed to remain in the Academy. Hauptmann, who wrote the story of the weavers, had already been through many " transformations." During the war he was one of the 93 intellectuals who signed a manifesto supporting the war-lords. After the war he became the official poet of the Weimar Republic. And now he maintained a determined silence when the Brown terror was driving the best bourgeois writers and scientists out of the country.

And now for the men whom Rust, the Nazi Minister of Education, has brought into the Prussian Academy of Poets. The leading figure is Hans Johst, who once eagerly supported the revolution. But the crime of November 1918 is now forgiven. He is the only National Socialist writer who has achieved a certain reputation. At present his *Schlageter* drama is being played, on instructions from the Hitler Government, in hundreds of German theatres ; its hero declares : " When I hear the word culture, I get my Browning ready ! "

Herr Rust's special attractions in the Academy, apart from Hans Carossa, are quite insignificant writers like Emil Strauss, Will Vesper, Wilhelm Schäfer, Agnes Miegel and Peter Dörfler. Hans Grimm wrote a novel on " the nation without room for expansion," and Börris von Münchhausen has written slight ballads expressing German sentiments.

In their endeavour to find names of any kind of significance the National Socialists even approached the poet Stefan George, the most snobbish and superior of all German poets, hoping to be able to use his name to grace Adolf Hitler's cultural policy.

Brown Poetry.   Dr. Josef Goebbels, Minister of Propaganda in the Third Empire, wrote a novel called *Michael : a German destiny in diary form.* Michael, the yearning German soul, has visions. Evil appears to him in the form of Ivan, the Russian, who tries to entice him into Bolshevism. Michael's soul struggles with the tempter :

> *But I am stronger than he.*
> *Now I have him by the throat.*
> *Now I hurl him to the ground.*
> *There he lies.*

The death rattle in his throat, and bloodshot eyes.
Perish, carrion ! I trample on his brains.
And now I am free !

That is the spirit which makes a man worthy of the Hitlerised Academy of Poets : " I trample on his brains ! Perish, carrion ! "

The notorious writer Hanns Heinz Ewers, who was appointed by Goebbels as head of the Association of German Authors after it had been " brought into conformity " has not yet been officially admitted to the Academy of Poets. His pornographic novels, *Alraune* and *Der Vampyr* were subsequently put on the list of " filthy and disgusting literature " by the Nazis themselves (and they were the only ones which really deserved it !) ; but he is the official biographer of Horst Wessel, the hero of National Socialism. On Hitler's birthday a " Horst Wessel " play by Ewers was broadcast by the German wireless. This writer's existence had been completely forgotten for many years until he was resurrected to be the official poet of the " Third Empire." In 1922 Ewers wrote a foreword, expressing great sympathy for the Jews, to Israel Zangwill's *Die Stimme von Jerusalem.* But the state of the market has altered since then, and Ewers has become an anti-Semite.

Thus the Prussian Academy of Poets has been reconstructed under the banner of the spirit which expresses itself in such an " awakening lyric " as the following :

All little birds are already there !
(Air : " Nun ade " and " All little birds.")

1. *Now adieu, my dear Fatherland.*
   At Strassburg
   A great lamentation begins.
   Hail to thee in thy crown of victory.
   A summons thunders through the land.
   Rosa Luxemburg is floating in the canal :
   Karl Liebknecht is hanging on the . . . tree !

2. *All little birds are already there!*
   All little birds, all,
   Thrush, finch and tit
   And the Reichsbanner black-red . . .
   What . . . a pity that there's no gold,
   For ever a pity!

[From *Germany Awake!* the small Nazi song book, Edition B, published by Paul Arend, Sulzbach, Oberpfalz, 8th (!) Edition.]

It must not be thought that this gem of Brown poetry, broadcast in the eighth edition, is not typical ; there is no difference between this and the most popular Nazi songs :

When Jewish blood spurts from under the knife,
Things will be twice as good as before.

Or :

The red brood, beat them to a pulp !
Storm troops are on the march—clear the way !

The Campaign against " un-German " Music.

Herr Josef Goebbels, Reich Minister of Propaganda, told the German theatre managers and actors on May 9th that : " Art comes from ability and not from the will." By way of illustrating this fine sentiment we give below a further list of losses to German art.

Bruno Walter, Otto Klemperer and Fritz Busch were always reckoned among the best creative artists of Germany. For some years Otto Klemperer directed the Kroll opera house in Berlin, and under him it became a centre of modern music ; it was he who brought forward Hindemith and Kurt Weill. Klemperer was subsequently appointed to the State Opera House in Berlin, where he continued his work along the same lines. Now he has been forced to give up his conductor's baton because he is of Jewish origin.

Bruno Walter, a conductor with a reputation throughout

the world, is a Jew. And as " Art comes from ability," he may no longer conduct in Germany. His place is taken by a certain Herr Fuhsel, official musician to the Nazis (he was commander of a large brass band), in connection with whom no one can use the terms art and ability ; but he will now show the awakened German nation how music is made.

Busch, the musical director in Dresden, is fair, and so his " Aryan " origin cannot be disputed. He is a conservative, but as it happens not a Nazi. He brought a new era of fame to the Dresden Opera House. During the " national revolt " a Nazi denunciator appeared on the stage in the middle of a performance, and demanded that Busch should resign his post.

> " Berlin, March 8th. Yesterday evening sixty Nazi storm troopers occupied the stage of the Municipal Opera House, during the performance of *Rigoletto*, led by the famous conductor Busch. According to the account given by the *Vossische Zeitung*, the leader of the Nazis told the audience that in future he himself would direct the theatre, and that the conductor Strieger would conduct the orchestra instead of Busch. As Busch nevertheless attempted to continue conducting, a terrific uproar arose among the Nazis who were present, and Busch was compelled to leave, while Strieger took his place at the conductor's desk."

The best known German pianist is Arthur Schnabel, who in the course of thirty years work has developed into an interpreter of the great music written for the piano. He conducted an advanced class for piano music at the Berlin Academy of Music ; and he has been turned out because he is a Jew. Two of his colleagues have also been turned out of the Academy : Emil Feuermann, who is now the only German 'cellist of any standing, and Leonid Kreutzer, a good pianist and teacher. The first-rate violinist Karl Flesch has been dismissed ; also the well-known conductors

Oskar Fried, Fritz Stiedry and Gustav Brecher, as well as the prominent pianist Bruno Eisner.

Of the creative musicians in Germany, Marx von Schillings immediately joined the Nazis ; his compositions are not original, and his conducting nowhere gets beyond the formal pattern. Schillings, who under the Republic accepted high positions, became president of the Academy after Max Liebermann's resignation. He has found a friend equally loyal to the Nazis in the composer Hans Pfitzner ; and another representative composer, Richard Strauss, has joined them. It is true that the latter's works, viewed from the Nazi standpoint, would satisfy the " wanton Jewish sensual appetites " ; but he is now on the way to becoming an official composer.

Hardly a single one of the modern German composers remains with the Nazis. Arnold Schönberg has been driven out of his post at the Academy of Music ; whatever one thinks of his music, he has certainly had the most important influence on the development of modern music. In politics a conservative, Schönberg was a formal revolutionary in music, and found a new and original musical language. But Nazi Germany cannot use this pioneer.

One of the best known German composers is Kurt Weill, whom Hitler's Germany has proscribed. He wrote the *Dreigroschen* opera, which achieved success throughout the world. But he is a Jew, and so he is now homeless.

Franz Schreker, the best known of whose operas is *Der Ferne Klang*, was ejected from the Association of the Academy of Music ; he is by no means particularly progressive, but his origin is " not above reproach."

The special hate of the Nazis was directed against the first proletarian revolutionary composer, Hans Eisler, who has also been driven out of Germany. In recent years he has provided the German working class with choral pieces (" Die Massnahme ") and popular fighting songs which were sung in meetings and on the streets, and will soon become known in other countries. His music was consciously and consistently made for the working class ;

Hitler's Germany offered him either the drilling of the concentration camps or a martyr's death in some Nazi barracks.

German music, which for some time has been in a general state of crisis, has now been deprived of its best forces. As a result of this action, the most famous conductor in the world, Arthuro Toscanini, who works in Mussolini's Italy, has refused to take part in the Bayreuth festival in connection with the anniversary of Richard Wagner. Early in June he sent the following telegram to Frau Winnifred Wagner :

" As events in Germany, which violate my feelings as an artist and as a man, in spite of my hopes show no change up to the present, I consider it to be my duty to break the silence which I have imposed on myself for the last two months, and to inform you that for my and your and everyone's peace of mind it is better not to think any more of my coming to Bayreuth. With sentiments of unalterable friendship for the house of Wagner : Arturo Toscanini."

Theatre—Painting—Films.   The chauvinistic glorification of Schlageter and the idealisation of Horst Wessel now dominate the German stage. Herr Goebbels has had his " well-known " drama *Der Wanderer* presented at a Berlin theatre.

All actors who had given proof of any artistic ability are no longer to be seen on the German stage. All State, municipal and private theatres have been " brought into conformity." The Actors' Associations have been brought under the control of Fascist commissioners. Fritz Kortner, Max Pallenberg, Massary and Bergner, and the stage managers Max Reinhardt and Jessner, have been driven out of Germany as " un-German."

The artistic abilities of the opera stars Lotte Schöne, Frieda Leider, Alexander Kipnis, among others, no longer count under the dictatorship of Rust's Brown culture. The proletarian singer and actor Ernst Busch, a highly-gifted artist, who popularised Eisler's proletarian songs and won a name for himself among the German workers, was hunted out of Germany.

Jewish Actors only to play in negative rôles. The UFA Film Company issued instructions that in their future films Jewish actors were only to be used in negative rôles, such as swindlers, criminals and pathological cases.

On June 6th a general meeting was held of the Union of Stage Directors, which has been incorporated in the National Socialist "League of Fighters for German Culture." The Government Commissioner, Hinkel, announced at this meeting that there would be a new "cleansing" campaign among professional actors.

"On the recommendation of the Prussian Ministry of Education to the head of the Government, Goering, the formation of a Prussian Theatre Commission has been announced. The work of this Commission, of which Hinkel will be chairman, will be to investigate the position of all stage managers, musical directors, conductors and soloists connected with all municipal theatres. Decrees will shortly be issued to facilitate the annulment, extension or alteration of agreements in order to ensure that no obstacles stand in the way of the artistic work which is essential in the German theatre. Legal measures will be taken to provide for the dissolution of private obligations where these are in conflict with the interests of the German theatre."

—(*Frankfurter Zeitung*, June 8th, 1933.)

The Nazi work of destruction is being carried on in every field of art. The president of the Academy of Arts, the painter Max Liebermann, a conservative in politics, was compelled to resign his post on the basis of the Aryan clause. It goes without saying that Käthe Kollwitz, the gifted artist of working-class life, was banished by the Nazis. The number of painters and artists who have fallen victims to the " German cleansing " is legion.

The best known and most progressive film directors have been forced to leave Germany to find employment. All film artists associated with the working-class movement and all proletarian or progressive films have been placed on the black list. The following are some of the films which were immediately prohibited by the Hitler Government :

Kuhle Wampe
Niemandsland
Kameradschaft
Mutter Krause
Die andere Seite
Das Testament des Dr. Mabuse
Im Westen Nichts Neues
Frauenglück—Frauennot
Hölzerne Kreuze (a French film).

Soviet films banned included :

The Path to Life
Storm over Asia
Mother
Menschenarsenal
Ten Days that Shook the World
The End of St. Petersburg.

Woe to those who are suspected of too close connection with working-class films ! An example of this is the imprisonment and maltreatment of Dr. A. Steigler by storm troopers and auxiliary police. Steigler was director of a film company in Berlin which in the course of its work rented Russian films. This was enough : the offices of the company were occupied by storm troops and police and the whole staff was arrested. All films were confiscated, and the offices sealed up. The staff was taken to the Maikäfer barracks in Berlin, where in the presence of his employees Dr. Steigler was subjected to the most terrible maltreatment and torture. Storm troopers attacked him with their fists, clubs and belts, and kicked him when he fell to the ground, covered with blood.

The Schools of the "Third Empire."

"'They say that in your schools boys and girls fight together naked and are thus trained as warriors and Amazons. But do they also learn anything? And are not their carnal desires excited when they see each other thus?'

"'Not at all, my friend, for we wear them out till they can no longer breathe, and when they are tired they can neither think nor feel carnal desire.

"'But how then do they acquire the sciences and arts which they must have, o wise lawgiver?'

"'They must not learn and they must not think, for whoever can think may think evil thoughts, but whoever is made perfect physically and made to toil the whole day long is capable of becoming a useful citizen.'"

(From a discussion on Spartan education in Greece.)

The Weimar Constitution made possible some, though inadequate, new experiments in school organisation. It enabled scholars, at least in the large towns, to pass through the public schools without religious instruction. It left undisturbed the educational privileges of the rich; but it did at least lead to some hesitating experiments in the admission of workers to the universities and in giving them special training for university work.

Now the schools have been once again transformed, from top to bottom, into drilling-grounds of the Christian religion. Experiments such as that made by the Karl Marx Realgymnasium in Neukölln—the use of modern teaching methods, the subdivision of courses into a number of separate groups based on the special interest of the pupils, and the systematic preparation of workers for the universities—have been stopped and prohibited.

In *My Fight* Hitler outlined his programme for the schools.

It was much the same as that of the Spartan cynic cited above. The meaning of Hitler's programme is that the schools of the " Third Empire " will not be expected to provide the children with knowledge and science, but to make them obedient to the leader. And Frick says in a less open form what Hitler says bluntly and without circumlocution.

On May 9th Frick laid down his programme at a meeting of the Ministers of Education of the various States. He told them that up to now the whole system has been wrong : that children " have been instructed, not educated." A fine distinction : but what is Frick aiming at ?

> "To-day we have more reason than ever to recall that, hand in hand with our kindred Germanic peoples of Northern Europe, and their daughter States beyond the seas, we have to fulfil tasks throughout the world which will give the Nordic race a wide field of constructive cultural work."

The " kindred " peoples are here not clearly defined. It would appear that Herr Frick hopes to unite them all against the " sub-men " in order to create a world-embracing " Third Empire " which will show the " inferior " peoples of Latin or other "races" how things are managed in a real Hitler empire.

> " Together with the development of purely physical suppleness and ability, special emphasis must be laid on the formation of will-power and the power to make decisions, as the essential basis for the development of a sense of pleasure in taking responsibility which lies at the root of character."

Though expressed in involved language, this corresponds closely enough with the maxims laid down by the Spartan cynic. The schools are to produce uneducated (" uninstructed ") but well-drilled, dauntless soldiers of the " Third Empire." In order to convince the children that nothing as good as the " Third Empire " exists in the world, the world must be completely distorted as it is shown to them. Hence history must be falsified and made National Socialist. The new history books must contain as little as possible. " Considerable abridgment is indispensable." It is therefore sufficient " to bring out the historical forces which have always been operative." The two last decades of our own age must be the main object of historical treatment. To make things plainer, Frick added that it would be particularly necessary to deal with " the beginning of the awakening of the nation in the struggle for the Ruhr, up to the victory of the idea of National Socialist freedom and the restoration of the German nation at the festival of Potsdam."

In addition to this type of historical science other subjects particularly insisted on for the schools are " racial science " and " the elementary study of the basic conceptions of family research." The Bavarian Ministry of Education issued instructions containing the following passage :

" At the beginning of the school year 1933-4—apart from all other subjects and lessons—all classes in the State of Bavaria must arrange for history lessons in the first four to six weeks covering the period 1918 to 1933.
" The remainder of the curriculum in this subject must be correspondingly shortened and allocated to the remaining months of the year. At the conclusion of this course the last lesson must be organised as an ennobling celebration, with short addresses by the teacher and one of the pupils on the national awakening, the singing of patriotic songs, etc. This theme, the national awakening, which is most important for the re-awakening of national sentiment among the Bavarian youth in the schools, is not only to be treated as a subject of study in history, health science, etc., but must also be dealt with fundamentally as a principle of education. If examinations are held at the end of the year, special attention must be paid to this theme."

The Government commissioner in Berlin, Dr. Mein-shausen, stated in a speech on the transformation of Berlin school life, which was published in the *Völkischer Beobachter* of May 6th, 1933, that :

> " A halt must be put to all liberal sentimental dreams.
> . . . In the Jewish question the principle must be :
> ' Sentimentality is high treason.' "

In accordance with this, the Nazi Minister of Education has completely re-shaped all pedagogical colleges, and dismissed all teachers who were " suspect." All secular schools are liquidated. Religious education is once again compulsory. The reintroduction of whipping was the first achievement of Brown school policy.

All modern tendencies in the schools have been completely rooted out. The pupils in the top class at the " unorganised " Karl Marx school in Neukölln have all been put back two years ; before they are allowed to proceed with their studies they have to be first drilled in the pure Nazi spirit.

Jewish students as well as Jewish professors were driven out of the universities. Henceforward only one and a half per cent of new entrants to the higher educational institutions may be " non-Aryan." (Instructions of the Prussian Ministry of Education, May 8th, 1933.)

All teachers are compelled to join the National Socialist Teachers' Union ; this is a condition of employment.

The following clauses are contained in the Act against the overcrowding and excessive proportion of persons of foreign race in the universities :

> 1. In all schools other than compulsory schools, the number of scholars and students is to be restricted so as to guarantee adequate education and to conform with the needs of the professions.
>
> 2. In accepting new entrants care must be taken that the number of those of German nationality who are of

non-Aryan origin within the meaning of the Law for the restoration of a professional civil service of April 7th, 1933, in relation to the total number of students in each institution and faculty, does not exceed the proportion of non-Aryans in the German population. This proportion is fixed for Germany as a whole as 1.5 per cent.

7. The Act comes into force from its promulgation.

Legal Examinations simplified for Nazis.   The Reich Commissioner for the Prussian Ministry of Justice, Kerl, issued instructions on April 5th that all candidates in legal examinations who have served the Fatherland for a certain period in one of the recognised national associations may, at their request, be allowed a shortened form of examination by way of compensation for the time lost to their studies. (*Deutsche Allgemeine Zeitung*, April 12th, 1933.)

The " Spirit " of the Students who burn books.

1. Language and literature grow from the nation.

2. To-day there is a contradiction between literature and the German nation. This is a shameful state of things.

3. Purity of language and literature depends on you !

4. Our most dangerous opponent is the Jew.

5. The Jew can only think Jewish. If he writes German, he is lying. The German who writes German and thinks Jewish is a traitor.

6. We mean to put an end to this lie, we mean to brand this treachery.

7. We mean to treat the Jew as a foreigner, and we mean to take the nation seriously. We therefore demand from the censorship the following : Jewish works must be published in Hebrew. If published in German, they must be described as translations. Only Germans have

the right to write in German. The un-German spirit
must be eradicated from public libraries . . .

The German Student Organisation.
(From the twelve theses " Against the un-German
spirit " posted in Berlin University on April 13th, 1933.)

Bringing the Press " into Conformity."

On the eve-
ning of January 30th, 1933—the day when the Hitler-
Hugenberg Government was formed—the new Minister,
Frick, summoned the representatives of the Berlin Press to
a conference, at which he promised that the new Government would be distinguished from its forerunners by its
maintenance of the freedom of the Press. A few days after
" the word of a German man " had been given, a wave of
prohibitions of the Communist and Social Democratic Press
swept through Germany. By the middle of February
practically the whole of the German Communist Press had
been closed down. Prohibitions of Social Democratic and
Democratic papers descended like hail. In the course of the
Reichstag election campaign, storm troops went into the
printing offices of the Centre newspapers in the Rhineland,
compelled them to print the speeches of National Socialist
Ministers, and, with the support of the police authorities,
exercised a rigid censorship over what was to appear.

In the course of the last few days before the burning of
the Reichstag Frick's " freedom of the Press " had been
almost completely crushed out by the storm troops and
police. The destruction of working-class printing works and
newspaper offices was only prevented by defensive guards.
When the Nazis succeeded in bringing off their monstrous
act of provocation in the Reichstag and the Brown terror
began to rage, the last remaining of the Communist and
Social Democratic papers were wiped out.

Communist, Social Democratic and bourgeois journalists
of Left tendencies were cast into prison or delivered over to
sadistic tortures in Nazi barracks. The democratic bourgeois press and the Centre newspapers began to be

" brought into conformity " with the new pogrom régime. The democratic publishing houses of Ullstein and Mosse and the liberal Press throughout Germany began the " voluntary " removal of Jewish, pacifist or other members of their editorial staffs who were not liked by the Nazis. And this press too celebrated the " fateful events of these days," and declared in support of the " awakening " of the nation, for Hitler. It suppressed the reports of the massacres in the working-class quarters. It suppressed the acts of brutality which were taking place daily only a few minutes away from the editorial offices. The " Jewish papers " denied the persecution of the Jews.

The foreign Press, which was not so accommodating in the matter of suppressing the inhuman cruelties which were taking place, soon came into conflict with the Hitler Government. On March 7th an official Government *communiqué* was issued :

" In view of the malicious reports in the foreign press as to what is taking place in Germany, serious measures against a number of foreign correspondents are in preparation. Some of the correspondents concerned have escaped the hands of the police by leaving the country. As far as the other correspondents are concerned, they will have to guarantee that in future they will avoid any malicious tendencies in their reports and any ambiguous statements. In consideration of this, the correspondents in question have not been expelled for the time being ; they have been granted a probationary period of two months."

On April 5th the Hitler Government suffered a defeat at the hands of the Foreign Press Association. It had threatened the Association with a boycott if it did not remove its president, Mawrer, correspondent of the *Chicago Daily News*. The general meeting of the Association decided by 60 votes to 7, with three abstentions, not to accept Mawrer's resignation. In the course of the following weeks public opinion abroad compelled the Hitler Government to make further retreats in its dealings with the foreign Press correspondents in Germany.

The German Press Association was " brought into conformity " by the appointment of the Nazi Press chief, Dietrich, as president ; similar measures were applied to the German Newspaper Proprietors Association and the Association of Publishers of Periodicals. All district organisations of publishers and journalists were " brought into conformity." The German Press Association under its new president decided that in future no Jewish or Marxist journalists would be admitted to membership.

The " *Germanising* " of its editorial staff and its humble submission to Hitlerite policy was not of much avail to the Rudolf Mosse Publishing Co., which owns the *Berliner Tageblatt*. Early in April the company was virtually expropriated and taken over by a newly-formed company controlled by a Nazi Commissioner ; a new editorial staff which could furnish the necessary guarantees of loyalty to Hitler was appointed.

Another example of the many cases in which non-working-class papers have been " brought into conformity " is that of the *Dortmunder General Anzeiger*, which was " voluntarily " transformed into an organ of the National Socialist Party. This paper has the largest printing works in Europe and the biggest circulation of all German newspapers outside of Berlin. As its circulation was mainly in the thickly populated industrial areas of the Rhine and Westphalia, its contents made some concessions to the anti-capitalist and anti-Fascist feelings of the workers there. On the formation of the Hitler Government the former editorial staff was dismissed, to enable the paper to be " brought voluntarily into conformity " along the usual lines. But this did not satisfy the Brown rulers. In the issue of April 20th, among various hymns of praise for the occasion of Hitler's birthday, there appeared a drawing of Hitler which the Nazi leaders declared was a caricature. They therefore seized the issue and closed the offices of the paper. The

Dortmund police president entrusted the editor of the Nazi journal *Red Earth* with the management of the printing works. The Nazis then threatened the proprietor with the permanent prohibition of the *Dortmunder General Anzeiger*, on which the proprietor declared his readiness to transform the paper into an official Nazi organ. And thus the Nazis conquered this great printing establishment.

It is not possible to enumerate all the prohibitions and warnings which have been directed against bourgeois papers and periodicals. The campaign of " bringing into conformity " led to a dictatorial transformation of the whole of the German Press services. Readers of the newspapers which still appear in Germany are hermetically sealed off from all reliable foreign news. Over 250 foreign newspapers are forbidden in Germany, from the following countries : United States, 9, Argentine 2, Belgium 7, Canada 2, Danzig 3, Great Britain 5, France 31, Holland 9, Lithuania 2, Latvia 1, Luxemburg 5, Austria 37, Poland 24, Rumania 1, Saar Territory 4, Sweden 1, Switzerland 26, Soviet Union 9, Spain 2, Czecho-Slovakia 66.

Germany was the country which had the greatest literary output. The following announcement is significant of the fall in production during the first few weeks of the Hitler régime :

" According to the *Frankfurter Zeitung* of April 15th, 1933, in the course of the ' national revolution ' production in paper mills sank in many cases to 25 per cent. The *Deutsche Allgemeine Zeitung* of April 22nd reports that the publishing output in the first quarter of 1933 was 30 per cent lower than in the same quarter of 1931. The export trade continues to register a decline. The German book trade has been deprived of its best customers and of a whole range of science and literature."

CHAPTER VII: BRUTALITY AND TORTURE

THE NATIONAL SOCIALIST GERMAN LABOUR PARTY, which for years has been maintained by the German Cæsars of industry and agriculture, has studied history to guide it in playing its part in the period of social decline. It learnt arson from Nero, the persecution of the Jews from the Middle Ages, the murder of Socialists from Mussolini. For many years the official documents of the National Socialist Party have been proclaiming the coming of a St. Bartholomew's Night; the official description has been "the night of the long knife." This Night began with the burning of the Reichstag, and it is not yet over. The workers and peasants have shown too much resistance ; too many millions have rallied behind the banner of freedom. The National Socialist Labour Party has had to turn the St. Bartholomew's Night into a St. Bartholomew's year, and it is the first quarter of this year which is covered in the following report.

The friends of the Hitler Government are always ready to repeat the government's declaration that peace and order reign in Germany. *Démentis* are issued to calm feeling outside of Germany, and festivals and parades are staged to distract attention from what is actually taking place. The few foreign tourists who still care to visit Germany under the present tyranny are not taken into storm troop barracks or into concentration camps. It is only by chance that the foreign visitor may be an eye-witness of the nightly tortures, shootings " while trying to escape " and secretly organised murders. Every message from foreign journalists to their newspapers, every telephone conversation, every visit they make, is carefully noted, and they are threatened with immediate expulsion. And when the cries of tortured victims in the cellars of storm troop barracks reach the ears of neighbours, when the wife of some tortured prisoner speaks out, when the brutality of the Nazis is actually seen by hundreds of witnesses, then the official explanation is given that " this is an exceptional case." But at Essen on March 7th, 1933, Minister Goering officially proclaimed, to the applauding howls of a great mass meeting, that " when wood is being planed there are always shavings."

In reply it must be stated that these " shavings " have been organised for many years ; that the methods of the Middle Ages now employed by the Nazis have been worked out and advocated for years by the National Socialist leaders. It is the National Socialist leaders who have organised the pogroms and lynchings, the burnings and the pillories, the tortures of the first, second and third degrees. The methods of the Middle Ages have been employed publicly in so far as they were effective for propaganda. But the tortures have been carried out in private, in the darkness of the night. Even now millions of Germans are ignorant of them.

The Terror by Night. The secret terror has raged continuously since February 27th, 1933. There is a general " settlement of accounts." Arrests are made systematically, tortures carefully arranged. And the Ministerial reply to scruples about torturing is to lay down how far these tortures can go :

> " So long as I do not see any Communists running round with their ears and noses cut off there is no reason to get excited."

Tortures up to this point are therefore authorised. There is no need to examine the victims too closely or to investigate the denunciations ; the Nazis in their arrests can follow the instructions of the French cardinal who told the faithful on the original St. Bartholomew's Night : " Kill them all, God will be able to pick out his Christians ! "

Every day we are being visited by new victims of these

tortures by night, who show us their still open wounds. We print below declarations made on oath and reports which we have investigated with the utmost care.

The Torture Chambers.   One report makes it clear that the Nazis have established a regular tariff for beating prisoners : " Simple membership of the Social Democratic Party is punished with thirty blows with a rubber truncheon on the naked body. Membership of the Communist Party is usually punished with forty blows. The penalty is increased when the prisoner has been an official of a political party or trade union. The punishment is to be modified in accordance with the conduct of the prisoner."

One prisoner, Bernstein, was given fifty lashes because he was a Communist, and then a further fifty lashes because he was " also a Jew." There are therefore several degrees of torture, a fact which is brought out in the various declarations which are in our possession.

The torture begins from the moment when the victim is " fetched " from his home. The person who opens the door is threatened with revolvers ; the members of the family are threatened ; furniture and books are destroyed or thrown out into the street. Authors' manuscripts, the fruit of many months of work, are destroyed. In the case of workers, whatever remains of their wages is confiscated. The family is made to witness the proceedings. The children see their father struck in his face by unknown young men ; the wife sees her husband's face streaming with blood. She asks what they are going to do with him. She gets only an insult in reply. Then the prisoner is kicked out of the room and down the steps to the car which is waiting for him.

One report states that after an arrest had been made the Nazis began to beat their prisoner on the way down the stairs. The leader of the storm troop suddenly ordered them to stop beating the prisoner, who then saw that people in the house opposite had been roused. The storm troopers are " disciplined " in public.

But from the moment when the prisoner enters the Nazi

barracks he is as much an outlaw as the Nazi leaders have been threatening for years to make him. Any Nazi who meets the prisoner on the stairs or in the passages kicks or strikes him. Cowards have become murderers : day after day they wait outside the doors of the rooms where the first degree of torture is applied, and make the prisoners run the gauntlet of whips and boots and rubber truncheons. Then the prisoner is admitted to the presence of the storm troop leader or higher officer, and the " trial " begins.

The " Court." The judge sits behind a table ; three stars on his storm troop uniform give him judicial powers over all prisoners. Daggers and bayonets are stuck into the table, and there are flickering candles at each end. The prisoner is pushed forward to the table ; Nazis press closely round him. When he answers, they hit him ; if he declares his innocence they kick him. Any attempt to defend himself is useless. There is no question of what the truth is ; the trial is only a farce to provide a pretext for making another martyr.

The prisoner hears the source of the denunciation which was the cause of his arrest, and thinks that he can at once disprove the charge ; he begins to say something, and then blows are rained down on him, and he is told not to speak unless he is asked a question. They ask him for addresses. They think that they will be able to make capital of the story that the leaders of the workers' movement have betrayed each other. But the prisoner refuses to say anything. Then the rubber truncheons are used again with furious rage.

It is to the eternal honour of the German working-class movement that thousands of workers have not flinched in spite of all the brutality and torture inflicted on them ; they have refused to give new victims to their torturers.

The Cellars. From the Court the prisoners are taken to the cellars, where they can see, in the semi-darkness, the flogging-benches standing ready. The air is thick with the smell of dried blood and sweat. The prisoner is thrown on to the flogging-bench, and steel rods hammer down on his back. Four of the Nazis do the beating. Each new blow cuts the raw flesh to pieces. Then they get tired, and push him into the next cellar, where he is no longer alone. Fellow victims are cowering in the corners ; the worst mutilated victims are writhing on straw sacks on the ground. Some have lost control and are crying out. From the next room come the cries of the next victim.

The prisoners in the adjoining room can now see everything, as someone has thought it right to leave the doors open. The next victim starts up at the first blow from the steel rods. His face is pale ; a new command makes him bow down again. His movement was " criminal," and the punishment was made more severe ; he was forced to count the blows in a loud voice, till the numbers could no longer be distinguished from his cries of pain.

The half-unconscious prisoner is then pulled from the flogging-bench, and the storm troop leader walks forward and announces to the victim : " Now you will be shot." The prisoner is placed with his face to the wall ; there is silence, broken only by the Nazis releasing the safety-catches of their revolvers. Then shots : the prisoner hears the whizz of bullets past his ears, and begins to realise that they are not hitting him. At last he sinks in a swoon, and before he loses consciousness he hears the Nazis laughing.

We have many reports of similar treatment, and give the following as typical :

" I lived in the Jüdenstrasse, near number 50, where a storm troop detachment was quartered. On March 19th the arbitrary arrests I previously reported were resumed. About 9 p.m., shortly after another prisoner had been taken in, the neighbours heard a shot through the open window of the Nazi office. I was determined to see what was happening, and discovered that there was a man, presumably the prisoner, standing doubled up

against the window. Then more shots rang out, but the
bullets did not hit the man. Then I saw him fall to the
ground, and Nazis bent down over him laughing. One
voice shouted several times : ' Now then, get up ! Go
home ! ' The prisoner seemed not to hear this shout ;
he had fainted with fear. Is it strange that one should
hear of men being driven mad by this ? ''

Hundreds of prisoners have been through this. They have
been dragged from the torture-chambers and thrown into
the " waiting-room " among their comrades. At the last
moment before they sink down exhausted on their straw
sacks they are told that they are to be shot the following
morning. They are in such pain that they are indifferent
to the new threat. But when they come to themselves some
time afterwards, they begin to think about it. They have
no reason to doubt that the threat will be carried out. So
they sit there among their groaning friends, waiting for their
last morning to come. During the night the guard leans
against the door and sings : " Dawn, dawn, you light my
way to early death." (A report from the Hedemannstrasse
barracks in Berlin gives this detail.) Sworn declarations
repeatedly show that in many cases the prisoners have been
left for days with this threat hanging over them. They hear
the beatings beginning again in the adjoining room. The
doors are kicked open, so that they can see the tortures.
From time to time one of the victims is called out and
" tried " again.

The Nazis delight in Filth.   A new prisoner, who
looks like an intellectual, is pushed into the torture-
chamber. The Nazis hold his head, force his teeth apart,
and then pour a bottle of castor oil down his throat.
Then they ask him politely to take down his trousers ;
he unbuttons his braces, and his trousers drop. The
Nazis do not put him on the flogging-bench ; they make
him stand doubled up. The Nazis wait a quarter of an
hour. Then they pick up the steel rods, and begin to

beat him. He screams and stands upright ; the Nazis press him down and beat him again. Then suddenly his bowels empty.

The Nazi leaders will deny these loathsome cruelties. But our archives show that these statements are true. And we have not only the declarations made by intellectuals and workers who have experienced this, but there is also in our possession a report of a confidential meeting of Nazis in Berlin, at which Dr. Goebbels, the Minister for Enlightenment, explained how he would deal with editors who happened to have different opinions from his :

> " The protective corps men must go to the offices of the paper concerned, and give each member of the editorial staff a litre of castor oil."

The Nazis therefore only act in accordance with instructions.

The " Red Cross " in Nazi Cellars. The Nazi doctors as a rule are only present at the actual torturing ; they are not to render any medical aid, but only to determine whether the prisoner may still be beaten. They are like the doctors of the Inquisition : the torture is stopped when there is danger of the victim dying.

All reports show that medical aid is only given when the victim appears to be dying. Injections are only made at the last minute. The victims are only carried away to the hospital when the medical expert certifies that they are dying.

Propaganda to Justify the Terror. For years the National Socialist leaders had been preparing the ground for the terror by systematic propaganda. This was directed in the first place against " the November criminals "—the revolutionaries of November 1918—who were represented as having been responsible for all the sufferings of Germany since 1918. Intensive propaganda was also directed against the Soviet Union. In *My Fight*, Hitler wrote :

" It must never be forgotten that the rulers of present-day Russia are bloodstained common criminals, the scum of humanity."

And on March 10th, 1933, German wireless stations broadcast a " Horst-Wessel " play in which Hitler's lies about the Soviet Union were repeated : that since 1917 two million people had been murdered in Russia ; that the Soviets are the embodiment of lies and deceit, looting and robbery.

Then there was the systematic propaganda against the " hereditary foe," France. Hatred of France was carefully nurtured, and the idea of revenge developed.

The propaganda against the Jews is dealt with in another chapter : one example shows its effect in the brutalities shown to Jewish victims of the terror :

" A doctor was beaten up in a Nazi barracks and was lying, seriously injured and covered with blood, on the straw. Someone who came into the room called attention to how serious the doctor's condition was. This made the Nazi guard furious with indignation, and from his excited statements it was possible to gather that his section-leader had told the men the following legend : all doctors who are Jews have for years been taking revenge on German women who come under their care in hospitals by secretly cutting out their ovaries, so that only Jewish women could bear children and thus the Jews would rule Germany. The Nazi guard followed up this story by kicking the severely injured man in the stomach."

The Blood Guilt of the Nazi Leaders.   The responsibility of the Nazi leaders not only for the methods of their organised gangs but for the murderous feelings among their followers is made clear from statements made by the leaders both before and after their seizure of power. The present Minister of the Interior, Frick, declared that :

" It is not a bad thing if a few tens of thousands of Marxist functionaries come to harm."

Stöhr, the former vice-president of the Reichstag, told a mass meeting :

" We will make the hemp industry prosper."

Immediately after the new cabinet of Oldenburg was formed, the premier, Röver, announced :

" We will put the Marxists and the people of the Centre on the gallows to feed the ravens."

On March 10th, 1933, Minister Goering spoke at a mass meeting in Essen :

" I would rather shoot a few times too short and too wide, but at any rate I would shoot."

Goering's words fell on fruitful soil. At the end of April the police president of Dortmund issued an instruction :

" In the last few days many Communist leaflets have been distributed. I order the police to make immediate use of their weapons against any attempt to distribute Communist leaflets."

The Terror was Organised.

1. On the night of the burning of the Reichstag 30 Nazi barracks were prepared for carrying out tortures in Berlin alone. Steel rods, whips, chains, cords for tying up prisoners, water-pails and castor oil were bought and taken to the barracks. That same night they were used. Doctors were allocated to each barracks.

Nazi Punitive Expedition against the working-class quarter of Düsseldorf-Bilk.
Hundreds of workers were arrested and terribly maltreated.
The young worker on the right of the picture had suffered such injuries that he could not raise his arms.

2. We are in possession of reports from a number of German towns showing that on that same evening the Nazis were fully mobilised, and guards were put round houses where working-class leaders lived, as well as at railway stations and post offices.

3. A similar selection of victims was made in all towns.

4. The arrests were almost everywhere left to the storm troops and their special detachments. The police merely accompanied them, as the Nazis were not at that time quite sure of their attitude.

5. The enrolment of storm troopers as auxiliary police began on February 22nd ; this is a definite indication that action on a large scale was contemplated and that it was proposed to keep the appearance of legality as long as possible.

6. In his capacity as Commissioner for Prussia, Goering, officially, by an order issued on February 17th, authorised shooting without any form of trial :

" Every man who, in pursuance of this duty, makes use of his weapons, will be protected by me regardless of the consequences of his action. On the other hand, every man who from any false scruples does not use his weapons can anticipate criminal proceedings against himself. Every officer must at all times remember that omission to take the necessary measures is more serious than a mistake made in applying such measures."

7. High officials of the National Socialist Party have constantly been present in the torture-cellars of the Hedemannstrasse in Berlin and in other barracks. They directed the acts of brutality, and conducted trials. We have definite evidence, for example, that Count Helldorf, leader of the Nazi storm troops, who was and remains in daily communication with Goering and Hitler, held parades of the victims of the brutalities.

Our Documents.   We have in our archives 536 declarations made by persons who had been severely ill-treated.

The statements have been checked and found to be correct.

One hundred and thirty-seven certificates show that the victims have received serious permanent injuries. Three hundred and seventy-five declarations mention that the victims, before being allowed to leave the torture-houses, were forced to sign statements that they had been " well treated."

Our material from the towns and villages of the Third Empire supports the conclusion that since February 27th about sixty thousand people have been subjected to violence.

An Unemployed Worker.

" On Monday, March 6th, 5 p.m., two storm troopers and a leader came to the door of the flat occupied by the Reichstag deputy ' X,' and demanded admittance. I was in the flat sorting out the washing. I opened the door, at first on the chain. A revolver was thrust through the opening, and I was ordered to open the door immediately. I was asked where ' X ' was living, but could give no information. Then they took me off with them. They took me in a side-car to the Böttcherstrasse. There they began to ill-use me. I still have, at the time of writing this, the marks of what they did to me : both eyes beaten blue, a bite on my left temple, my hands still swollen and scratched. They called me a ' young murderer ' and similar names, without the slightest ground. Then they made me wash off the blood which was streaming from my forehead, mouth and nose. I had hardly washed it off when I was taken into the front room and again they started beating me. I covered my face with my hands, or they would certainly have broken my jaws.

" But that did not satisfy them. Together with two other prisoners I was taken in a taxi to the Hedemannstrasse, with two motor cyclists as escort. I was told I should be thankful that they were so humane, as they ' worked ' differently in the lower groups. I nearly had to laugh when they told me this.

"At the Hedemannstrasse I stated when they examined me that I had been begging and had always got something at the door where ' X ' lived. Because of this I had gone there many times, also to talk politics, and eventually Frau ' X ' gave me some housework to do, beating carpets and so on. I told the Nazis that I had been very glad to get such treatment from Communists. I told them that I was a Communist sympathiser and had voted List 3. Then the man in charge said : ' We can always do with people who tell the truth. It is not you we want, it is your leaders we want to destroy and settle accounts with.' "

But Workers are Brutally Beaten. " On the evening of March 5th I was with six other workers in a public-house in Berlin North ; we were waiting to hear the election results. A group of uniformed storm troop men came in, pointed their revolvers at us and made us go with them, with our hands above our heads, to the storm troop quarters in the X-Strasse. There we were first beaten up as ' Communist sows.' Then we were put into a car and taken to the Nazi headquarters in Hedemannstrasse. We were chased up to the fourth floor, and driven along a corridor with repeated blows and lashes with riding whips. The corridor was ' decorated ' from top to bottom with ' conquered ' Social Democratic banners and posters. There was a figure against the wall which was supposed to represent Ernst Thaelmann, in the uniform of the Red Front, hanging on a gallows.

" We were driven with blows into a general room. We were forced to go down on our knees and shout ' Heil Hitler,' also to say the ' Our Father ' and sing the *Horst-Wessel* song. Anyone who did not obey instantaneously was beaten till he was unconscious. Later we were placed against the wall of the room, and continuous volleys were fired close above our heads. After they had left us alone for a little, we were put through the first 'interrogation.' Each of us was summoned alone into a room where there were about six Nazis with riding whips. We had to strip, and were then told that we should be beaten until we told everything. They demanded that we should confess the most impossible things. We were asked to give the names and addresses of Communist officials, and to reveal imaginary hiding places of arms and duplicating machines. During the interrogation we were beaten the whole time. Then we were given half an hour to think things over, and then the torture began again.

"Some anti-Fascists who had formerly belonged to the Nazis had their heads shaved except for a forelock which was tied together. We were told that these people were to be shot next morning ; when we arrived, they were lying unconscious on the floor of the general room. Besides ourselves, there were about 50 other Communist and Social Democratic workers in the room. When we were released, a document was put in front of us stating that we had left the building without any injury to our health. We signed. I found two of those who had been with me some time after in the 'Am Friedrichshain' hospital. One of them had a bullet wound in the neck."

Other Typical Cases.

"J.M., a worker living in the Werderstrasse, Berlin, was taken away by storm troop men during the night of March 27th–28th and severely ill-treated in the Nazi barracks in the Rudowerstrasse. His whole body is covered with open wounds.

.   .   .   .

"R., a worker living in Schöneburg, who was known to do political work, was found in his flat and there severely injured with steel rods, then being taken to a Nazi barracks. At the time when this report was being written it was not yet known what had become of him. His flat was completely smashed up by the Nazis when they came to arrest him."

. . . .

" Max F., a worker in W., Brandenburg, was attacked during the night by about 40 armed storm troop men. The door of his flat was broken in, and they started shooting wildly into the flat. He was hit in the back, but managed to jump through a window and escape ; as he ran he was hit again in the arm, and another shot grazed his body. He got away, and was taken in by a hospital. It had to be kept secret that he was in the hospital ; every day his relatives were threatened."

. . . .

" Paul Paprocki, a worker of 36 years of age, living in number 23, Malplakstrasse, was taken from his room at 3 a.m. on the night of March 26th–27th. A strong detachment of storm troop men took him to their headquarters in the Utrechterstrasse ; when he refused to give any addresses they began to ill-use him. Some hours later he was released with serious injuries from blows."

. . . .

" The 18-year old worker Kirt Hackenbusch, Grünthalerstrasse 63, was arrested with three of his friends on March 26th and taken to the Nazi quarters in the Prinzenstrasse. They were beaten with heavy leather straps. The prisoners refused to say the ' Our Father.' Further beating. Some hours later the prisoners were taken to an accident station, where they were forced by threats to state that the Nazis had rescued them from an attack. In addition to cuts in his face and back, Hackenbusch has a severe wound on his head."

. . . .

" Jacob Ickler, a worker living in Cassel, Kettengasse 4, 20 years old, was carried off on March 20th, 1933 by

Nazis who searched his father's flat. He was taken to the town hall, laid on a flogging-bench, and then beaten with rubber truncheons. Some blows struck the lower half of his face and his temples. His back and upper legs were streaming with blood. A doctor's certificate testifies to the condition in which he was found. The doctor's name is not given here, as in Germany of the Third Empire it is no longer safe to give medical attention to a man who has been injured."

Urine for Thirst. Wilhelm Sollmann, a Social Democratic member of the Reichstag and a former Minister of the Reich, writes as under of his ill-usage at the hands of storm troop and protective corps men :

" On Thursday, March 9th, shortly after three o'clock in the afternoon, three cars filled with storm troop and protective corps men pulled up at my house. As at that moment I was speaking on the telephone to a member of the town council, I was able to tell him : ' Nazis are forcing their way in, give the mobile police the alarm.'

" At that moment a number of men armed with loaded revolvers, sticks and knives forced their way into my study. Before I could say a word I was struck down at my desk. The men were in a kind of frenzy of hate and joy at being able to take revenge on me. Most of the men went to the other rooms in the house and in a few minutes literally smashed everything to splinters. . . . I was hit and thrown into an open car. My wife called out : ' Where are you taking my husband ? ' One of them answered jeeringly : ' You'll soon know that ! ' First they drove me over the grass towards the wood. As there was a storm troop man sitting in front of me and flourishing a revolver the whole time, I thought that they were going to shoot me in the nearest wood. But they drove on, abusing me all the time—some of the abuse was quite insane—and then we crossed the bridge near Kalk. There they drove slowly, and all along the High Street, which was full of people, I was exhibited to the crowd : ' This is the great Sollmann ! See how small he is ! ' I was taken to the district head-quarters of the National Socialists in the Mozartstrasse. I was chased up the stairs with blows and kicks and lashes, and then into the conference room. They had lowered the blinds so that the room was half in darkness. I was to be put before the tribunal. A large swastika banner was spread over the table. I saw that my colleague, Efferoth, was sitting near the window, in the same plight as myself. I had hardly taken a seat near him when the tortures began, and they went on for two hours.

" First a man in storm troop uniform, whom my colleague said was Councillor Ebele, made a short speech attack-ing Efferoth, saying that retribution was now to come. Then protective corps men began attacking us with their fists. For about half an hour Efferoth and I lay on the floor, so exhausted that we could not get up. All the time we were being hit and kicked, and now and then our hair was pulled and our heads knocked together.

" Eventually we were pulled up and forced into chairs ; a man held our hands behind the chair, while another forced us to open our teeth and poured a quarter of a litre of castor oil down our throats. One of our tormen-tors shouted for salts to increase our torture, but appar-ently salts could not be got quickly enough. Then they gave us a short rest again. I begged for a glass of water. When it was given to me I saw its colour and therefore only used it to pour over my hands, which were covered with blood. One of the men shouted : ' Why don't you drink the water ? ' At the same moment he threw the glass with what was left of its contents into my face. Then we were struck and kicked again.

" All at once our tormentors seemed to get uneasy. I thought that the police must have been notified of our being attacked and carried off. About 5 o'clock the protective corps men took hold of us and with a shout of ' Into the coal cellar ! ' literally flung us down the stairs. Apparently the coal cellar was locked, and they seemed to be in a hurry to get rid of us. They therefore pushed us across the street, with blows and kicks—our faces were already a bloody pulp—to a motor. We were made to squat on the floor.

" The ill-treatment was carried on in the closed motor ; one blow struck me in the right eye. We pulled up at police headquarters. Although we were in a state of collapse we were forced to run in and up the stairs. . . . One of the Nazis said that next day we would have to walk in front of the Nazis' torchlight procession and at the finish we would be thrown on to the heap of torches. . . . The president of police advised us to let ourselves be put under protective arrest. I referred to my parliamentary immunity ; he agreed with what I said, but nevertheless advised that Efferoth and I should go into the prison hospital.

" In the hospital we were sewn up and bandaged. During the torturing one of the protective corps men had slowly and deliberately pressed a knife into Efferoth's side. The doctor stated that it would have been dangerous if it had gone a centimetre deeper. . . . Next day the Press published a report that we had been attacked by political opponents and suffered ' slight ' injuries."

A Doctor and his Wife tortured.

" On June 3rd, at four in the morning, there was a ring at the door of the flat. A number of men shouted : ' Police ! Open the door ! ' My wife replied : ' Please come in the morning, I don't open the door at night.' Then there were heavy blows against the door ; it was broken in, and five men in storm troop uniform, without police badges, forced their way into the flat, holding revolvers out at us. I asked what they wanted, and they replied with a shower of blows with their fists and rubber truncheons. ' Hold your mouth, who asked you to speak ? ' They ordered ' Hands up ! ' Some of them

seized my throat and pressed me against the wall.
' It's all up with you Jews, you Bolshevik rabble ! '
When I tried to say something they struck me again.

" They searched the flat, smashed in the drawers of my
desk, filled a trunk with books, manuscripts and letters,
and ordered me to ' Get out of it ! ' My wife, who did
not want to leave me in the hands of these bandits,
came with me, although she was not told to. . . . They
kicked me down the steps. When my wife protested
against their treating a sick man like that, she was
cursed and pushed off the seat of the car : ' You impu-
dent sow, keep quiet, or you'll get it too ! ' The car
pulled up at a house, in front of which there was a
group of storm troop and protective corps men. As
soon as we got out of the car we were driven along with
rubber truncheons and dog-whips, and up the stairs to
the fourth floor. I was hardly able to climb up, as I had
had influenza and my heart was weak, so they beat me
furiously until I reached the top. I was pushed into a
corridor, and my wife and I were made to run the
gauntlet through Nazis who struck at us as we passed.
I was then taken to a separate room. I stated that there
must be some mistake and asked to be allowed to clear
it up."

The prisoner, who had worked at a Berlin hospital for
seven years, and had since been chief doctor in a section of
the Municipal Hospital in Neukölln, learnt in the course of
a long interrogation that the absurd charge was made
against him that he was the head of the Communist propaganda activities in the Reich. When he protested his
innocence he was beaten. He continues his report :

" They threw themselves on me with bestial fury, using
rubber truncheons, leather whips and steel rods. They
hit particularly at my head, jumping up on tables and
chairs and hitting mercilessly at me from above my
head. My face was streaming with blood. My cries for

help soon stopped : a few blows with an iron rod, and I doubled up and fell unconscious."

The victim further reports that he was soon in a condition in which he might die at any moment, and the Nazis felt compelled to summon medical aid. He was able, however, to keep track of what was happening, and his account includes the following :

" There were young men sitting in the room. Their faces were pale, and many had bandages round their heads. They were waiting to be interrogated. Now and then Nazis would come into the room and insist on all the prisoners jumping up and greeting them with ' Heil Hitler.' Those who did not obey the order promptly enough were lashed with whips and forced to stand up and sit down again. They had to do this ten or more times in quick succession.

" Storm troop men came in and took revolvers and ammunition from the drawers of the desk. The drawers were full of revolvers and each Nazi selected the one he liked best. Other Nazis came in looking for the list of volunteers for Austria (!).

" A man who had sworn at a storm troop man some days before was pulled out of his bed that night and arrested. A woman, who had said that a man who had gone over from the Communists to the Nazis was mad, was arrested at her flat and brought to the Nazi headquarters.

" All at once someone shouted out ' Pieck and Ullstein have been arrested and will be brought here ! ' The storm troop men raved with delight, and swung their rubber truncheons round them. ' Let them come ! ' Someone said that the worker Schulze had come. All the Nazis went out of the room. For a quarter of an hour I heard them raging out in the corridor. Then a short man about thirty years of age was pushed into the room. His right eye was full of blood. In the interrogation he admitted that he was a member of the Red Aid.

He was accused of having been present when a storm troop man was murdered. He denied this. He said that he had already been arrested on suspicion of this charge and then set free again. He was beaten with dog-whips and ordered to answer ' Yes ' to every question put to him. He was beaten until he answered ' Yes.' ' Are you a murderer, you scoundrel ? ' He answered ' No.' He was then beaten harder. His whole face was covered with blood. He wiped his face with his sleeve. ' You've admitted it now.' He replied : ' It was you who compelled me to say it.' They beat him again. He was asked how many children he had brought into the world and with how many women he had slept, and whether all his children were such idiots as he was.

" Then he was sent into the kitchen to have his head shaved. When he came back, he was pushed in front of a fragile old man, a clergyman from Lichterfelde. The white-haired old gentleman was told to hold out his hand to him and say : ' Good-day, comrade.' The old man held out his hand and said : ' I shake your hand, you are a suffering human being.' They all laughed : ' That's how you greet a murderer ! ' The old man answered : ' And even if he is, he is a man who has been tortured, and you are the embodiment of force, and force is not eternal. You cannot break my convictions with rubber truncheons : you are national and I an international.' This courageous act of the white-haired old man made some of the Nazis look abashed, and when some of them rushed at him the others held them back.

" After midnight I was taken to the interrogation room, where I saw my wife, who was as pale as a ghost. She whispered to me : ' I can't bear it any longer : I must throw myself out of the window ! They are going to say that you are a spy of the Cheka and shoot you ! ' ' Don't do anything stupid, pull yourself together ! ' This exchange of words was enough to rouse the Nazi in charge to fury ; he was so tired (or drunk) that he could hardly sit up. My wife was led away. My condition grew worse, and I asked for a doctor. I was taken to the room of the officer in charge, and my wife was allowed to give me something to drink."

In spite of the victim's critical condition the storm troop detachment was determined to force the doctor to " confess " :

" The man pulled out his revolver and yelled : ' Three bullets, one in your forehead, one in your mouth, one in your stomach, and then it's all over and you'll be thrown on the dung-heap.' I lay silent and quite still. . . . He raised his fist and struck me in the face : ' In a couple of minutes it will be all over with you. I'll hang you from the window. I've hanged people in Kiev like that. Only a few minutes more : when I leave the room it will be too late, whether you say it or not. You miserable scoundrel ! What is the Cheka doing ? What is the Ogpu doing ? Are you going to talk or not ? ' I lay still, and he kicked me in the stomach as hard as he could. I lost consciousness."

A Doctor Decoyed into a Trap. Although every victim of the Nazis deserves equal mention, we must quote the case of another doctor on account of its special features. The following report is taken from the Saarbrück *Arbeiter Stimme* :

" On March 17th there was a regular meeting of the Berlin Medical Association. After the lecture the chairman, Professor Goldscheider, head of the University Clinic, a man seventy years of age, asked his colleagues to remain for a few minutes, as he wanted to show them a particularly interesting case. Then a patient completely swathed in bandages was brought in, and Professor Goldscheider explained : ' Gentlemen, this patient is our colleague Dr. Lust. The day before yesterday he received a telephone call in the evening summoning him to a patient in Lichterfelde. When he reached there he was met by storm troop men and ill-treated in this terrible way.' These words caused great indignation in the meeting. The well-known Professor Sauerbruch, a German Nationalist, jumped up and declared that he was prepared to take the victim of the Nazis into his clinic. As a result of this experience something like a panic has spread through Berlin doctors, many of whom fear that when they are called to a patient they may meet a similar terrible fate."

A Woman 46 Years Old Whipped.

During the night of Monday, March 20th–Tuesday, March 21st the Social Democratic woman councillor, Marie Jankowski, was attacked in her flat (Bergmannstrasse 18, Köpenick, Berlin). A laundry van pulled up in front of the house ; twenty storm troop men broke in the house-door and occupied the stairs. Six men forced their way into her flat, with revolvers ready. Frau Jankowski was taken in the van, with two Communist officials who were already in it, to the Transport Headquarters of the Nazis in Köpenick. In a shed in the courtyard she was forced to take off her clothes and lie on a wooden bench which was covered with a black-red-gold flag. Four men held her down, one pressing her face into a bundle of old rags. For two hours this woman, forty six years old, was beaten mercilessly with truncheons, steel rods and whips.

After this torture Frau Jankowski was put out into the street. At about five in the morning some passers-by found her, and took her to her home in a taxi. The doctor certified that her condition was dangerous. One kidney had been broken by blows. There was literally not a sound spot left on her body. In the Antonius Hospital in Karlshorst, Frau Jankowski made the following deposition :

" While I was being beaten I was told again and again to give the names and addresses of workers. They made me count the colours of the Republic and say foul

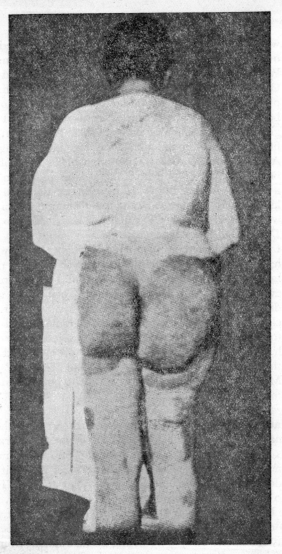

FRAU MARIA JANKOWSKI, district Social Welfare director, who was taken from her home by Brown Shirts to the Nazi station in Köpenick and there beaten for two hours with rubber truncheons, steel rods and whips. The photograph shows the result of this appalling brutality.

PLATE NO. II.

words instead of Black-Red-Gold. They asked me questions like : Have you had any money from the Welfare Department ? Have you housed and fed Communists ? Have you stolen shoes from unemployed workers ? Have you made a list of Nazi shops to be boycotted ? Every time I answered ' No ' I was given a new shower of blows. When I cried out, the fifth of my tormentors pressed my face into the rags.

" After I had had at least a hundred blows I fell off the bench. I was then pulled off the ground and given such a blow in my face that I fell in a corner, damaging my knee. Then together with the two Communist workers, who were also being tortured, I was forced to sing *Deutschland, Deutschland über Alles.*

" I was compelled to sign a declaration that I would leave the Social Democratic Party, that I would never take part in politics again, and that I would report every Thursday to the Nazi office. Then I was given different treatment. I was given a glass of water. My clothes were brushed and given back to me. The leader told one of the men to ' take the lady out.' The man held me up when I was about to fall down, and shut the door after me with a polite ' Good evening ! '

" My husband reported the facts to the police, but was told that they were powerless."

What was it that made these young lads carry out the inhuman cruelties recorded above and in the photograph ? This hate was directed against a woman who for years had been in a responsible position, giving relief where it was needed, a woman old enough to be their mother. There is no question of this having been a private act of revenge. The lads not only made the woman strip and beat her, they also demanded names and addresses of Social Democratic Party members. They were acting on instructions from the Nazi leaders. The leaders not only hushed up this crime, but when it had become known abroad started proceedings against her for spreading " atrocity stories."

Nerve Specialist Exiled After Being Beaten. On Tuesday March 21st the nerve specialist Dr. Fraenkel, whose patients are mainly working-class people, was arrested in his flat in Berlin by a large detachment of storm troop men. He was taken to the Nazi barracks in the General-Papestrasse and kept there till Thursday. In these two days he was interrogated several times and on each occasion beaten with steel rods and dog-whips. The results of this ill-treatment, including damage to an eye by a lash from a whip, were established beyond question when he was released. Dr. Fraenkel was released on March 23rd, after he had signed an undertaking for himself and his wife, that they would immediately leave Germany and never return. Dr. Fraenkel, who is now living abroad, reported as follows on some of the details of his treatment :

" While I was there about 15 young workers were brought into the room where I had been put. I can testify that these young workers were most cruelly ill-treated. As a doctor, I am of the opinion that at least eight of them must have succumbed to the injuries they received. After they had been tied up and lighted cigarettes had been pressed into the soles of their feet, the storm troop men continued torturing them cruelly for hours. A doctor Philippsthal, of Biesdorf, Berlin, was brought in at the same time as I was. He was seriously wounded. I am very doubtful whether he got through alive." (Editorial note : On March 23rd, Dr. Philippsthal was taken to the Urbank Hospital, where he did in fact die.)

Reichsbanner and Social Democrat Officials. The *démentis* issued by the Nazi Government always try to represent the excesses in the Nazi barracks as the arbitrary acts of individuals. We print here a number of reports from Cassel, which make it perfectly clear how closely the brutal acts are connected with the Nazi leadership. The Nazis did not take much trouble to distinguish between " trials " and torturings which took place in different rooms of the same house. A deposition made by Hans Quer, a Reichsbanner leader, contains the following :

" On March 24th, 1933, at about one o'clock, I was arrested by four storm troop men and one civilian, and taken to the Town Hall. They said : ' Herr Quer, you must come with us,' and then I was taken along, two men holding my arms. I was taken down the outside steps, several Nazis who were at the top calling out to the public : ' Here comes the Reichsbanner general Quer ! ' I was taken to the public hall. The storm troop leader who took me is a commercial traveller, selling gin. He was formerly employed in the Welfare Department ; he stole some money and was dismissed and sentenced to four months' imprisonment. One of the storm troop men then took my particulars, including what Party I belonged to. Then I was informed that I could go.

" As I went out two Nazis got hold of me and prevented me from going. One of them went in to the man who had taken my particulars. Soon after, he came back and waved his hand, indicating that I was to be taken down to the cellar. There I was met by ten to fifteen storm troop men, who ordered me to take off my hat and coat. Then I was taken into a dark cellar, where there was a bench ; one of the men went in front with an electric torch. The torch went out. I was forced down on to the bench, and for ten or fifteen minutes was beaten with rubber truncheons in a most brutal and inhuman way. When I fell off the bench half unconscious and begged them not to be so inhuman, they jeered at me and started beating me harder than ever. When I was coming out of the cellar I did not walk quickly enough for them, and I was told : ' You've had too little, if you don't hurry up you'll be brought back in again.' "

Other Cases in Cassel.

" Martin Meyer, aged 30, a municipal official, of Böttner-strasse 4, was taken out of the Municipal Offices where he was working, at 12.30 on March 24th, by storm troop men, and taken to the public hall in the Karl-strasse. There he was taken into a dark cellar, laid on a bench, and beaten with rubber truncheons for half an hour, with one short interval. One blow hit his nose, and another his right eye."

. . . .

" Kaschel Seppel, trade union secretary, Schillstrasse 14, Cassel, was taken from the trade union house, along with Gerke, another trade union secretary, by eight storm troop men, on March 23rd, 1933, 5 p.m. They were told they were to be tried at the public hall. They were put into the large hall. They heard cries coming from the rooms below. They waited an hour. They were then taken by eight men into a dark cellar, laid across a table, and beaten by six men with rubber truncheons. They are now still confined to bed and under medical treatment. Their kidneys appear to be injured ; their urine is mixed with blood. Their backs, buttocks and legs are injured."

. . . .

" Ball, Heinrich, a shopkeeper of Ludwigstrasse 2, Cassel, was arrested in his shop at about 3 p.m. on March 24th, 1933, by four storm troop men, and taken to the public hall. He was beaten in the street, and threatened that he would be shot if he tried to escape. Maltreated in the public hall. He was made to take down his trousers, and beaten for quarter of an hour with rubber truncheons. Since then he has been in Cassel Hospital."

. . . .

" Christian Wittrock, age over 40, manager of the local health insurance department at Cassel, was taken out of his office by two storm troop men on March 24th,

1933. He was taken down the outside steps, then through a crowd of people to the public hall in the Karlstrasse. There he was asked particulars about himself, and then the Nazi in charge said : ' Wittrock is discharged.' He was then taken out as if he was going to be set free, but then taken into a dark cellar, laid on a bench there, and beaten with rubber truncheons. Two blows on his head ; his skin cut on his back, his buttocks and his legs. His clothes were stained with blood, and partly torn, also his shoes. Then he was taken back into the hall and there beaten again. He is now under medical treatment."

Even an Officer Maltreated.

" In the second week of March a retired lieutenant, Anhalt, now district surveyor, living at Germaniastrasse 12, Tempelhof, Berlin, was arrested in his flat by three storm troop men and one civilian. He immediately gave the alarm to the police, who arrived at his flat but refused to interfere. The storm troop men took Anhalt to the Hedemannstrasse. There he was first struck by the civilian for having called the police. Then he was taken into a room where there were already 12 or 13 men lying on straw. A storm troop man, whom they called ' Oberfahrer,' took charge of the lieutenant. There was no mention of the fact that Anhalt was charged with anything ; ' Oberfahrer ' only knew that he had a former officer in front of him. He began to deliver punishment, with two accomplices, and did not stop beating Anhalt until blood was streaming from his mouth and nose. Then he lifted up the injured man and showed him to the other prisoners lying groaning on the floor, saying : ' See here, this swine is a lieutenant, and is in such a fright that he can't stand straight.' As Anhalt then stood up, the storm troop man then kicked him behind his knees, and repeated this till Anhalt fell down. Another beating followed, which however did not seem to break the prisoner's spirit to the desired extent. Anhalt endured the blows in silence, and the storm troop man shouted in fury : ' You'll howl, you dog ! ' and hit at Anhalt until he lost consciousness. Then he threw him on the straw by the other prisoners."

.   .   .   .

" Otto Gerke, arrived at the Trade Union House, Cassel, at 3.30. Three auxiliary police said : No. 1 : ' That's one of them.' No. 2 : ' We'll come for him.' No 3 : ' That's Gerke of the Metalworkers' Union.' At 4.30 four storm troop men entered the office. ' Herr Gerke ? ' ' Yes.' ' Put on your coat. You must come with us to be interrogated.' In reply to my question whether the police president knew of this, I was told ' Yes.' Eight storm troop men took me to the public hall. I was first taken to the guard-room, then up into the hall and searched for arms. At about 5.30 I was summoned, and taken by two storm troop men down the steps into the cellar, where there were a number of bicycles in the passage. They told me to leave my hat and coat there. I was then taken down twelve steps into a lower cellar. In this cellar, I was thrown on to a table. My head and arms were held down, and I was beaten with rubber truncheons for 15 to 20 minutes. I was then pulled up and told to say ' Heil Hitler,' which I could not do. A doctor was summoned immediately, and he certified that I was suffering from loss of blood and nervous collapse."

" *Cassel, March 28, 1933.*

" I certify that I have treated Herr Otto Gerke, Yussowstrasse, Cassel, for wounds on both arms, buttocks, legs and calves. The wounds extend to the region of the kidneys. I have had Herr Gerke under treatment since March 24th. He is unable to carry out his duties and must be confined to bed."

(*Signed.*)

Propaganda Film instead of Dinner.

"At 6.30 a.m. on Monday, April 3rd, I was arrested by two protective corps men. Although my interrogation showed that there was no ground for my arrest, I was taken with two other prisoners to an ice cellar—an underground room 15 feet by 6, with no opening for either air or light. On Thursday at about 11.30 p.m. we were brought out of the cellar and put in a schoolroom. On Friday we thought that we were going to be released, but they had evidently only decided to make a spectacle of us. As we were put into a car, we were surrounded by a crowd of Fascists who jeered at us. To our surprise we were taken to a cinema, where we were shown a film 'Bleeding Germany.' It was a film of incitement against France, and included the shooting of Schlageter. One of the Nazis present began a speech. He imagined that he could win us over. But the main thing in our minds was that we had had no dinner that day.

"At midnight on Friday I was again fetched out by two storm troop men and taken to the police station. I was not able to answer their questions to their satisfaction, and the police inspector ordered me to be taken out again. An hour later two protective corps men came for me, but they did not take me back to where I had been imprisoned. They drove the car out to a wood and pulled up there. I was pulled out and then thrown on the ground ; then they asked me, 'Where are the arms?' I said : 'I don't know of any.' Then they started to beat me with rubber truncheons, one man holding my face pressed into the sand. After a while they paused and again demanded : 'Where are the arms?' I thought of trying to run, as I felt that nothing mattered any more, but then I noticed that they were getting tired. The man who was holding down my head let go, and then I felt a terrible blow on my head and lost consciousness. When I came to I crept home."

Tagore's Experience.   In the last week of April the

nephew of the Indian poet Rabindranath Tagore was arrested on suspicion of having plotted to assassinate Hitler. He was afterwards released, and gave the following account of his experiences :

" The room in which I was put was underground, dark and without any air. Twenty-two prisoners were already imprisoned there, all of them members of Left Parties, mostly Communists. Many of them had already been there more than a month and had not yet even been interrogated. From time to time one of them would be summoned and taken out of the cell. We would hear terrible cries, and then our companion would be pushed back into the room. He would show us the traces of what had been done to him. A Communist member of the Reichstag showed me the marks of ill-usage on his body, saying simply : ' Look, this is called national German culture.' On the day when I was arrested a young man of the name of Rahm was called out, and returned with cut and bleeding thighs. The storm troop men had beaten him with steel rods because he had refused to give false evidence against his comrades. Early on Tuesday morning a man was thrown into our cell who could hardly stand ; his arm was swollen and in a sling, and his face was covered with blood. He was a trade union official of the name of Fuhler. Storm troop men had forced their way into the Trade Union House, and as Fuhler could not produce the arms which they demanded he should give up, they attacked him, broke his arm, pushed a stick into his side, ripped his cheek open nearly to his eye, knocked him down and kicked him.

" It was impossible to sleep at night ; all the time the place was filled with the cries of the prisoners and the singing and laughter of our tormentors. In the next cell one prisoner was crying out for his mother without cessation. Often the storm troop men would come into the cells to carry out their brutalities."

Hᴛ

Documents which not even Goebbels can Dispute. Kurt Haas, a film critic who took absolutely no part in politics, was arrested by civilians in his flat on the night of February 28th. He refused to go with the men, who produced no official document apart from storm troop credentials. They then threatened that they would shoot him, and they beat him on his bed, tied him up and carried him, severely injured, to a car. Some police stopped the car on the way, and rescued Haas. His wounds were bandaged in hospital and then he was released.

Up to this point there is nothing exceptional in this story. But Haas made a complaint to the Ministry of the Interior, and what followed gives the case importance. Although the storm troop men were quite unable to produce any proof that they were acting on behalf of the authorities, they were subsequently fully protected by the Ministry. Here is the reply sent by Goering's Ministry :

" Prussian Ministry of the Interior.
" Storm Troop Connections Department No. 29/33.
" Berlin, 13th March, 1933.

" *To Herr Curt Haas, Berlin-Wilmersdorf.*

" Your letter dated 4/3/1933, addressed to the Minister of the Interior, has been passed to me as the appropriate officer to investigate and decide the matter.

" I have ascertained that the particulars given in your letter are inaccurate and distorted in essential points. The storm troop was completely in the right and acted with authority to take you into protective arrest. In accordance with the information I have received, after the storm troop men had produced their credentials, as you yourself admit, they acted as the circumstances required. After putting on your clothes at their request, you yourself are responsible for having made it necessary to break your resistance by force, inasmuch as you suddenly began to shout and bluster, and attacked the storm troop members, biting one man's thumb so severely that the wound is not yet healed. From the facts in my possession the degree of force used was not greater than was required to break your resistance.

" I see no grounds for taking any action against the storm troop leader and men concerned, but must rather reserve to the injured storm troop man the right to take proceedings against you.

> " Head of the Storm Troop Connections Department in the Prussian Ministry of the Interior.
>> " (*signed*) DR. HEYL."

This document should be of historical value. It can as little be disputed as the official announcement from Bielefeld :

" Bielefeld, 3rd April, 1933. The Social Democratic Member of the Reichstag and Town Councillor, Schreck, was arrested yesterday ; at present he is in hospital."

Chapter VIII: THE PERSECUTION OF JEWS

One of the first acts of the new Nationalist Government of Thuringia was the dissolution of the Central Union of German Citizens of Jewish faith within the territory of the Thuringian State. The following statement was issued by the Government in explanation : " One of the chief objects of the Central Union is to fight anti-Semitism. As there is no anti-Semitism in Germany, the Central Union no longer has any justification for its existence. It is therefore dissolved as from to-day."

WE ARE here dealing with questions of fact. Authentic reports and depositions relating to tortures, acts of brutality, and outlawry directed against Jews living in Germany will show clearly enough where the boundary lies between " atrocity stories " and the appalling reality. It will become evident that although in some particular cases the so-called " atrocity stories " may have been inexact and exaggerated, yet they have also to some extent understated the actual facts of brutality. For example, there has been a report that a certain Herr Cohn had his hairs pulled out one by one. But it turned out that this Herr Cohn had been out of Germany for some time, and had not suffered at all ; but on the other hand, that a certain Herr Levy not only had his hair pulled out, but had one of his eyes put out and has been in a hospital for some weeks in danger of death. Mistakes in names and in places where incidents took place have come to light ; but for every case reported which on investigation proved to be incorrect or exaggerated, there are a hundred cases of torture, murder and robbery which have not come to light at all, for the reason that the people concerned have been threatened with death if they tell the truth about the crimes which are being committed every day in Hitler's Germany.

The reports of actual incidents can stand by themselves without any reference to the problems of " the Jewish question." Many attempts, written from various standpoints, have been made to present an analysis of the situation in Germany in regard to the Jews. Here we deal with this wider question very briefly ; but it is essential to say something of the inseparable connection which exists between the Hitler movement and anti-Semitism.

Anti-Semitism as one of the Foundations of National Socialism.

It is an old practice of the ruling class to distract the attention of the people from their actual sufferings. It is not possible here to deal in a scientific way with the reasons why attacks on the Jews have for many centuries served as the basis for distracting the people in this way ; why throughout the Middle Ages the Jews were attacked as a religious community, and more recently for the most part as a " race." The analysis made by Marx in *The Jewish Question* has been followed by many subsequent writers who have treated the question from a social standpoint. At the present time it is impossible to approach " the Jewish question " as a confused complex of race, nationality, people and religion ; it must be regarded as a *social* question containing racial, national and religious elements.

Anti-Semitism in Modern Germany.

Hitlerism is a characteristic form of the process of dissolution of the lower middle class in the age of industrial capitalism ; and it has its parallel in the past. Anti-Semitism in modern Germany dates from the movement which developed under Adolf Stöcker, a court chaplain, in the last quarter of last century. The basis of that movement was economic. There was a period of unrestricted speculation in the years when German industry was being built up after the victorious war of 1870–71, and this was followed by a severe economic crisis which directly affected the lower middle class as well as the working class. Adolf Stöcker found the new gospel of salvation in a campaign against the Jews. Ernst Ottwalt, in his brilliant study *Germany, Awake !* writes of Stöcker as follows :

" Without any regard to fundamental economic facts, Stöcker ascribed to Jewish influence everything within the German Empire which seemed to him unhealthy and harmful : in the indebtedness of the peasant population of the provinces of East Prussia, which was an inevitable consequence of the increasing world production of grain, Stöcker could see only the Jew who gave credit to the peasant in order to drive him from hearth and home a short time afterwards, out of diabolical wickedness. He saw in the wretched position of the German industrial workers not the greed of a type of capitalist which had been brought into being by the advance made in the means of production, but the existence of Jewish capitalists—and the Jews were responsible for everything."

Bismarck the " Servant of the Jews."   The anti-Semite propaganda achieved a certain success : the first revolutionary upheaval of the duped lower middle class was concentrated on the weakest point, that is to say, the Jewish minority. But when Adolf Stöcker began to attack rich and powerful Jews also, the solidarity of the possessing class was roused ; Bismarck himself intervened, and the court chaplain who had become an agitator fell out of favour. It is amusing to find that the anti-Semitic movement of that period also attacked Bismarck, denouncing him as " the servant of the Jews." A pamphlet published in 1878 contains the following :

" The credit for having raised the Jews and their associates into a ruling clique in Germany must be given to Prince Bismarck. . . . The protection of the Jews is one of the blackest pages in Bismarck's glorious Empire, with its consequences in the impoverishment of the

working class, the demoralisation of all sections of
society and the disgusting fusion of money with the
aristocracy by birth. . . . Prince Bismarck succumbed
to the influence of the Jews. The society in which he
moved was composed of Jews and the associates of
Jews ; they were always with him, and were his political
advisers and the champions of civilisation on whom he
mainly relied."

This " popular movement " of the time inevitably found
expression in excesses. The signal was given by the burning
down of the synagogue in the little Pomeranian town of
Neustettin. (Then too the " national " indignation was
roused by an act of incendiarism ; and then too it was not
the incendiaries who were brought to trial, but Jews, who
were alleged to have burnt down their own temple out of
vindictiveness.) Pogroms followed. And when the " popular
movement " had already begun to flag—when the economic crisis was over—this anti-Semitism took legal shape
in the form of Parties, and also found people who could
supply the necessary ideology : Professor Eugen Dühring
with his work on *The Jewish Question as a Question of Racial
Character* opened a new era of anti-Semitism, racial anti-
Semitism. Since then a great deal of ink has flowed in order
to prove that the Jews are a race, and an outlandish,
inferior and criminal race at that. Apart from Chamber-
lain's ingenious assertions, this " science " has for the most
part been content with coarse jests. Now, in Hitler's
Germany, the science celebrates its triumph, and no
doubt there are a good many people who will be able to
earn their bread in this shameful way in the Third Empire.

Anti-Semitic Parties.   Germany was the country in
which anti-Semitism was first organised on a party basis.
These parties were the " German Social Party," the " Anti-
Semite People's Party," and later the " German Reform
Party " : they had no other object than anti-Semitism,
which was the sole aim and purpose of their existence. It

was characteristic that their fortunes varied with the economic situation ; but in any case anti-Semitism remained " parliamentary " for nearly three decades. During this period it was a sociological rather than a social phenomenon. With the economic catastrophe of the post-war period, however, anti-Semite parliamentarism once more developed into a " popular movement." The traditional anti-Semitic Parties disappeared, but there were no fewer than 260 anti-Semitic organisations in post-war Germany. These were all united by the National Socialists.

The National Socialist Workers' Party of Germany is indissolubly linked with anti-Semitism ; in fact, it is quite unthinkable without it. Anti-Semitism was one of the foundations and the constant companion of National Socialism from triumph to triumph up to the seizure of power.

Forms of anti-Semitic agitation.   Recent German anti-Semitism, of which Hitler's victory is the fulfilment, has never worried itself overmuch to find " scientific " justification. It is one of the special characteristics of this movement that from the very beginning it has never proved anything, but always merely asserted. Its success depends on confusing and distracting people from the actual state of things. This anti-Semitism has always found expression in the most repulsive forms of incitement. During the Kapp *Putsch* early in 1920 the curious anti-Semitic symbol, the *Hakenkreuz* (swastika), was first publicly exhibited, on the steel helmets of the Ehrhardt brigade. On that occasion, too, the Nazi songs were first publicly sung. Then also, a real " national " man made speeches entirely composed of expressions such as " Rathenau, the Jewish sow." On the streets the children were learning anti-Semitic songs. Now, in the Third Empire, they all know the glorious battle-song whose refrain runs : " When Jewish blood spurts from under the knife, things will be twice as good as before."

For fifteen years, in tens of thousands of meetings and tens of thousands of articles in the press, the Jew has been presented by Hitler's Party to the duped masses as the most utter abomination. The Jew is responsible for everything. For the war as well as the peace, for capitalism as well as the revolution, for poverty as well as wealth—the National Socialist agitation sees the Jew lurking everywhere and helping on the work of Judaism to reach its aim of world domination : and to Hitler and his followers this is equivalent to the destruction of the world. Here we can only give some examples of the absurdity and vileness of this anti-Semitism.

Hitler on the Jews. We take these examples from the most official statement of National Socialism, Hitler's book *My Fight*, which is now circulating in many hundreds of thousands of copies. There we find :

" The black-haired Jewish youth lies in wait for hours, satanic joy in his face, for the unsuspecting girl, whom he defiles with his blood and thereby robs from her own race " . . . " They were and are Jews who brought negroes to the Rhine, always with the same aim and idea in their minds of destroying, through the bastardisation that must inevitably result, the white race which they hate—of bringing it down from its high cultural and political level and themselves getting the mastery over it. . . . In culture the Jew defiles art, literature and the theatre, destroys natural sentiments, undermines all ideas of beauty and dignity, of nobility and goodness, and drags humanity down under the spell of his own base mode of life " . . . " If the Jews were alone on this world, they would smother themselves in dirt and filth just the same in their attempts to get advantages over each other and destroy each other, in so far as their complete lack of any sense of self-sacrifice, which finds expression in their cowardice, did not turn the fight into a farce " . . . " When the Jew wins political power he casts aside the few wrappings which he still has. The democratic Jew of the people becomes the Jew of blood and tyranny. He tries in a few years to root out the national carriers of intelligence, and by robbing the peoples of their natural intellectual leadership, prepares them for their lot as slaves in permanent subjection."

It must be borne in mind that these phrases occur in a book which is certainly representative and was written with the consciousness that it was representative. The extracts given in fact illustrate only the mildest and most restrained form of anti-Semitic agitation. A different and much clearer language is used in meetings and in articles in the Press. For years the typical headlines in the National Socialist papers have been : " At the udders of the Jewish sow," " The Jewish Plague in the World," and so forth. And finally it must not be forgotten that the main battle-cry of the Hitler movement is : " Perish Judah ! "

In the " Guide and Instructional Letter for Function-aries " of the National Socialists, dated March 15, 1931, we find :

" The natural hostility of the peasant against the Jews, and his hostility against the Freemason as a servant of the Jew, must be worked up to a frenzy."

" Day of Reckoning."   It is necessary to recall all this in order to realise the ridiculous character of the *démentis* issued by the National Socialist members of the Govern-ment in connection with the reports of the persecution of Jews and the grotesque nature of the statement that the Jews would suffer no harm under Adolf Hitler's protecting rule. For fifteen years the Jews have been spoken of as a world plague, as the most brutish of sub-men, and the adherents of the National Socialist movement have been given license to calumniate and persecute the Jews. Hatred of the Jews has been systematically nurtured. For fifteen years a " day of reckoning " has been promised. Is it strange that this sowing of murder should bear fruit when the so-called National Revolution developed ? Every young National Socialist has been ceaselessly told that it is a moral act, and his highest duty as a national German, to extirpate the Jews. How is it possible to make these young National Socialists understand that now, when they are in power, they are to protect the Jews ? So they are given a free hand—and very willingly, too, for of all the things which they have been promised the only thing they can be given is : the satisfaction of their lust for murder. The Government cannot give all National Socialist supporters bread and work, nor can it improve the economic situation or redeem any of the promises it made ; but so long as it allows the lower middle class to persecute and beat up the Jews it can distract them from the tremendous imposture of which they too have been the victims. For this reason the campaign against the Jews is given its head in Hitler's Germany. It would be a terrible mistake to think that the persecution of the Jews was only a transitory phenomenon of the period when Hitler took power. It is a political measure systematically carried out, and necessary for the tremendous deception of the people. Minister Goebbels, in a pamphlet called *The Nazi-Sozi*, says that " The liberation of the German nation can only be carried out against the Jews. It is true that the Jew is also a man . . . but the flea is also an animal—but not a pleasant one . . . our duty to ourselves and to our conscience requires us . . . to make him harmless."

Jews are Watching You ! To show that the anti-Semitic propaganda has not in any way stopped, but that it is being carried on in an organised way, making use of every available means, we quote only one of the publications which have appeared since Hitler took power. It is a book by Dr. Johann von Leers, with the title *Jews are Watching You !* It is a somewhat random collection of photographs which are presented to " the German people " by way of a warning. Among some 60 photographs of Germans and people of other nationalities there are pictures of Karl Liebknecht, who was a descendant of

Martin Luther, of the Catholic leader Erzberger, of Willy Münzenberg, in whom there is not a drop of " Jewish blood," of Gresinski, of the Catholic Mayor of Cologne, Adenauer, of Erwin Piskator, son of a clergyman—who are all, on the National Socialist racial theory, " Germans of pure race." But this is characteristic. In Hitler's Germany no one takes the trouble to check up even the most simple facts which are supposed to be the basis of statements made. It is quite enough to make assertions and calumniations. Anyone who is inconvenient to the Hitler régime is a " Jew " so far as this régime is concerned. That is all there is to it. The conception of " responsibility " is completely alien to these National Socialist " writers." If anyone asks for any proof, the National Socialist storm troops are good enough to silence any inconvenient questioner. This is the reason why no one dares to challenge even the most nonsensical statements ; and as no one contradicts them, the masses believe everything.

This book, which we hope will get a very wide circulation, as it is really a revelation of the " spirit " of the new régime, contains also photographs of Rosa Luxemburg, Professor Einstein, Georg Bernhard, Lion Feuchtwanger, Theodor Wolff, Emil Ludwig, Max Reinhardt, Charlie Chaplin, Alfred Kerr and the American banker Otto H. Kahn. No one who is not a National Socialist will find anything repulsive in these photographs. For the most part they are splendid heads of clever and serious people of real intellectual standing. The only repulsive things about the photographs are the titles which Dr. Von Leers has provided. Under Rosa Luxemburg is printed : " Executed." Levine : " Executed." Erzberger : " Executed at last. The young Germans who shot him were released from persecution after the national revolution of 1933." For Einstein there is the laconic remark : " Unhanged." This is a favourite observation of the compiler of the book ; he uses it for everyone who has not yet been murdered. For Reinhardt : " His second-rate and soulless art, etc." Chaplin is described as " a little sprawling Jew, as boring as he is repulsive." It is said of Toller : " Promptly locked up after Adolf Hitler's seizure of power "—but not even this is true, as by that time Ernst Toller was already out of Germany. Erwin Piskator is called a "Bolshevistic artistic Jew." The bankers Max Warburg and Dr. Karl Melchior are said to be " Extremely dangerous ! "

Among these " Jews " there is a young man of the name of Schlesinger, who once in desperation carried out an attack on a train which cost many lives. Later on he was released on an amnesty. In the course of the trial it came out that Schlesinger was not a Jew but a German " of pure race." Anti-Semitic propaganda made use of the name at the time, but subsequently had to drop its attacks when it was proved beyond question that this Schlesinger was " of pure race." But Dr. von Leers writes under his photograph : " Moved by greed and unconcealed race hatred, he caused the terrible railway accident at Leiferde." But what does it matter ? One lie more or less makes no difference to these people.

" Perish Judah ! " Herr Hanfstaengl, " Foreign Press Chief " of the National Socialists, gave a semi-official interview on March 27th, 1933, to the American representative of the semi-official Telegraph Union Press Service. In reply to the question : " Are the reports of alleged maltreatment of Jews true or false ? " he said : " A few minutes ago, when I met the Chancellor at the Munich airport on his arrival from Berlin, he authorised me to tell you that these reports are one and all base lies." Hanfstaengl's answer to detailed questions about the persecution of Jews was : " The Berlin Embassies of Sweden and Holland have investigated and have found that not a single Jew has been killed."

43 Murdered. The list of Jews shot or beaten to death by the storm troops has been checked by us, and it shows a total of 43. These 43 are cases in which the victims were murdered primarily because they were Jews, not because they were " Marxists." These 43 authentic cases, which have been examined in every detail, represent only a small part, a fraction, of the real number, which will undoubtedly come to light in the course of time, when it becomes possible to get more exact information on the actual incidents which have taken place in Hitler's Germany. These 43 names are selected from many hundreds of names ; all cases which up to now it has been impossible to check satisfactorily are left out of account. We do not want to " estimate " or " think," but to prove actual facts : a few detailed examples are taken from the mass of material before us.

On the 18th of March 1933, a tragic doom claimed our dearly beloved and promising son,
SIEGBERT KINDERMANN,
baker's apprentice, who had just completed his 18th year.

Moritz Kindermann, Sign Painter, and his wife. Franseckystrasse 5.

Funeral : Sunday, March 26th. 1933, 2 p.m., Weissensee.

No visits of condolence, by request.

The Jewish apprentice Kindermann, whose " tragic doom " this inconspicuous notice announces, was attacked in 1932 by National Socialists, because he was a member of the completely non-political Jewish Sports Society " Bar-Kochba." In connection with this attack a National Socialist was charged and convicted. In order to " revenge " this conviction, after Hitler's seizure of power young Kindermann was dragged to the Nazi barracks in the Hedemannstrasse in Berlin and there literally beaten to death, his body being then thrown out into the street. A large *hakenkreuz* was cut in his chest.

An Example from Cassel. Dr. O. M., of Cassel, reports as follows: " On Friday, March 17th, 1933, bands of Nazis went all over the town of Cassel, dragging off members of the Jewish community whom for any reason they did not like, in order to bring them to ' trial.' It should be noted that the victims were not persons who had been prominent in politics of any kind ; the reason for their ill-treatment was as a rule some petty spite on the part of the Nazi leaders. The following were particularly bad cases :

" Dr. Max Plaut, a lawyer, was dragged out of his office by a large gang of Nazis and taken away in a closed car which drove along the main street. As they drove along he was forced to shout ' Heil Hitler ' by blows with rubber batons, and each time he shouted the Nazis roared with glee. Plaut was taken to the Nazi headquarters, where a so-called court-martial was held and sentenced him, for alleged professional shortcomings, to 200 blows with rubber batons. He was then taken down to a cellar and strapped to a bench for the sentence to be carried out. He was then most terribly mishandled for almost two hours. After some time Plaut fainted ; water was then thrown over him until he revived, when he was given some alcohol by so-called ' sisters.' When he had come to himself the mishandling was resumed. By the time the brutal punishment had been concluded he had completely lost consciousness, and was left, covered with blood, lying in a corner. Plaut was then taken to his flat, where he died ten days later. The doctors who were called to attend him, Dr. Scholl, a nerve specialist, and Prof. Tönnisen, head doctor of the State Hospital, found the most terrible injuries, including serious damage to the internal organs, especially kidneys and lungs. His back and legs gradually turned completely black. Plaut had to be kept on his bed in a permanent state of narcosis, as when he came to consciousness he screamed so terribly that he was heard in the street. After ten days of this he died.

" On the same occasion another lawyer, Herr Dalberg, was most brutally treated in the same way as Plaut, and at the same place. It should be noted that some time previously he had had a conflict in court with a lawyer who is now in an official position; this dispute was brought up against him while he was being mishandled. There can be no doubt therefore that the tortures inflicted on Dalberg were due to direct instructions from this high Prussian official, who had previously been in command of the Cassel National Socialists. Dalberg was so badly injured that for some days the doctors were afraid that one leg would have to be amputated, but fortunately it was found possible to save it. Dalberg is still severely affected by the results of his ill-treatment.

Another particularly bad case was that of a young Jewish merchant, Mossbach, against whom, so far as I know, the only accusation was that he had had relations with a Christian girl, though these had been discontinued. Nazis broke into his flat and in the presence of his mother beat him so brutally that his head and spine were terribly injured. A doctor was called, Dr. Stephan, who is politically on the extreme Right, and he stated that even during the war he had never seen such an appalling sight. For a long time Mossbach hovered between life and death, but his life was eventually saved.

On the same day, also at the Nazi headquarters, two merchants, Freudenstein and Ball, were beaten and severely injured, both of them being dangerously ill for some time after. In both cases the ill-treatment was an act of personal revenge on the part of certain Nazis, but I have no details.

There was also a case of a banker named Plaut being severely handled, but his injuries were not so severe ; he was sixty years of age.

The crimes of the Nazis in Hesse were certainly not restricted to Cassel. It would not be an exaggeration to say that in every village in the province of Cassel where any Jews live, there have been similar cases, some of them appalling. I know that in some villages all the male members of the Jewish community have left their homes and only returned, if they have returned at all, after a long interval."

Forced to sign a Statement.

Leo Krell, 25 years of age, living in the Skalitzerstrasse, Berlin, was attacked by a Nazi Storm Detachment and carried off to a Nazi barracks where he was murdered. His body was then dropped in front of the Jewish cemetery. We mention this case because of what followed. His aged mother received a letter asking her to go and identify her son in the mortuary. It was difficult for her to identify the body, which was mutilated in every way. The *hakenkreuz* had been carved in his face and all over his body and burnt into the flesh ; all that was left of her son was a mass of bleeding pulp. Faced with this mutilated body, the mother was compelled to sign a statement that her son had died " after a long illness in hospital."

Such statements are always demanded from relatives in the case of people who have been beaten to death. If any of the relatives ever hint, even in private, at what actually happened, they can look forward to being brought before a court and sentenced to many months, if not years, of imprisonment, for taking part in an " atrocity campaign." As a rule the Storm Detachment people concerned tell the relatives that they will suffer the same fate if they do not " keep their mouths shut."

A deep silence lies over Germany. The people who are suffering dare not even call for help : that would be treason.

Forty-three mutilated corpses of Jews who had been beaten to death with rubber batons, steel rods and leather whips, have been recorded up to now—people whose only crime was that they were Jews. We do not know the total number of such corpses that have been secretly buried. Perhaps five hundred ; perhaps a thousand ; perhaps even more. The future will bring it to light. It is only after some years that it will be realised that all the reports of the brutalities carried out by Hitler's bandits which have so far been published fall far short of the appalling reality.

300 Proved Cases of Barbarous Cruelty.   Forty-three mutilated corpses, identified and authenticated up to the present—and how many cases of people beaten almost to death or injured for life ? Up to now we have records of 301 cases of severe bodily injuries inflicted on Jews—cases in which we have been in a position to verify the place and date of the crime and the identity of the person injured. The actual number of Jews who have suffered ill-usage must already be considerably over ten thousand. Of the three hundred cases which we have been able to verify we give the following examples.

In the middle of April a number of papers reported that Rabbi Jonas Fränkel, who is over 80, had been attacked and severely ill-treated by Storm Detachment men at his home in Berlin, Dragonerstrasse 37.

The Government issued a denial of this report.

The Rabbi's daughter, Ella Fränkel, reports the following details :

How my Father was to be Murdered
By ELLA FRÄNKEL

" At about 7.30 on the evening of March 7th three Storm Troop auxiliary policemen forced their way into our flat at Dragonerstrasse 37. Two of them held me prisoner, with their revolvers pointed at my forehead and my breast. The third shot at my father, who was sitting at his desk. Two bullets struck his head, and my father, streaming with blood, sank unconscious to the floor. One of the Nazis shouted : ' That's fixed him ! ' Then they broke open the desk and stole all the money in it—my dowry of 5,000 dollars and 2,000 marks. Before leaving they warned me against calling for help, and smashed the electricity connection so that the flat was left in darkness. We later ascertained that these ' auxiliary police ' were members of the Dragonerstrasse Storm Troops.

" I lifted my father from where he was by the desk to the window, and for half an hour was calling for help. The street was cordoned off by Nazis and several squads of police. Anyone who attempted to leave his house was driven back with blows from rubber batons. Eventually some police officers came up, followed by officials of the Humane Society, with whom our neighbours had got into touch. They wanted to take my father to hospital, but I would not agree. Two days later we were visited by an official from the Polish Consulate ; he found the flat still splashed with blood.

"For two weeks my father lay helpless ; we were afraid every hour that he was going to die. On April 8th some Nazis again came to the flat and demanded to see my father. They stated that if my father was willing to certify in writing that he had not been attacked by Nazis, but by Jews, he would not be interfered with again. I told them that my father was too ill to write, and that they must come back again in two days' time. They drew their revolvers and forced both of us to give our words of honour that we would give them the certificate two days later. As my father was determined in no case to give such a declaration, the only course left to us was to get away as quickly as possible. Two friends wrapped him up in a rug, and took him away in broad daylight to friends living in a distant part of the town. I was almost out of my mind with anxiety. We had previously taken away the two Scrolls of the Law[1], but we left everything else in the flat. I left the house in indoor clothes and without a hat, as our porter was a Nazi, and he would immediately have denounced us. We took the train to Vienna. My father, whose head was covered with bandages, was represented as being very old and deaf. I said that I was travelling to Vienna and had promised to look after the old man on the way. Soon after the train left Berlin a spy came and sat with us and put questions to me, but he left the compartment when we reached Dresden as my answers had not made him suspicious. After Dresden the examination of passengers began. German officials went from compartment to compartment asking ' Are you Jews ? ' I took up my position at the door of the compartment, in which there

[1] A Scroll of the Law consists of two " tables of stone," round which is wound a parchment on which the Pentateuch is inscribed.

were only the two Scrolls of the Law besides my father. The officials had however already been given a report by the spy, and they greeted me politely and said : ' Ah, you are the young lady travelling to Vienna and looking after the deaf old gentleman. We have this information already.' So we succeeded in getting here, and stopped at Reichenberg, as my father was quite unable to travel any further then. Later we came on to Prague. My father is still lying here ill."

We have given this case in detail as it is a very typical one, and we refer the reader to the accompanying photographs. A Rabbi eighty years of age attacked and left for dead, and his flat robbed—but the *démenti* machine has the effrontery to announce to the press of the world that there was no such person as this Rabbi. This case is typical of a thousand *démentis* of a régime which lies with an unscrupulous brutality equal to that with which it murders.

Attacked in the Synagogue.   We want to state another case, the scene of which was a synagogue. Rabbi Bereisch was in the synagogue in Duisburg at divine service when he was attacked and brutally handled. He was dragged out through the street and after being wrapped in the black-red-gold flag was made to run the gauntlet through a crowd of shouting men. Finally he was arrested and the charge made against him was " being responsible for public disorder in the street."

The Rabbi of Gelsenkirchen was driven out of the synagogue during the Sabbath service and with a number of other Jews was taken through the streets to the Nazi barracks. There they were all forced to turn their faces to the wall and make genuflections. When the Rabbi protested against this he was laid across a ladder and beaten with a stick. Later, he was set free, and succeeded in escaping across the Dutch frontier. He arrived at Amsterdam so severely injured that he was unable to stand. Before the Nazis set him free, they forced him to sign a declaration that " his imprisonment had been due to a misunderstanding."

Dementi einer Greuelhetze.

Berlin, 25. April. (Wolff.) Das „Prager Tagblatt" verbreitet heute eine Greuelmeldung und behauptet, der Berliner Groß Rabbiner Jonas Fränkel sei heute in Prag eingetroffen und berichte über scheußliche Greuel an Juden in Deutschland. So behauptet er u. a., er sei von SA.-Leuten überfallen und um 2000 Rmk. bestohlen worden. Die SA.-Leute hätten ihn und seine Tochter mit Revolvern bedroht, ihn niedergeschlagen und schwer verletzt. Er habe in Decken gehüllt in ein anderes Stadtviertel geschmuggelt werden müssen, und er habe sich dann so nach Prag durchgeschlagen. Er leide noch jetzt an Gleichgewichtsstörungen und an einer Gehirnerschütterung. Er habe die Absicht, nach Palästina weiterzureisen und nehme überall die Hilfe der jüdischen Hilfskomitees in Anspruch.

Wie dazu von zuständiger jüdischer Stelle in Berlin festgestellt wird, gibt es in Berlin überhaupt keinen Groß-Rabbiner. Ein Rabbiner oder anderer jüdischer Geistlicher namens Fränkel oder ähnlichen Namens ist nirgends vorhanden. Es handelt sich also wieder einmal um eine der üblichen Greuelmeldungen aus Prag, deren Quellen (WTB. zufolge) im allgemeinen deutsche marxistische Kreise sind.

Official denial issued through Wolff Telegraph Bureau that any such person as Rabbi Fraenkel existed.

PLATE NO. 12a.

Der Reichspräsident

Berlin, den 5. Januar 1933.

Herzlichen Dank für die mir zum Jahreswechsel übermittelten Glückwünsche, die ich bestens erwidere.

Mit freundlichem Gruß!

von Hindenburg

Herrn
Gross-Rabbiner Jonas Fränkel
Berlin C.

Letter from Hindenburg, dated Jan. 5th, 1933, to Rabbi Fraenkel, which proves his existence.

PLATE NO. 12b.

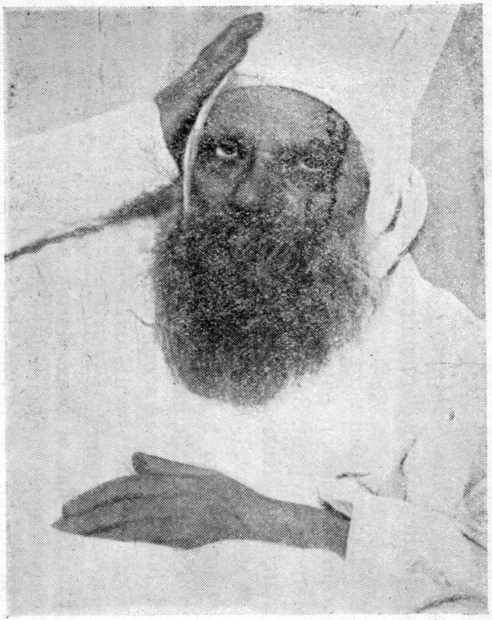

RABBI JONAS FRAENKEL after being brutally assaulted by Nazis.

PLATE NO. 12.

Pogroms.   The *Frankfurter Zeitung* of April 24th, 1933, contains the following announcement :

" Wiesbaden, April 23rd. Two assaults with fatal results occurred here on Saturday evening. The two victims were a merchant, Salomon Rosenstrauch, and a dairy-man, Max Kassel. The police report on the murder of Max Kassel runs as follows : ' On Saturday at 23.30 cries for help were heard coming from a flat in No. 43 Webergasse. At the same time a number of shots rang out. A motor lorry driver who was passing along the street went and informed the police. The police ascertained that the cries for help had come from the flat of Max Kassel, a dairyman, fifty-nine years of age. On entering the officers found Kassel lying dead on the floor of one of the rooms. On examination the body showed bullet wounds which had proved fatal. Further investigations showed that several persons by breaking in a door panel had forced their way into the flat and shot down the man as he was running towards the window. The shots had been fired from an army revolver. The investigations did not produce any evidence showing that the motive of the crime was robbery, and the indications are that it was an act of revenge.' "

The official report of the second case states that on that Saturday at 21.45 the police were called to the flat of a merchant, R., 58 years old, living in Wilhelmstrasse 20. R. was lying on the ground only just breathing. The body showed no injuries. A doctor ordered the man to be taken to hospital, but he died on the way from heart failure. The housekeeper who was still in the flat stated that at 21.10 two young men had rung at the door of the flat and asked for R. When he came to the door the two men pushed their way into the flat and one of them pointed a revolver at R. R. fled into another room and fell to the ground. The two attackers then left the flat without giving any further explanation. According to the woman's description they were two lads of between twenty and twenty-three years of age.

We mention these cases because they seem to us typical of the actual pogrom which is being carried out.

Living Targets.   These are a few of the cases which the authorities have themselves made public : but this does not mean that thousands of similar acts of brutality have not taken place, although nothing is said of them. One day in the middle of a Berlin street the son of an attendant at a Synagogue was attacked by a Nazi troop in the presence of his father. The lad was held by the Nazis and one of them fired his revolver twice through the lad's right calf and twice through his left calf. The lad has now been in hospital for three months, and it is probable that he will be lame for life.

A Case from the Provinces.   The following statement which we have received has been checked up by us in detail. It is typical of hundreds of similar reports which are in the possession of editors outside Germany and also in the hands of many private individuals.

" In the little town of Niederstetten, in Würtemberg State, a small Jewish community has lived for centuries. Its members are for the most part merchants who, as might be expected, in so far as they take any interest in politics, belong to the Parties of the Right rather than to the Socialists or Communists. Friendly relations existed until quite recently between the Christian and the Jewish sections of the population. A week before Easter a Nazi detachment arrived in the town early one morning and occupied the Town Hall, also taking control of the police. Then the houses of the Jews were searched for Communist documents, naturally without any result. In spite of this ten Jews, all respected citizens, were taken to the Town Hall and there, one by one, taken to a room. Each of them was then gagged, thrown across a chair and beaten with steel rods until he was practically unconscious. Then the victims, who could hardly stand, were taken to the Council Chamber and made to stand up against the wall—' The Wailing Wall,' as the Nazis called it. After they had been forced to give the Fascist salute, they were allowed to leave the Town Hall. Most of them, however, were so weak after the ill-treatment they had received that they had to be carried home by their relatives. All the victims were ill for some weeks and one of them has lost his speech. It should be mentioned that the non-Jewish population of the town, most of whom had voted Nationalist in the election of March 5th, were very indignant at what had taken place. An old peasant said : ' Hitler certainly would not have wanted this to be done.' The old man apparently did not have a wireless, or else he would have known that these ' German men ' have only carried out what the leading people in Germany have broadcast as their aim in thundering speeches every evening."

The following appeal, issued by the " Action Committee for fighting Judah in Neustadt " was published in the local paper dated May 18th, 1933 :

" Our aim is to liberate Neustadt from Jews and servants of the Jews. We must lay this down once again in plain language, in case the people who are affected by it have not yet understood it . . . if anyone still thinks that he can defend the Jews, in our eyes he is a scoundrel with whom we shall deal in the same way as we deal with the Jews."

In the Nazi Barracks.   K. W., of Berlin, reports as follows on his experience in a Nazi Barracks :

" A twenty-six year old Jew was brought in with me. He told me later that he had been arrested on his motor cycle, although he had never paid any attention to politics and has never voted. First his hair was cut off with nail scissors, and then the auxiliary police had a dispute as to who was to beat him. The auxiliary policeman who had brought him in said, ' I need not have brought the Jew in at all if I am not going to be allowed to beat him.' The others said, ' You are drunk ! Go and sleep it off.' Most of the auxiliary police smelt strongly of alcohol. After that the Jew was beaten up like the others, with cow-hide whips, steel rods and rubber batons. Then a dagger was placed against his chest and he was told : ' Now you are going to be stabbed to death ! ' He was actually only scratched and then he was told that he would be stabbed to death early the following morning. At a quarter to six I was brought to trial. As they could produce nothing against me, I was taken to the sleeping hall where about forty men were lying. I myself, was only given a few kicks and blows with rubber batons. There was also what they called a murder-cell. The three men who were in this cell had been beaten black from head to foot. At seven o'clock in the morning the Nazi officer in charge arrived and we were given breakfast, coffee and dry bread. Then we were drilled in the courtyard, after we had been forced to say, ' Hail to our Chancellor, Adolf Hitler.' While we were being drilled we had to sing *Deutschland über Alles* and other similar songs. Then we were asked whether we would defend the Fatherland if there was a war against Poland. We replied that we would. After that we were asked what we would do if we were set free, and whether we would join the Nazis, and to this we also replied in the affirmative."

Polish Protests. We cite the following, which is one of many official announcements and protests made by foreign countries.

" Berlin, March 30th. The Polish Ambassador in Berlin has lodged a protest with the German Government against the persecution of Polish Israelites by Hitler's bands. The Ambassador mentioned among other cases the following which had occurred in Berlin. On March 4th Herr Israel Weiss was taken from his flat and dragged off to a garage, where he was so brutally treated that he lost consciousness. After that he was taken to the police station where he was kept until March 6th. While he was being assaulted Hitler's followers took from him his passport and his ring and he never recovered these. On March 6th, Herr A. L. Mittelmann was attacked and taken into a restaurant where he was very severely injured. As a result of his treatment he is quite unable to work. In Chemnitz and Plauen, Hitler's followers have perpetrated terrible brutalities against the Jews. All the Polish Israelites who were arrested in Chemnitz were taken under guard through the town, being made to wash out all the inscriptions which had been written on the walls during the last election. A Polish citizen, Adalbert Dafner, was given 50 lashes with a riding-whip, being forced after every blow to say ' Thank you.' Terrible cruelties were carried out against a number of Israelites in the prison at Plauen.''

United States Complaints. A message from Berlin dated March 9th states that the American Ambassador has lodged a protest against the ill-treatment of American citizens. He cites a number of cases which have occurred in Berlin alone in the course of a few days. '' In Berlin many Jews, including some of American nationality, have been brutally treated. For example, an American citizen, Herr Max Schüssler, who is the owner of a house and had secured the eviction from his house of a Nazi tenant, was visited by Nazis one night. In order to gain entry to his flat they represented themselves to be police. Then they demanded that Herr Schüssler should sign a declaration allowing the return of his National-Socialist tenant.''

Official Statement from Czechoslovakia. The official press bureau announces under date of April

2nd : " In the hospital at Warnsdorf four refugees from Germany who have been brutally treated are now lying. Last night, at one o'clock they were taken from a place in Saxony which is now a concentration camp to another village not far from Warnsdorf, being accompanied by 12 Nazis. They were four Jews, one of whom is an Austrian citizen, two being Poles and the fourth having no nationality. A hundred yards from the frontier near Warnsdorf the four men were taken out of the lorry and beaten up until they were covered with blood, and when they ran towards the frontier of Czechoslovakia shots were fired after them. All four are seriously injured ; one of them, in addition to other wounds, has a serious fracture of the skull and is unconscious. It must be noted that two of them had been settled in Leipzig for 25 years, where they were in business, and the other two had been 12 years in Dresden. It is announced from Germany that the refugees had refused to leave Germany and had conducted themselves in an offensive manner to the guards who were accompanying them."

At the Frontier.   The following message comes from Prague. " The Berlin-Athens Express, which every day brings several hundred people to Prague, arrived there an hour late on April 1st, and with only three passengers. The passengers made depositions which they signed before a Notary, regarding what had happened in Dresden. At the station in Dresden a cordon of Nazis had been drawn up on both sides of the train, and another detachment came through the compartments giving the order ' Jews out of the train.' All Jewish passengers, including foreigners, were forced to leave the train. After this the passports of the other passengers on the train were examined, and they were also forced to get out. They were forced to line up on the platform and then they were ordered to march. The column of passengers, guarded by Nazis, went off towards the exit from the station. After this nothing more has been heard of them ; they included many women and children."

Another report runs as follows : " The National Socialists even come on to Czechoslovakian territory and promise a reward for any refugees who can be brought on to German territory under any pretext. The reward promised for an ordinary refugee is one hundred crowns, for a Jewish refugee, however, the amount is two hundred crowns. These facts have been certified by the Czechoslovakian authorities."

The following laconic announcement from Warsaw throws further light on the position of refugees : " Warsaw, March 15th. Forty-eight Jewish families from Germany, consisting in all of 150 persons, have crossed the frontier of East Prussia and taken refuge in Poland. There were terrible scenes at the frontier, the refugees being horribly ill-treated by the German frontier guards. They were beaten and kicked and everything they had with them was taken from them by the guards."

The Chief Rabbi of France issues a Statement.   In connection with the denials issued by the German author-ities, the Chief Rabbi of France has issued the following statement in connection with the anti-Semitic excesses in Germany :

" I am unfortunately compelled to say that the statements regarding atrocities are absolutely correct. We have evidence that cannot be disputed and also photographic documents. Do not think that we believe what we are told by refugees without further examination. We have ways of checking up their statements. We are in pos-session of documents which have come to us from an absolutely reliable source, which I am not able to name. I can, however, say that some of these documents have an official character and have been prepared by foreign Governments. The incidents in question are not cases of simple abuse, but cruel persecutions which have created victims and martyrs. If we are compelled to publish these documents, we shall do so. The conscience of the world," the Chief Rabbi continues, " is deeply troubled and is horrified at the revival of barbarism which the anti-Semitism of the Nazis represents. In the name of humanity and civilisation the whole world protests with us. It fears that the restoration of world peace will be endangered through these new attacks of brutal force against right."

The correspondent of the English *Manchester Guardian* has made an extremely detailed and objective report (published April 8th, 1933) which is certainly not coloured either by love or by hatred of national Socialism but only by a human horror of brutality.

" The samples of outrages committed by Brown Shirts since the elections make it more evident than ever that the Terror has been much worse than was at first believed. The British, French, and American press, so far from exaggerating it (as the German press complains), has understated the truth, although this is natural enough, seeing that only a small fraction of the truth is accessible. The Terror seems to have been worst of all—worse even than in Berlin—in Cassel, in Silesia (where Heines, who was imprisoned on a charge of manslaughter and released by an amnesty, is in charge of the Brown Shirts), in Worms, and in many villages.

" A precise account of what has happened in the villages of Oberhessen alone during the last four weeks would make a terrible story. But it is impossible to establish more than a few cases, enquiry being made difficult by the general fear not only of reprisals but also of imprisonment. A few days ago a man was sentenced to a year's imprisonment for spreading the ' false rumour ' that a Jew had been hanged by Brown Shirts—the ' rumour,' as a matter of fact, was true : the Jew, a certain Mr. ———, was beaten by Brown Shirts and hanged by his feet, so that his head was suspended off the ground. When the Brown Shirts had finished with him he was dead.

" Any German who dare say a true word about the Terror in his own country runs the risk of a fearful beating, or long imprisonment or even death, and no one can reasonably be expected to run such a risk. But, as one of the victims of the Terror said to your correspondent to-day, it is impossible to remain silent even under threats. There is no reason why opinion in England and the United States should be hoodwinked, and it is necessary to point out that letters or statements by German Jewish or Republican organisations or Societies saying that the Terror has been exaggerated are products of fear and intimidation and are therefore altogether unworthy of credence.

" Thousands upon thousands of Germans have only one wish—to get out of the country. But the frontiers are being closed by the new passport regulations and escape is impossible except at great risk. Thus all Germany is being converted into a huge prison."

Einstein's Appeal.   We will end this section with the appeal issued by Professor Einstein after he had been driven out of Germany. Professor Einstein arrived at Havre on March 27th on the steamer *Belgenland*. He was met by a delegation of the International League against anti-Semitism and gave it the following statement written by his own hand.

" The actual facts of brutal force and oppression against every free-minded person and against the Jews, the facts of what has taken place and is still taking place in Germany, have fortunately aroused the conscience of every country which remains true to the ideals of humanity and political freedom. . . . All friends of our civilisation which is so seriously menaced should concentrate all their efforts in order to rid the world of this psychological disease."

THE BOYCOTT

A Defensive Movement. From its early days National Socialism has made use of the method of representing itself as attacked, persecuted and menaced. The political terror which has been organised by Hitler has always worked hand in hand with organised lies.

The boycott against Jewish business concerns and the special acts against German Jews, of which we will speak later, give the best examples of the combined use of these methods. The National-Socialists might have said : It is in accord with our programme and with the demands which we have been making for many years that the Jews in Germany should be completely wiped out.

But what did the Nazis actually do by way of justifying their boycott of Jewish shops ? They cried out " We have been attacked. The Jews are trying to destroy us. What we are doing is in self-defence." This organised boycott was therefore called a defensive movement.

The boycott manifesto which was posted up everywhere runs as follows : " Men and women of the German nation ! The people who are guilty of this crime, this despicable atrocity campaign, are the Jews in Germany. They have called to their fellows abroad to fight against the German people. It is they who have issued lying statements and abuse. For that reason the leaders of the German movement of liberation have decided, by way of defence against this criminal campaign, to impose a boycott on all Jewish businesses, shops, etc., as from ten o'clock in the morning of April 1st, 1933. We call on you German men and women to make this boycott effective. Do not buy from Jewish businesses and shops ! Do not go to Jewish lawyers ! Have nothing to do with Jewish doctors ! Show the Jews that they cannot go unpunished if they humiliate and dishonour Germany. Anyone who opposes this manifesto thereby proves that he is on the side of the enemies of Germany."

On March 28th the national leaders of the National-Socialist Party published a manifesto to all Party organisations in which the German Jews are accused of having started the " atrocity campaign " against the National Government of Germany.

The Eleven Points of the Programme.

On the same day the famous eleven points for carrying through the boycott were published. We give them verbatim below :

(1) In each local group and section of the National-Socialist Party, Action Committees must be formed at once for the practical and systematic carrying out of the boycott of Jewish shops, Jewish goods, Jewish doctors and Jewish lawyers. The Action Committees are responsible for seeing that the boycott does not harm any innocent person but that it hits all the harder all those who are guilty.

(2) The Action Committees are responsible for protecting all foreigners without regard to their religion or race. The boycott is a purely defensive measure, and it is exclusively directed against German Jews.

(3) The Action Committees must immediately popularise the boycott by propaganda and explanatory statements. The principle of the boycott is that no German should buy from any Jew or be served by any Jew or his assistants. The boycott must be general. It must be carried out by the whole people and must hit Judah in its most sensitive spot.

(4) In cases of doubt the boycott of businesses must be postponed pending a decision from the Central Committee in Munich.

(5) The Action Committees must closely watch the newspapers from the standpoint of how far they take part in the enlightenment campaign of the German people against the atrocity campaign of the Jews. If the newspapers do not do

this or only do it to a limited extent steps must be taken to see that they are immediately prevented from reaching any house in which Germans live. No German man and no German business must give them advertisements. They must be given to understand that they incur only public contempt and that they are written for people of Jewish race but not for Germans.

(6) The Action Committees must carry into the factories their propaganda of enlightenment as to the consequences to German labour of the Jewish atrocity campaign, and they must explain to the workers that the national boycott was necessary as a protective measure on behalf of German labour.

(7) The Action Committees must carry their activities into the smallest villages in order to strike particularly at the Jewish traders in the countryside.

(8) The boycott must not be introduced gradually, but at a single blow. All preparatory measures must therefore be taken immediately with this in view. Instructions must be given to the storm troops to post pickets to warn the population against entering Jewish shops from the moment when the boycott begins. This will be April 1st punctually at ten o'clock in the morning. It will be carried on until instructions are received from the party leadership.

(9) The Action Committees must immediately popularise at thousands of mass meetings, which must reach even the smallest village, the demand that Jews shall only be admitted to every profession in proportion to the number of Jews in the community. In order to make this action more effective the demand should at first be restricted to three sections :

  A. Students in the intermediate schools and universities.
  B. The medical profession.
  C. The legal profession.

(10) The Action Committees are furthermore charged to see that every German who has any connection whatever

It

with people in other countries should make use of this, in letters, telegrams, and telephonic communications, to spread the truth that peace and order reign in Germany, that the German people has no more ardent wish than to continue its work in peace and to live in peace with the rest of the world, and that its fight against the Jewish atrocity campaign is purely defensive.

(11) The Action Committees are responsible for seeing that the whole fight is carried out absolutely peacefully and with the strictest discipline. Henceforth no Jew must have even a hair of his head harmed. We must finish with this atrocity campaign purely through the effectiveness of the measures outlined above.

This manifesto was accompanied by a long-winded explanation each word of which was evidence of a bad conscience. The explanation concluded with the words " National Socialists ! On Saturday at 10 o'clock, the Jews will know who it is that they are fighting."

The lords of the Third Empire appointed to take charge of this defensive action a man named Julius Streicher, the editor of a newspaper called *Der Stürmer*. The outside world will not know what sort of a paper this is although from time to time its circulation runs into hundreds of thousands. For his services in editing this Herr Streicher has been appointed commissioner in charge of the boycott movement.

Herr Streicher had hardly taken up his post when he gave an interview to the press at a conference of " national journalists " on March 30th. In the course of this interview he said :

" I shall not hesitate to prohibit by force the holding of divine service by the German Jews, or to prevent them from gaining entry to the synagogues by the use of armed storm troops. The stone has now begun to roll ; whether the atrocity propaganda ceases or not makes no difference.

This foreign propaganda against Hitler has given us the opportunity which we welcome, and the action will be carried through. It would be a complete illusion to imagine that the Nazis will allow themselves to be held back." (He, Streicher, was completely satisfied with the way things had developed ; his only care in the past week had been to see that the war of destruction against the Jews did not weaken.) " Had this happened—this is my firm conviction—the national revolution would have collapsed owing to its own weakness. This danger has now finally been averted and the German people can trust in me to carry out the whole of the necessary work in connection with the Jews."

Preparations for the Boycott.   Incitements to Jew-baiting were systematically developed during the last few days before the boycott. An example of this was the speech given by the newly appointed Chief of Police in Frankfort, reported in the *Frankfurter Volksblatt* of March 30th :

" No Nazi will have anything to do with a Jew, because he knows that the Jew is of inferior race. And I am no longer going to permit animals born on German soil to be killed by the sadistic Asiatic methods of slaughter used by the Jews. If the Jew cannot eat our meat then let him eat potatoes and turnips as you did in the hungry winters of the war. Germany is awake. You Jews, you have no need to tremble, we shall remain legal, so legal that perhaps legality will be uncomfortable for you, and then you can go to Palestine and fleece each other."

The instructions from the Nazi leaders issued in a steady stream. Action Committees were set up everywhere and they were given the task of ascertaining which shops, stores, lawyers' offices, etc., were in the hands of Jews. The Central Committee for the boycott of Jewish concerns laid down the following principles for action :

" The Action Committees must hand over to the storm-troops the list of shops which have been ascertained to be Jewish, in order that these may be picketed from ten o'clock in the morning of Saturday, April 1st, 1933. The pickets are charged with informing the public that the shops at which they are posted are Jewish. They are forbidden to take any physical measures of restraint. They are also forbidden to close the shop. In order to make it clear which shops are Jewish, posters or placards with yellow spots on a black ground must be posted at the entrance doors. The Jewish shops which are boy-cotted must not dismiss their non-Jewish employees and workers, or give them notice. The Action Committees, in agreement with the political leaders of the district, must organise mass demonstrations and processions in all areas on Friday evening. On the Saturday morning at ten o'clock at latest, the posters with the boycott pro-clamation must be put up on all advertising spaces. At the same time lorries, or better still furniture vans, must be driven through the streets with posters bearing the following words in the order given :

' In defence against the Jewish atrocity and boycott campaign ! '
' Boycott all Jewish shops ! '
' Don't buy from Jewish stores ! '
' Don't go to Jewish lawyers ! '
' Avoid Jewish doctors ! '
' The Jews are our bane ! '

" The Committees must organise collections in the German shops to finance this movement of defence."

During the days preceding April 1st the following announcement was posted on all advertisement spaces throughout Germany :

" The Jews have time to reflect until Saturday morning at 10 o'clock. Then the fight begins. The Jews of the whole

Storm troop pickets at the entrance to a
Woolworth store in Berlin.

PLATE NO. 13.

world are trying to destroy Germany. German people, defend yourselves ! Don't buy from the Jews ! "

Several of the Government Departments also issued instructions as to the measures which were to be taken in connection with the boycott. All sections of the Nazi organisation also issued detailed instructions ; there was no party official who failed to take the opportunity to make himself important by issuing an instruction of some kind.

Treatment of Judges.

An eyewitness has given us the following report :

" On Friday, March 31st, an extraordinary scene took place in front of the High Court in Cologne. Nazi lads forced their way into the court buildings and dragged out the Jewish lawyers and judges. Then these were put into a refuse cart and made the laughing stock of the crowd. Many of the lawyers and judges were still wearing their robes. The police looked on without interfering. The cart was then taken to the main police station, which is a considerable distance from the court.

" The official report, which is an absolute lie, was as follows : ' In Cologne, members of the Nazi storm troop, in conjunction with the police, arrested a number of Jewish judges and lawyers for their personal safety, as a large crowd had collected in front of the Law Courts.' "

The boycott had a limit—namely, at the point when it endangered profit. In effect, all these measures only hurt the Jewish middle class and working class but not the big Jewish capitalists. And when it was a question of trade with foreigners, all prejudice and race-hatred had to fall into the background, and the Jews were not treated as " Sub-men " or " World Pests " but only as extremely welcome paying guests. Here is a report published in the *Frankfurter Zeitung* :

" Wiesbaden, May 31st. Up to the present this year, the number of visitors has fallen below expectations. The number of foreign visitors during the first week of May, which is always the height of the season for Wiesbaden, was 1,744, and in the festival week following, it rose only to 1,808, falling again to 1,760 in the third week. The total number of visitors up to the middle of May has only been 27,000. It is therefore in the interests of this health resort that the local magistrates, the directors of the Kurhaus, and the National district leaders should make it known to everyone concerned both in the country and abroad that the mineral springs of Wiesbaden are as before available without hindrance to all visitors from all countries, and that peace and order have never been disturbed in this town. . . . The authorities of Wiesbaden should feel their responsibility both to the population and also to foreign visitors, and should guarantee to all who are either permanently in Wiesbaden or make a temporary stay there, without regard to their religion or political outlook, a secure and pleasant visit."

Laws of Exception.   The open boycott ended on April 1st, although the National Socialist press, the official leaders of the party, as well as their spokesmen, had assured the whole organisation that this historic Saturday must be regarded as " merely a test preparatory to a whole series of other measures," which " would be carried out unless the opinion of the world, which at the moment was hostile, underwent a complete change."

Opinion in other countries certainly changed radically, but in a direction unfavourable to the Third Empire. The Government in Germany was quick to notice this ; in fact they noted it even before the boycott, and they realised that this open demonstration against the Jews was bad business. The National Socialists have principles, but they have always been prepared to sell them.

The Retreat. In the course of the week before the boy-cott even Herr Streicher, evidently under instructions from the Government, stated that it would not be necessary to resume the boycott. And the Minister for Propaganda and National Enlightenment told the representatives of the foreign Press on March 31st:

" That the Government had decided provisionally to restrict the boycott against the Jews to Saturday, April 1st, when it would operate from ten o'clock in the morning till eight in the evening. After that no further action would be taken until Wednesday. If the international press had by then stopped its agitation against Germany no further action would be taken, but if this were not the case, a boycott would be started at ten o'clock on Wednesday morning and this boycott would drive the Jews of Germany into absolute ruin. The instructions that two months' wages and salaries of employees of Jewish firms must be paid in advance from April 1st is cancelled."

The last sentence of this announcement shows that under the pressure of events the National Socialists had been forced to repeal their own decrees. It had originally been decided that all owners of Jewish shops must pay all their Christian employees two months' salary in advance. The consequence of this was a run on the banks which might have led to a catastrophe if this decree had not been withdrawn at the earliest possible moment.

The Silent Boycott. The public boycott was a demonstration, and as a demonstration it failed and was not resumed. On the other hand, the silent boycott was continued, a boycott which cost nothing and hit not so much the rich and powerful Jewish firms as the tens of thousands of Jewish employees, doctors, lawyers, teachers, officials, university professors, etc. Hundreds of thousands of Jews have been deprived of their living; but this has given hundreds of thousands of places for Nazi hangers-on.

Jewish Lawyers not Allowed to Practise. In Berlin at first out of 1,200 Jewish lawyers, only thirty-five were permitted to practise, and the number allowed to continue their practice in Cologne was only four. All Jewish judges have been given " leave of absence."

The Commissioner of the Prussian Ministry of Justice issued the following instructions on March 31st :

" The irritation of the people at the presumptuous attitude of Jewish lawyers and doctors has reached such a height that it is necessary to take into account the possibility that the people may take the law into their own hands, especially during the period of the defence campaign of the German people against the Jewish atrocity propaganda. This would endanger the authority of the administration of justice. I therefore request you to suggest to all Jewish judges now in office that they should at once apply for leave of absence, and this should immediately be granted to them. Please arrange with the Lawyers' Association or other local organisations of the legal profession that from 10 o'clock tomorrow morning the number of Jewish lawyers permitted to practise is fixed in a proportion which is the same as that of the Jewish population to the rest of the population. It is unnecessary to point out that Jewish lawyers should not be employed as junior counsel, nor should they be allowed to take dock briefs, or be appointed receivers in bankruptcy or trustees. All engagements of Jewish lawyers in connection with official cases must immediately be withdrawn. The Executives of Associations of Lawyers must be induced to resign. If the provincial and local leaders of the National Socialists express the desire to supervise the maintenance of security and order within the court buildings by sending armed pickets to these places, their wishes should be complied with."

Similar instructions were issued against Jewish doctors. In the first place they were excluded from Health Insurance practice, which of course, covered the great majority of all cases.

The teachers and lecturers in Prussian educational institutions were required by the Minister of Culture, Rust, to fill out a questionnaire as to their racial origin.

The Civil Service.   As for Government officials, the following decree was published in the beginning of April :

" Anyone of non-Aryan descent, particularly if their parents or grandparents were Jewish, is to be regarded as non-Aryan. One parent or one grandparent who is non-Aryan is sufficient. This is particularly to be assumed when one parent or grandparent has been a member of the Jewish religious community. Furthermore, every official who has joined the service since August 1st, 1914, must prove that he is of Aryan descent or that he fought at the front or that his son or father fell in the world war. Birth certificates and marriage certificates of parents, in addition to military papers, must be sent in. If the Aryan descent of an official is doubtful, a decision must be made by the office of experts for racial investigation attached to the Ministry of the Interior. In deciding whether the provisions of Section 4, par. 1, apply, the whole political activity of the official concerned, particularly since Nov. 9th, 1918, must be taken into account. Every official is under an obligation to inform his superior authorities to what political party he has hitherto belonged and what his political activities have been. The Reichsbanner, the Republican Richterbund, and the League for the Rights of Man are to be considered political parties within the meaning of this paragraph. This decree finally and definitely puts an end to the scandal of the November system, which aims at the destruction of the honest professional Government servant by the

THE PERSECUTION OF JEWS 267

introduction of party officials and office seekers. The consequences of this criminal policy have been the innumerable scandals of corruption, in which the people concerned were always representatives of the parties which, in November 1918, by treason and cowardice had put themselves at the head of a clean and untarnished State. It is well-known and does not require to be proved here in detail that the most prominent supporters of the November Republic had been involved in the worst of these affairs. That period is now gone for ever, and the new Germany will once more be administered by really efficient officials, as the world knows it was before the war."

The special importance of this decree is that subsequently almost all categories of university-trained people (doctors, lawyers, teachers in high schools, etc.), and also bank officials and commercial employees, were put through a sieve in accordance with the principles laid down in this decree.

The Attack on Jewish Doctors.   The following manifesto was published in the Medical Journal of Greater Berlin, dated May 20th, 1933. The writer, a certain Dr. Ruppin, is not just a nobody ; he is Commissioner of the Provincial Medical Association of the provinces of Brandenburg and Grenzmark. The article is headed " Away with Jewish Doctors ! " The text is as follows :

" The complete removal of Jews from all academic professions is necessary. Members of the free academic professions, particularly doctors, come into personal contact with very wide circles of the population and occupy a position of confidence in relation to their patients which gives them influence over the outlook of the people with whom they are in contact. The Provincial Executive of the Doctors of Brandenburg therefore considers it unthinkable that in our National State a Jew should have the possibility of spreading the poison of

Jewish thought in this way. Undoubtedly, the earlier ideal conception of professional duty has given way in wide circles of the profession to the Jewish commercial outlook, and this is due to the over-loading of the profession with Jews. This commercial attitude must be driven out of the medical profession and we must make its re-introduction impossible. In so far as corruption has penetrated the profession, it must be rooted out by the most decisive measures. We German doctors therefore demand the exclusion of all Jews from the possibility of giving medical treatment to our German people, because the Jew is the incarnation of lies and deceit. Furthermore, we demand legislation to punish with imprisonment and immediate removal from the profession the offences and crimes which are associated with the positions of confidence filled by the profession. We doctors ask all National professional organisations in Germany to support our demand."

By way of supplement to the above we give the following decree of Commissioner Dr. Wagner, who is in control of the German Medical Associations :

" In pursuance of the boycott against the Jews, the Berlin Health department, by agreement with the Mayor, instructed its sections not to meet any claims from its members where Jewish doctors have been called in to treat cases on or after April 1st. Where a Jewish doctor had previously been called in, it is suggested that members should consider whether to continue to make use of him. The Health Insurance Institute hopes that a sense of national duty will prevent the members from making use of Jewish chemists, dispensaries, opticians, or dentists."

Dismissal of Jewish Teachers.   We can give only a few examples of the many similar instructions which have been issued in connection with the various professions. The future position of Jewish teachers in Germany is indicated by a letter issued by one of the most prominent of the Nazi leaders, Dr. Löpelmann, a member of the Prussian Diet :

" We call your attention to the fact that it is intolerable that Jewish teachers should still fill posts in Prussian educational institutions, while German soldiers who fought at the front have to wander round as underpaid auxiliary teachers in their own Fatherland. Furthermore, we consider it an impossible situation that any regard should be paid to the exaggerated claims of male and female Jewish scholars. On behalf of the National Socialist Parliamentary fraction in Prussia we expect you to take the following measures :

(1) All Jewish teachers, that is, teachers of Jewish descent, must immediately be dismissed or sent on leave from all Prussian educational institutions.

(2) In the case of male and female scholars who are Jews, the proportionate clause must be applied, so that the percentage of pupils of Jewish origin in any institution must correspond with the proportion of Jews to the whole German population ; that is to say, only one per cent of the students at any institution may be Jews or of Jewish descent."

In accordance with this circular, almost all Jewish teachers employed in the public educational system were immediately " granted leave." An instruction issued by the chief official of Brandenburg and Berlin extended these measures also to Jewish private teachers.

A Cabinet Meeting on April 25th passed an Act " against the excessive number of students of foreign race in German schools and universities."

The same principals were applied to the staffs of universities. In an earlier chapter some of the best known Jewish lecturers who have been dismissed are mentioned.

Removal of Jewish Editors and Journalists.　The *Neue Freie Presse* of April 13th, 1933, reports :

" In the extraordinary general meeting of members of the Berlin district organisation of the National Union of the German Press, it was unanimously decided to nominate Dr. Dietrich, at the general delegate meeting, for the presidency of the Union. After the general meeting of the Berlin organisation the new committee met, and adopted unanimously a motion that in future no Jewish or Marxist editors were to be admitted to membership. A further motion for the general delegate meeting was also adopted unanimously, demanding that Jewish and Marxist editors be not permitted to enter or belong to the National Union of the German Press."

Almost all Jewish editors of German papers have been dismissed, and contributions from independent journalists of Jewish faith or Jewish origin are not accepted. It must be noted that in this connection even Jewish newspaper proprietors have achieved inglorious distinction ; for example, Gütermann, the Jewish proprietor of the *Neue Badische Landeszeitung* in Mannheim, dismissed all his Jewish editorial staff and employees as early as March 1st.

Debarred from Lists of Assessors and Juries.　The silent boycott of the Jews continues in every sphere ; they are being banished from all public life. The *Neue Freie Presse* of April 12th reports the exclusion of Jews from the lists of assessors, jurymen and arbitrators :

" The Government has decided to shorten the current period of office of all assessors and jurymen to June 30th, at which date the period of office of commercial arbitrators will also be brought to a close. The new lists of assessors and jurymen will be differently constituted in future, as in present circumstances the municipal authorities will naturally send people of a different outlook to participate in the electoral colleges. There will no longer be any Communist assessors and jurymen. The number of Social Democrats nominated will be considerably smaller than hitherto, and it is probable that no Jews will be elected. The appointment of the new commercial arbitrators will also be on the same lines. The decree just issued provides that, until new elections of assessors and jurymen are held, judges need not adhere to the existing rules for bringing in lay assistants ; for example, they may pass over certain names on the lists."

Jews as "Outcasts" in Sport. Even in sport every Jew is an "outcast." Although even in America coloured boxers are allowed to take part in championship fights, German boxers of Jewish faith or origin are no longer allowed to appear in the boxing ring in Germany. The holder of the middle weight championship in Germany, Erich Seelig, was prevented from defending his title in Germany ; he was, however, able to show his form in France. Daniel Prenn, who is far and away the best tennis player in Germany, can no longer be selected to represent Germany in international matches. We await with interest the steps which are to be taken against Helene Mayer, the champion woman fencer. Although probably no one looks more " pure-blooded " and Nordic than she does, she is the daughter of a Jewish doctor in Offenbach.

We quote the following as a good example of many similar announcements ; it was printed in the *Neue Freie Presse* of April 28th, 1933 :

" The German Swimming Association issues the following statement : ' The German Swimming Association has adopted the Aryan clause. In what form the membership of Jews in all sports associations, and therefore in the Swimming Association, will be regulated, and whether the Aryan clause will be incorporated in the

Statutes of the Association, will be determined in accordance with instructions issued by the Government. Meanwhile, I order that Jews shall be removed from all leading positions in the association and put into the background ; and they must not appear as representatives in displays or take part in sports meetings.—GEORGE HAX.'

The German Swimming Association is at present affiliated to the International Swimming Association, and the Aryan clause conflicts with the statutes of the latter body, which prescribe equality of rights for everyone. The president of the International Swimming Association is, however, Binner, who was 'removed from the Executive of the German Association because of his international outlook.'

Pending the final decision of the Government Commissioner of Sport, the regulations relating to official posts will be applied to Jewish members of the DSB Union. This means that only those Jews (by race, not religion) who enjoy protection under the Civil Service Law will be allowed to take part in sports meetings."

Malicious Rumours.   But when business questions come in, in this connection also loyalty to principle takes second place. The Government-controlled *12-Uhr-Mittags-Blatt* of April 19th, 1933, under the heading " Malicious Rumours " gives an assurance that the race question will not be raised at the Eleventh Olympiad, which is to take place in Berlin in 1936 :

" The foreign boycott-propaganda against Germany has even penetrated sport. Many foreign papers have repeatedly stated during the last few weeks that efforts are being made, especially in the United States, to transfer to another country the Olympic Games which have been arranged for Berlin in 1936, on the alleged grounds that measures will be taken in Germany to prevent Jewish sportsmen from taking part in international competitions. In reply to an official enquiry, Avery Brundage, chairman of the American Olympic committee, stated that the International Olympic Committee had the right to select where the Olympiad would be held. The Committee, which is to meet in Vienna in June, would undoubtedly consider the question ; his personal opinion was that the Olympic Games should not be held in a country where the fundamental Olympic principle of the equality of all races was being violated. In connection with the premature declaration made by this leading American sportsman, it must be stated that no measures have been or will be taken in Germany which make participation in international sporting events dependent on the question of race. The world can be confident that every individual who is sent to Berlin to represent his country in the Olympic Games will be received and treated as a guest, irrespective of his race or nationality."

Passports. Special regulations are also in force for Jewish holders of passports. The Breslau chief of police has issued instructions

" that German citizens of Jewish faith or formerly of Jewish faith who are in possession of passports must present these in person at the police headquarters of the area in which they live, not later than April 3rd, 1933. The passports will be returned after they have been altered so as to make them valid only for internal travelling in Germany."

Special Hours for the Baths. There is hardly any possible regulation calculated to bring Jewish citizens into disrepute of which some person in authority or some administrative body has not thought. The town of Speyer in the Palatinate will live in the history of these times for its unique inventive powers. It has the glory of being the first German municipal authority to issue a regulation

" that in the interests of public order Jews may only use
the municipal baths at certain hours of the day."

Other German municipal authorities were quick to
follow this example. The *Frankfurter Zeitung* of May 24th,
1933, reports :

" At the Tübingen council meeting on May 15th it was
moved by a National Socialist that ' Jews and persons
of foreign race be excluded from the use of the free
municipal baths.' The motion was adopted with only
three voting against it."

Shortly afterwards, the Upper Silesian newspapers
published similar regulations.

Dismissal of Jewish Employees.   It would be a mistake
to think that German Jews were only thrown out of the
professions. A good deal is said, and rightly so, about the
outlawry of Jewish professors, doctors, lawyers, teachers and
artists ; but unfortunately not so much attention is paid to
the treatment of Jewish employees, small traders and
workers. But the main part of the Jewish population is
covered by these categories ; and the economic position of
these Jews is just as difficult as that of the non-Jewish lower
middle class and working class. The Nazi factory cell
organisations have been most assiduous in depriving the
Jewish clerks, small traders and workers of their livelihood.
A Berlin message of March 31st runs :

" On the instructions of the National Socialist Party
Executive, the factory cell organisation instructs
National Socialist factory cell committees, together with
the workers' organisations, to visit the Jewish shops and
demand two months' payment in advance for Christian
workers and employees. The demand should also be
made that all Jewish employees be dismissed. Anyone refusing to comply with these demands must be

immediately reported to the party leadership, which will take the necessary steps. Punctually at three o'clock to-morrow afternoon all employees and workers in Jewish shops must leave work and take part in warning off customers. Newspapers and vital industries are excepted, but in any case all Jewish employees must be dismissed. In the Ullstein publishing house the whole of the responsible editorial staff of Jewish race has been granted leave of absence."

The *Frankfurter Zeitung* of May 28th, 1933, states :

" It is reported in the *Pössnecker Händlerblatt*, the official journal of the Association of German Merchants, Showmen and Commercial Travellers, whose headquarters are at Dresden, that at a provincial conference of the Union of Traders the question was raised whether Jewish merchants and traders would be allowed access to the markets in future. The president of the provincial organisation put forward the view that ' the Jews must be completely rooted out.' "

Business is Business—even for anti-Semites. The *Völkischer Beobachter* of April 2nd, proclaims the " spontaneous rise of prices on the Stock Exchange, now rid of Jews," as the most obvious result of the boycott movement. We know why such a point is made of this ; it is to show that the fight is not against the existing system, not against capitalism and not even against the excesses of capitalism, but that it is a competitive fight of the national profiteers against the Jewish profiteers. The members of the Stock Exchange can do business even on a " Stock Exchange now rid of Jews." The fight is not against capitalism, not against private property, but against the small man ; against the " Aryan " workers and middle class who are being hoaxed ; against the Jewish employees and small traders, who are being ruined, to the delight of the capitalists of " Aryan " and Jewish blood.

The " Aryan " principles are regulated everywhere by the size of a man's purse. In a statement printed in the *Berliner Tageblatt* of March 31st, 1933, Herr Oskar Wassermann, a director of the Deutsche Bank und Diskontogesellschaft, correctly stated that he had not suffered the least inconvenience, and that the change of things had not made any noticeable difference so far as he was concerned, even from a social standpoint. The other Jewish capitalists may equally congratulate themselves : the National Socialist Government is doing its utmost for their material wellbeing. It has issued reproofs to those in its lower organisations who thought that the basis of anti-Semitism was the National Socialist hostility to capitalism. It protects, if not the Jews, at least Jewish capital. Business first ! Capitalism, whether " Aryan " or represented by Jews, is not to fall a victim to the spiritual revival which the " National Revolution " has brought to boiling point. The *Frankfurter Zeitung* and the *Völkischer Beobachter* of March 27th publish the following letter, addressed by the " Commissioner for Trade," Dr. Wagner, to the president of the " National Socialist Party Office for Municipal Politics," Mayor Fiehler of Munich :

" I have recently received from a number of business firms copies of circulars issued by various local authorities to a large number of manufacturers and other business concerns, with a view to ascertaining whether the concerns can be regarded as ' German undertakings.' The questions put in the circulars are intended to discover to what extent the capital of the firm concerned is German, to what extent non-Aryan and non-German principals are connected with it, and so forth. While I am of course completely in agreement with the view that the municipalities particularly should only obtain their requirements from German firms, I nevertheless consider it necessary that a stop should be put to the measures which have been taken. The whole complex of questions raised in these circulars is not so simple that decisions can be made by a mere ' Yes ' or ' No ' or on the basis of figures. It is rather the Government's task to see that *every undertaking in Germany, no matter where its capital comes from or who controls it,* finds its place in the German economic system, and that the management of each undertaking is in future conducted exclusively from a German economic standpoint. In carrying through this necessary task the Government can however only be hindered, if through the action of certain authorities a situation is created which reacts unfavourably on economic life. Our aim cannot be to ruin existing economic undertakings in Germany, even if they are worked with foreign capital and have hitherto been directed to some extent by foreign individuals, but rather to compel them to act in a German way and in conformity with the great principle laid down by our leader—' the common good before private interests.' I must therefore request you to use your influence, as the leader of the Department of Municipal Politics, to prevent further circulars of this type being issued in future, and to explain that such measures will cause a dislocation in the whole of the country's economic life which, with the best will in the world, we do not want at the present time."

" With the best will in the world "—they do not want any capitalist to suffer loss in this " national revolution." We knew this long ago. The people who still swear by the " Socialist " Adolf Hitler, and expect him to perform the miracle of securing for the peasants higher prices and at the same time lower prices for the consumer, higher wages for the workers and at the same time greater profits for the employers, higher salaries for civil servants together with economies to the State—these misled and incited " miracle believers " will before long be roused from their hypnotised state by the undeniable and inexorable fact that in the " Third Empire " no one gains anything but the capitalists, whether they are of Jewish or non-Jewish faith. They will learn from what they have still to experience in the " Third Empire " that the whole campaign against the Jews has only served to distract them from the struggle against the people who are really responsible for their conditions.

The Aryan Clause and Race Officials.

We have seen that the anti-Semitism of the New Germany has a biological basis : that it is racial anti-Semitism. This biological anti-Semitism dates back to the anti-Semitic campaign led by the court chaplain Stöcker, which derived its " ideology," that is, its pseudo-scientific justification, from Eugen Dühring's *The Jewish Question as a question of Racial Character*. " Race science," which used to be a hobby-horse of freak writers and was never taken seriously, has now in the New Germany been declared an official " science "—which means that it is now a lucrative profession.

The Jews as a " Race."

It is true that in spite of all its efforts this " science " has not yet succeeded in proving that the Germans are a race ; on the contrary, it is evident that the Germans are a mixed people and are very far from having any right to call themselves " Nordic." But these curious research-workers have not yet even succeeded in proving that the Jews are really a " race."

We will come to their aid : there is something in the talk of a Jewish race. But in this case too it is necessary to stand things on their head in order to examine the matter, which is extremely complex. That is to say, we must treat race, not as an original factor, but as an artificial product, not as the beginning, but as the result of a process of evolution. To attempt to trace back the Jews of the present day to the original Jews of the Bible would be a hazardous and absurd undertaking. In the course of Jewish history there was a constant mingling of races which it is not easy to disentangle. But from about A.D. 1000, at the end of the period of proselytism (that is, the entry of people of other faiths into the Jewish religious community), the religion and laws of the Jews themselves, and the social relations in which they lived, maintained an " in-breeding " which in duration and degree has no parallel in European history. The anthropological characteristics of race originated during this period, which in the course of more than eight hundred years produced a new type of human being, namely, the Jew.

But what is to be gained even by proving the existence of Jewish racial characteristics is quite another matter. The special characteristics of the Jews against which the anti-Semites pretend they are fighting are not in any way the product of race, but of the social conditions in which they live : the fact that they are a *caste* whose conditions of existence are prescribed by the world around them. When these imposed conditions no longer exist, then the characteristics disappear immediately, that is to say, at least in the second generation which has not had to live in these conditions.

But such theoretical discussions take us a long way from the actual practice of National Socialism. In this sphere everything is much simpler and more straightforward. There is not a single question in which National Socialism has acted in accordance with its own arguments ; on the contrary, it has always *post factum* found venal persons to justify its own barbarities as " acts of culture." And if in Germany to-day " racial research " sets itself up as " science," the real purpose is only to provide a new cloak for the bestialities of the existing régime.

" Race Officials."   The *Frankfurter Zeitung* of May 5th, 1933, reports :

> " Dortmund, May 4th. (TU). The Government Commissioner of Dortmund has issued instructions for the immediate organisation of a Race Department in Dortmund. The Assistant Commissioner for Health, Dr. Brauss, who is to take charge of the department, has made an important statement to the press on the question of racial hygiene. He indicated that medical

material relating to the 80,000 schoolchildren in Dortmund, which provided partial material for statistics of race hygiene, was already available. Thus the department would first deal with the young persons who would constitute the next generation. At the same time, the investigations laid down under the recently published regulations would be undertaken, that is, in connection with the candidates for official positions and the students in the higher schools and universities. Investigation of the whole population would be a task for future years.

" *The early publication of laws for the separation of the race and its division into types was to be anticipated.*

" The essential feature of this legislation would be the prohibition of any intermingling of races in Germany ; the population would also have to be divided into families whose offspring would be welcome to the State, and those whose offspring would be regarded as a burden on the nation. The logical consequence would be the demand for the compulsory sterilisation of criminals and other anti-social elements. The fact that all the Medical Associations of Prussia had recently declared in favour of the sterilisation of criminals, in the interests of the nation as a whole, proved that this demand put forward by the National Socialists was already recognised as justified by wide circles of the nation. The fundamental aim of the organisation of racial hygiene could only be reached after some generations, but a Government which was conscious of its responsibility was obliged to think in terms of generations."

Dr. Achim Gercke, a pushing young man, got himself appointed " Ministerial Adviser and Expert for Racial Research in the Ministry of the Interior."

Men and " Sub-Men."   All of this seems relatively " harmless." It is primarily directed to bring about the economic destruction of the Jewish population, but not to threaten life and limb. The following leaflet is not so harmless ; it was distributed in thousands in all restaurants, and in particular was given to every German girl who was seen in company with a Jew.

This document threatens every girl who is suspected of the terrible crime of being friendly with a Jew that her face will be branded with the initials J.H.—*Juden-Hure*, Jewish prostitute. The assurance is given that this is no mere empty threat, but that in any circumstances it will be carried out if the girl is seen again in company with a Jew.

In this we have a clearer example of the National Socialist distinction between men and " sub-men," sub-men being everyone who does not think and feel as the National Socialists do. The National Socialists divide the " men " and the " sub-men " into different groups. In Group I are the " pure representatives of the Nordic race." In Group II (according to *Ziel und Weg*, the journal of the National Socialist doctors) are, along with " inebriates, drug-takers, habitual criminals and prostitutes, all persons of foreign race, particularly Jews."

The National Socialist " race theoretician," Professor Stämmler, proposed on behalf of the National Socialist doctors the following law for the " Division of the Race " :

" 1. Every person who is of foreign racial blood to the extent of one-half—that is, one of whose parents or two of whose grand-parents were of foreign race, irrespective of their religion—is regarded as of foreign race. Foreign race means all coloured races, near-Asiatic and oriental races including the Jew.

" 2. In conformity with this every adult German citizen must declare on oath, at the registration office for his area, to what race he belongs. In the case of persons under age, the declaration must be made by their legal representatives. False declarations will be punished with imprisonment and confiscation of property.

" 3. Persons ascertained to be of foreign race must in

future describe themselves not as Germans but as of foreign race (Jews from Germany, etc.).

"4. Persons born after the day of grace are to rank as Germans only when both parents are German. Younger brothers or sisters, however, rank as of the same nationality as their elder brothers or sisters whose nationality has been established by declaration."

"Breeding Farms."   Professor Stämmler, whose name has already been mentioned, writes that "The aim of breeding is a physically, morally and mentally sound person of Nordic race." To help towards the achievement of this aim "breeding farms" are to be provided. The outpourings of a certain Professor Ernst Bergmann indicate what kind of breeding farms they have in mind :

"There are quite enough *willing* and *industrious* (!) men and youths to provide mates for the available women and girls, and fortunately *one* lively lad suffices for 10 to 20 girls who have not yet killed their desire for a child, were it not for the civilised nonsense, so contrary to nature, of monogamous and permanent marriage." (Professor Ernst Bergmann, in *Erkenntnisgeist und Muttergeist*.)

We conclude these examples with yet another "Bill for the Preservation of Race Purity," which contains the following :

"1. Marriages between Germans and persons of foreign races are prohibited. Those which have already been contracted remain valid ; but new marriages must not be entered into and will not be recognised.

"2. Extra-matrimonial sexual intercourse between Germans and persons of foreign race will be punished with penal servitude for the person of foreign race and imprisonment for the German party. Prostitutes do not come under this law.

"3. The entry into Germany of persons of foreign race is

only allowed in special circumstances. The settlement in
Germany of persons of foreign race is prohibited.
" 4. Changes of name, which in most cases are for the
sole purpose of concealing the race of the person concerned, are prohibited until further notice. Changes of
name made since 1914 are cancelled."

It may be objected that this kind of nonsense has no
real connection with the mass movement, that these " race
hygienists " are only on the edge of the movement, which
cannot be regarded as responsible for them. This suggestion
is not well founded. A man like Professor Stämmler is the
official adviser on these questions. The " Bills " drafted
by him were introduced by the National Socialist fraction in
the Reichstag. They are therefore typical, and must be
taken seriously as agitation material.

Liquidation of the Jewish Question.   We have given a
small number of examples out of the mass of incidents in
the war of extermination which is being waged against
600,000 German Jews. These documents and facts are
typical of the artificially nurtured hatred of the Jews, who
have once more in Europe's history been given the rôle of
scapegoats. We have tried to show that, in general, this
fanaticism is not directed against those who were first made
the object of hatred : the big bankers, merchants and
speculators. The " wrath of the people " has once more
been turned aside, against the lesser fry, against the Jewish
middle class and the Jewish working class.

Forced Denials.   What action did the Jews in Germany
take ? They protested against the foreign " atrocity propaganda." Under the pressure of the storm troopers they
sent out into the world documents which were the product
of mortal fear. Often their fear has made them go further
than was necessary. No one can blame them. Not every
man is a born hero. And eventually an enterprising man got
the idea of publishing these denials which had been forced

from the Jews, in book form, under the title : *The Atrocity Propaganda.* The Government-controlled *Berliner Tageblatt* devotes two columns to this " extremely welcome book " ; but no one in the world will let himself be led to believe that it was not written by men in fear of their lives and their liberty, and that they were not compelled against their better knowledge to spread the lie that there is no persecution of Jews in Germany.

Jews who support Hitler.   There are even Jews who support Hitler. In the *Jewish Press* (Wien, Bratislava, of March 31st), the organ of the orthodox Jews, a Rabbi, Professor Dr. Weinberg, writes as follows :

" In Jewish circles generally, and particularly in orthodox circles, there is more sympathy and understanding for the national revival in Germany than the leaders of this movement realise. The religious Jews know how particularly grateful they must be to Hitler for his energetic and thoroughgoing fight against Communism."

The central organ of German Zionists, the *Jüdische Rundschau,* adopts the same attitude :

" Jewish history will understand even Hitler. It will cite him as evidence of the fact that history is made up of the imponderables of human endeavour towards an ideal, no matter what this may be."

We have already quoted the statement made by the third partner in the alliance with Jewish orthodoxy and Jewish nationalism : Jewish capitalism—the statement made by Oskar Wassermann, Director of the Deutsche Bank und Diskontogesellschaft, that he has not suffered the least inconvenience and that he has hardly been able to notice the change in things.

Lenin on anti-Semitism.   We have not hushed up these statements. On the contrary, they seem to us convincing proof that in the last analysis the Jewish question too is not a question of race, but a class question. The similar experience in Russia under the Tsardom is summarised by Lenin as follows :

" The propagation of hostility against the Jews is described as anti-Semitism. When the accursed Tsarist monarchy was at its last gasp, it tried to incite the ignorant workers and peasants against the Jews. The Tsar's police, in league with the landlords and the capitalists, organised pogroms. They tried to deflect the hatred of the workers and peasants, crushed down by want, from the landlords and exploiters, and turn it against the Jews. It has often been the same in other countries too : the capitalists have roused up hostility against the Jews in order to throw dust in the eyes of the workers and distract them from the real enemy of the toiling people, capital. . . .

" It is not the Jews who are the enemy of the toiling people. The enemies of the workers are the capitalists of every country. There are workers, toilers, among the Jews : these form the majority. They are our brothers, our comrades in the fight for socialism, because they are oppressed by capital. There are *kulaks*, exploiters, capitalists, among the Jews as among all other peoples. The capitalists strive to arouse hostility between the workers of different religious beliefs, of different nations and races. The rich Jews, like the rich Russians and the rich people of all countries, all in league with each other, trample on, oppress and contaminate the workers.

" Shame and contempt upon the accursed Tsarism which tortured and persecuted the Jews ! Shame and contempt upon those who sow hostility against the Jews and hatred against other nations ! "

CHAPTER IX: THE CONCENTRATION CAMPS

ON THE basis of statements published in the Press the total number of political prisoners in Hitler's Germany at the beginning of June 1933 must be put at about sixty to seventy thousand. Of this total, between thirty-five and forty thousand men and women have been taken to concentration camps. It goes without saying that there is no legal justification for the establishment of concentration camps. There are no laws or regulations determining the rights of prisoners in concentration camps. Nor is there any law or regulation governing the length of their detention in the camps.

"Till our leader takes pity on them." The *Neue Züricher Zeitung*, in an article on the concentration camps in Germany published on May 8th, 1933, states that the prisoners will be divided into two groups—those whom it is easy and those whom it is difficult to train as citizens—and that the former will be kept in the camps one year, the latter three years. But this is merely the personal opinion of the reporter, not an official statement. Banishment to the concentration camps and also the length of the period of detention are entirely determined by the arbitrary will of the Fascist chiefs, central and local. Lieutenant Kaufmann, one of the Nazi controllers of the concentration camp at Heuberg in Baden, put the position very clearly in an interview which he gave at the end of April to a reporter of the Danish paper *Politiken*. In reply to the question : " How long will you keep the prisoners here ? " the Lieutenant replied : " Till our leader takes pity on them."

The *Deutsche Allgemeine Zeitung* of April 30th, 1933, confirms this statement by Lieutenant Kaufmann in so far as it says : " It will be a long while before many of the prisoners get their freedom, for the will of the prisoners is not easy to break."

" If I even knew why I am here." The men and women who have been interned in the concentration camps are completely innocent, even within the meaning of the principle of the Fascist State. All Socialist and Communist workers and leaders who in the Government's view have done anything against the laws of the Fascist régime are not put into the concentration camps, but are locked up in prisons and penal settlements and brought before special courts and sentenced. The people who are interned in the concentration camps are only men and women whose political views are regarded by the Fascists as suspect, though even the Fascist prosecutors cannot find any pretext for a criminal prosecution against them. Most of them were arrested immediately after the burning of the Reichstag and the elections on March 5th, so that they could not conceivably have carried on any activity hostile to the Fascist régime. Towards the end of April the *Politiken* published some letters from prisoners in concentration camps. One young worker writes : " If I only knew why I am here." A doctor writes : " Only anonymous and personal revenge can be the reason for my imprisonment." Another man writes : " I have nothing to reproach myself with. I have no idea why I was arrested."

The trivial things which suffice to bring people into the concentration camps are well illustrated by the case of the Jewish religious teacher Karl Krebs, who is a citizen of Czecho-Slovakia and has been in Germany since he was a year old. The following order was issued for his arrest :

" The Jewish teacher of religion Karl Krebs, of Dinkes-bühl, a Czecho-Slovakian subject, is to be arrested. On March 29th, 1933, Krebs killed some hens, creating great dissatisfaction among the population. Although this was not a criminal act, in view of the great excitement among the population in connection with the atrocity campaign of the Jews abroad, Krebs should not have carried out such an act. The excitement among the population is so great that Krebs must be put under arrest in order to protect him from attacks. The order for his protective arrest is issued in agreement with the Commissioner Burgomaster Ittameyer in Wassertrüdingen.

Dinkelsbühl, March 29th, 1933.

Krebs is still in prison.

What the concentration camps are for.   Captain Buck, Nazi chief of the Heuberg concentration camp, told the reporter of the *Politiken* that the purpose of the concentration camps was " to punish the prisoners." In some of the camps, as prisoners who have been released report, the prisoners have to register as " Convict " X. In accordance with the regulations for penal settlements, their heads have even been shaved. The London *Daily Telegraph* of April 27th, 1933, confirms this, in a cable from its Vienna correspondent R. G. Geyde. The " convicts " have not seen a judge and will not see one. The National Socialist leaders have repeatedly stated that internment in the concentration camps is a purely administrative measure, that it is a question of protective detention. The Nazis told the *Politiken* correspondent : " We have had to intern many of these individuals in order to protect them from the vengeance of the people. They would have been lynched by the patriotic mob, who regard these ' criminals ' as the instigators of the November revolution."

This statement is an outright lie. The extraordinarily strict watch on the camps is not for the sake of protecting the interned Socialists and Communists. The machine guns in front of the camps are to make any attempts at flight or rescue impossible. Wherever there have been so-called demonstrations against arrested persons, the tumult and rioting has been organised by the Fascists. The transfer of the former Social Democratic Minister Remmele to a concentration camp, which was organised as a great popular

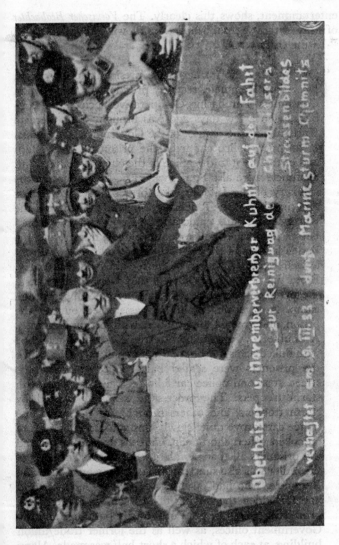

HERR KUHNT, the former Premier of Oldenburg and Social Democratic Member of the Reichstag, was arrested by storm troops in Chemnitz on March 9th, 1933, and taken in triumph through the town.

PLATE NO. 14.

entertainment, shows this clearly. The *Völkischer Beobachter* of May 17th 1933 published the following report, headed " In the Pillory."

" On Tuesday the former State president and Minister, Dr. Adam Remmele, recently president of the German Consumers' Purchasing Co-operative Society in Hamburg, who a few days ago was brought from there to Karlsruhe at the request of the Government, was taken in an open police car from the prison at the western end of the town to the office of the chief of police. With Remmele were also Stenz, whom he had placed in the Ministry of the Interior, the former Baden councillor and member of the Reichstag, Marum, the editor of the Karlsruhe Social Democratic paper *Volksfreund*, Grünebaum, the former police commissioner, Furrer, and the Baden leaders of the Reichsbanner and the Iron Front as well as other members of the Social Democratic party. From the police headquarters they were then taken to the penal settlement at Kieslau, now a concentration camp. A gigantic crowd had assembled outside the prison, and greeted the prisoners with jeers and catcalls. A double row of Nazi protective corps men marched with linked arms in front of the first police car, on which the prisoners were seated bare-headed, to clear the street. A second police car followed the first, filled with storm troopers. The procession was also flanked by storm troopers, and others brought up the rear. The police cars drove quite slowly through a double wall of onlookers, often eight deep. Catcalls and abuse greeted the prisoners all the way along the streets. The song of the miller was also sung everywhere, by way of mocking Remmele, who had once been a miller's labourer and had forbidden the singing of this song in Baden. The procession passed in front of the Diet buildings and the Government offices, as well as the former trade union building, at each of which a short halt was made. Along the way bands also played the song of the miller. The

concourse was so immense that the whole of the tram-
way and motor traffic was stopped. A number of
persons who shouted ' Red Front ! ' were arrested on
the spot and taken along in the second police car."

The report shows clearly that this was an organised
demonstration with carefully prepared shouting—in short,
that it was one of those spectacles which the Reich Minister
of Propaganda, Goebbels, uses to entertain the crowd and
to make it for a while forget its hunger.

"Protective arrest."   Protective detention in Germany
is strictly governed by the law of 1849 on the restriction
of personal freedom. By this law only persons who are
themselves threatened may be taken into protective arrest.
This must not be continued longer than is necessary for the
purpose, and in no case longer than three months. The law
provides for the lodging of appeals and a decision by the
courts. But all those who are now imprisoned were arrested
not in their own interest but to protect the new rulers. They
are being kept longer than three months. And they have no
right to appeal.

Forty-Five Concentration Camps.   How many concentration camps are there, and how many people are detained
in them ? The German Government, probably with good
reason, avoids giving any exact information. On the basis of
a few reports in the German Press, occasional statements by
Nazi leaders and visits of foreign journalists, it is possible
to draw the conclusion that early in July 1933 there were
forty-five concentration camps with between 35,000 and
40,000 prisoners. The following are some of the camps :

Dachau, near Munich, Bavaria	..	5,000 prisoners
Heuberg, Upper Baden	..	..	2,000	,,
Kieslau, near Bruchsal, Baden	..	100	,,
Rastatt, Baden	..	..	300	,,
Bad Dürrheim, Baden	..	..	500	,,

Pfalz	..	..	..	..	2,000 prisoners
Mühlheim, Rhine	..		..	..	2,000 ,,
Hohenstein, Saxony		..	..		800 ,,
Ortenstein, Zwickau, Saxony			..		200 ,,
Zittau, Saxony	..		..	..	300 ,,
Ohrdruf, Thuringia		..	..		1,200 ,,
Oranienburg, near Berlin			..		1,500 ,,
Sonnenburg (Prussia)		..	..		414 ,,
Sennelager, Paderborn (900 men, 30 women)		..	..		930 ,,
Esterwegen, Westphalia		..		..	500 ,,
Wilsede, Lüneberger Heide			..		2,000 ,,
Königstein, Saxony		..		..	200 ,,

A concentration camp at Papenburg, Emsland, has been
equipped for 4,000 prisoners.

Other camps are at : Ginsheim and Rödelheim, near
Frankfurt ; Langen and Osthofen, in Hessen ; Cassel ; Fuhlsbüttel and Wittmoor, near Hamburg ; Bremen ; Braunschweig ; Grundau, near Königsberg, also another in East
Prussia ; Schleswig ; Pommerania ; Breslau ; there are six
camps in Brandenburg province, five in the Ruhr area, and
a number in central Germany. The number of prisoners in
these camps is not known.

In the middle of May the Government decided to open
ten new concentration camps. The *Frankfurter Zeitung* of
May 30th, 1933, reports that a second concentration camp
will be opened at Heuberg for such prisoners as are not to
be released before the winter.

Women and Intellectuals in the Camps.   There are
hundreds of women among the prisoners in the concentration camps. The Communist women members of the Reichstag and of the State Diets, in so far as they were found,
were first taken to the women's prison in the Barnimstrasse
in Berlin, before they were taken to the concentration camp.
This prison has been organised as a collecting and transit

Prisoners in the concentration camp at Oranienburg.
They are kept drilling for hours without a rest.

PLATE NO. 15.

station for arrested women. Early in June a special concentration camp for women was organised in South Germany. An official announcement dated June 8th, 1933,
states : " A detention camp for women has been organised
at Gotteszell, near Gemund in Württemburg." A second
concentration camp for women was opened in Saxony a
few days later. All reports agree that the women in the
prisons and concentration camps are being subjected to
exceptionally bad treatment and persecution.

All kinds of views and professions and ages are represented
among the prisoners in the concentration camps : Communists, Anarchists, Social Democrats, adherents of the
Centre Party, pacifists, Jews ; young and old people,
workers, intellectuals, artists, students, members of Parliamentary bodies, lawyers, doctors, writers, tradesmen ; well-
known names and unknown names ; Martin Buber, the
grey-haired Zionist poet ; Karl von Ossietzky, the revolutionary pacifist editor of the *Weltbühne* ; the anarchist, Erich
Mühsam ; the Bavarian Member of Parliament, Auer ; the
democratic Member of the Reichstag, Fischer ; the Social
Democrat Members of the Reichstag Rossmann and
Pflüger ; the barrister Hans Litten ; the doctors, Schminke
and Boenheim ; and many others of similar standing.

The Truth breaks through. The Hitler Government
has done its best to conceal the conditions in the concentration camps. The Committee for the Victims of Fascism has
nevertheless succeeded in obtaining from prisoners who
have succeeded in getting away, and from the relatives of
prisoners, a considerable amount of material which throws
light on the terrible condition of the prisoners in the concentration camps.

In spite of the Nazi guards and barbed wire the truth
has broken through to the outside world. Foreign journalists
have been allowed to see some of the " model " camps, such
as those of Heuberg, Dachau and Oranienburg. Nazi storm
troopers accompanied the press representatives everywhere ; there was no opportunity of separate conversation

with any of the prisoners. The descriptions given by these correspondents are therefore general impressions of the arrangement of the camps rather than observations of actual conditions. But where the journalists were able, even though in a very restricted way, to describe the objective conditions—or where, as in the case of Edmund Taylor of the *Chicago Daily Tribune*, they were able to put a few questions to prisoners in a foreign language—the truth also comes to light in the newspaper reports.

Anyone who wants to help to get the truth about the German concentration camps must support the demand for an international commission of members of all the Relief Committees to have the right to visit every camp—not under the control of the commandants of the camps and of Nazi guards, but to make their visits without warning, with the right to investigate conditions in every detail and to talk to every prisoner without interference.

The convict prisons of Sonnenburg and Fuhlsbüttel were closed down some years ago because they were buildings belonging to the Middle Ages and were absolutely unhygienic from a modern standpoint. Even habitual criminals were no longer sent there. In Fuhlbüttel there are no closets and no drains. Detention in this prison is acute torture, particularly in the hot part of the year. But these are the prisons which the Hitler Government has now established as concentration camps. Among the prisoners at Sonnenburg are Litten, Kasper, Ossietzky and Mühsam.

The concentration camp at Zittau was formerly a bookshop, so that the comforts of this " camp " can be imagined. The concentration camp at Dachau, according to a report in the *Daily Telegraph* of April 25th, 1933, consists of old half-decayed huts. Oranienburg is the model camp which has been shown to a number of foreign journalists, and of which the Nazis have broadcast photographs. " An abandoned factory, formerly a brewery : the works have fallen into ruin, the windows are simply broken glass, the yard is covered with grass and weeds." This is how the *Deutsche Allgemeine Zeitung* of April 30th, 1933, describes

Oranienburg. We are in possession of a confidential report from a German woman journalist who accompanied a foreign correspondent as interpreter when he visited the camp at Oranienburg :

> " Only one single pump in the courtyard. The prisoners, of whom there are between 100 and 200, have to wash in five old wash-basins which stand in the courtyard. The rooms where they sleep are old workshops which are in ruins ; a few inches of dirty straw cover the cement floor."

The *Deutsche Allgemeine Zeitung* of April 30th, 1933, confirms that the prisoners have to sleep on straw.

In Dachau, according to the description given by Geyde in the *Daily Telegraph* of April 25th, 1933, 54 prisoners sleep in a small hut on rough wooden boards covered with straw.

The interpreter who has already been mentioned describes the appalling conditions in such a dormitory at Oranienburg :

> " Already by evening, when the prisoners are locked in, the place stinks as if a herd of wild animals had spent the night there. But it is impossible to describe the air after it has been slept in by 50 or more men whose clothes are unwashed and whose sweating bodies fill the room with vapour."

The Model Camp at Heuberg.   The concentration camp at Heuberg is the show place among the camps. It is exhibited to all foreign reporters, who for the most part describe the external appearance of the camp and its environment but do not deal with the internal rooms and dormitories. At the end of May the *Frankfurter Zeitung* published a detailed report on a visit to the Heuberg camp, which testifies to the extremely close guard kept on the prisoners and the military drill imposed on them. The young Nazis are forbidden to enter into conversation with the prisoners, owing to the fear that they might be influenced politically. The report runs :

" The old parade ground is now used as a concentration camp. Going in through a lattice fence, we could see the whole camp spread out before us. First there are the offices, a post office and the officials' quarters with little gardens, then left and right the former quarters of the Reichswehr soldiers. Here, at a height of 2,700 feet, where there is little green to be seen, 2,000 prisoners are herded together in small rooms.

" The houses are shut in by iron railings. Tall barbed wire fences run round the buildings in a double line, so that there is a space between. The concentration camp is divided into sections. The storm troopers are on guard, with rifles, by the iron railings. Both sides of the barbed wire fences are guarded by auxiliary police. The windows are empty : it is forbidden to look out. At night search-lights play on the sides of the building. Each building is divided into two sections, A and B ; there is one latrine between them in the courtyard.

" Left and right of the staircase on each floor are large rooms, and between them the former sergeant-major's room, now labelled ' control officers.' There are three of these : one storm troop officer for each of the large rooms, and a police sergeant who maintains contact with the police officer in charge.

" At the entrance to the prisoners' room there is a register, containing the names of the 36 prisoners. Name, place of birth, address. The storm troop officer pulls out his key. We hear ' look out ! ' shouted inside, and the voices in the room are silent. Chairs are pushed back. The prisoners rise to their feet when the control officer enters.

" The prisoners sit on little stools at long smooth tables, playing chess. They have made the pieces themselves. There are practically no papers or books to be seen ; each room is provided with one newspaper, which is usually read aloud by someone. There are small square cupboards along the wall, in which eating utensils are kept.

" While the young Nazi auxiliary police, all of whom come from the countryside, are forbidden to have any dealings with the prisoners, the Nazi officers are charged with the duty of bringing their political influence to bear on the prisoners in the room under their control.

" Correspondence is controlled by the officials. Each prisoner can write a letter or card once a fortnight. The officer in charge has to determine from these letters, the general conduct of the prisoners, and official and private conversations with them, which of the prisoners shows any prospect of changing their political views."

We can supplement this report with information given us in a letter from the Heuberg camp. The writer's name cannot be disclosed, for the reason that he is still in the camp.

" There are 2,000 comrades in Heuberg, most of them Communists. They are kept in seven or eight two-storey buildings. Each double block and single block are separated off by barbed wire fences two metres high. In rooms 12 metres by 8, thirty men are housed ; in the top rooms four to twelve men according to the size of the rooms. The beds, in two tiers, consist of a straw sack and 2 blankets. There are no baths. (The reporter of *De Telegraaf*, the Amsterdam paper, says in a report of April 5th that the prisoners get a bath once a month. Evidently this does not apply to all prisoners.—THE EDITORS.) Soap is not provided ; anyone who wants it must buy it. Linen is not provided, and there is no washing. Towels are in short supply : one between two prisoners. Open razors are forbidden. Shaving is difficult, so beards are becoming the latest achievement of the German awakening. . . ."

Captain Buck, who is in control of the camp, told the *Politiken* reporter that Heuberg is not a sanatorium, either in comfort or in hygiene. He is right. These camps are breeding grounds of disease, and but few will leave them sound.

The Guards round the Camp.   The prisoners in the camps are kept under extraordinarily strict control. Nazi storm troopers are patrolling everywhere, armed with rubber truncheons, rifles and revolvers. Many of the patrols are accompanied by police dogs ; the official photographs show this. It is confirmed by the *Politiken*, the *Telegraaf* and the *Daily Telegraph*, and by every prisoner's letter. In the *Daily Telegraph* of April 27th, 1933, Geyde reports that the concentration camp at Dachau is surrounded by a high wire fence which is charged with high voltage electricity. Machine guns are kept ready at the main posts. The correspondents of the *Telegraaf* and *Politiken* were struck by the mass of barbed wire and railings from which escape was impossible. At night the camp is lighted up by gigantic searchlights ; the light prevents the prisoners from sleeping.

The *Telegraaf* of April 5th, 1933, says : " If anyone opens a window to get a breath of air, he is shot at."

The camp at Oranienburg has low factory walls on one side, and on the other, where the prisoners take exercise, quite low shrubbery. Do none of the prisoners try to get away ? The journalist who visited the camp with a foreign correspondent put this question.

> *The reply :* " There is no danger of flight here. The guards are armed and have strict instructions to shoot at once if any of the prisoners cross the boundary marked by the bushes. Besides, why should they try to get away ? Things are all right for them here. Even when they are allowed to go they don't want to."
> *The questioner :* " But that is impossible ? "
> *The reply :* " The day before yesterday we received instructions to set one man free. He would not go, and had to be taken to the station by force. Ask the others whether this is so or not."

The journalist continues her report :

" It is a fact that there have been cases of prisoners
not wanting their liberty. But why ? The orders for
release come as a rule at night or at a very early hour
of the morning. At that time it is easier to shoot a
prisoner on the way, and then the following day the
papers report : Marxist shot when trying to escape."

In fact, these low bushes are meant to tempt prisoners to
flight ; but flight means death.

Grouping of Prisoners.   The arbitrary decisions which
have brought the concentration camps into being have also
divided the prisoners into three categories :

A. Easily reformable (German Nationals, Bavarian
        Guards, and political followers).
B. Not easily reformable.
C. Unreformable.

Communist leaders and officials and intellectuals of Left
views are put in the last category, and the worst treatment
is meted out to them. In the report on the Heuberg camp
which has already been quoted this fact is confirmed :

" Prisoners who on the basis of documents and reports
are classed as unreformable are put into the " old
building," numbers 19 and 23. There everything is
much stricter. The controlling officer does not have
any conversation with them. The time allowed for exercise is restricted to ten minutes. Permission to smoke
and talk is given less frequently ; and they are not
allowed to work, which with the other prisoners gives
the opportunity for a few hours of physical activity and
entitles them to extra food."

The commandants of the camps compete with each
other in inventing more and more ingenious punishments.

Prisoners have their free time shortened. Permission to write letters is granted less often or taken away altogether. They are not permitted to have visitors for a long period. They are forbidden to take part in the general conversation during their free time. They are isolated and particularly sharply controlled. They are forbidden to smoke. They are given long periods of arrest with only ten minutes exercise, or are confined in a dark room. Disciplinary punishments which are frequently used are : additional exercise, continued for several hours, drilling, longer work hours, and particularly unaccustomed and irritating work. In some of the concentration camps prisoners against whom the Nazis have a particular grudge have even been kept in chains.

According to the *Daily Telegraph* report of April 27th, 1933, refractory prisoners, for example at Dachau, are not allowed out of the tiny huts and may not go into the open air.

The report of the woman journalist already referred to describes a cell in the Oranienburg camp, in which " not easily reformable " prisoners are kept.

" A hole in the wall, shut in by an iron door, and without any other ventilation but the door. We were shown one of these rooms empty. But this was an hour after we had begun to inspect the camp, so that evidently the prisoners had first been taken out. Then of the 120 prisoners in the camp 30 were missing. Were they perhaps behind that iron door, which we were not allowed to examine more closely ? "

At Heuberg an elderly lawyer complained of the bad food. For making this complaint he was condemned to sleep 15 nights on the roof of the barracks without any shelter.

Captain Buck however assured the *Telegraaf* reporter (April 5th, 1933) that there were no detention cells in the Heuberg camp.

Manhandled and Beaten.   All reports are unanimous on the fact that the "unimprovable" prisoners are being treated in such a way that their physical ruin is inevitable. The aim is the physical extermination of the organisers of the German working class. Captain Buck assured the representative of the *Politiken* that no one was mishandled in the concentration camps. " No blows, no punishments," he asserted. But the Government's Press itself indicates that this is not true. The *Angriff* of April 1st writes :

" A Reichsbanner man was interrogated . . . he gave an insolent reply. However, a friendly but pointed look at his own rubber truncheon sufficed to bring home to him the seriousness of the position."

The maltreatment that must go on in this camp if a glance at a rubber truncheon is enough to bring home to a prisoner " the seriousness of the position " is confirmed by the *Deutsche Allgemeine Zeitung* of April 30th, 1933 :

" For it was only by laying hold of them and carrying through the interrogation with merciless severity that we have succeeded in discovering the underground terror almost to its full extent . . . but the resistance of individual prisoners has still to be broken."

This report confirms that torture is used in the interrogations. We have a report of the correspondent of the *Chicago Daily Tribune*, Edmund Taylor. He managed to speak in English and French with some of the prisoners in the Heuberg camp, so that the storm troopers accompanying him did not know what was said. Many of the prisoners expressly stated that in that camp severe mishandling was a frequent occurrence.

Similar reports come from the Schloss Ortenstein camp near Zwickau. Visitors to this camp have declared on oath that they saw bleeding weals and green and blue patches on the arms and hands of prisoners. There can be no doubt whatever that these are the result of maltreatment. The mishandling was particularly severe when the storm troopers were in charge of the prisoners ; when they were replaced by police, the position became more bearable. But the storm troopers have been put into the Ortenstein camp again since the beginning of May.

The Hell of Sonnenburg.

The concentration camp at Sonnenburg must be dealt with separately. Letters and reports from prisoners, and even official statements, show beyond doubt that Sonnenburg is a real torture chamber. Working-class leaders and intellectuals are subjected to the most disgraceful maltreatment. Throughout Germany the camp is known as 'the Sonnenburg hell.' A letter from a worker who escaped from Sonnenburg gives a terrible description of the conditions there :

" The first batches of prisoners were met at Sonnenburg station by storm troop detachments and police. They were compelled to sing and were literally beaten to the camp. The inhabitants of Sonnenburg can testify to this. When they arrived at the camp, the prisoners were compelled to stand in the courtyard in streaming rain. Then the first ones were taken to the rooms. Each had to fetch straw for himself from another floor. Storm troopers were standing on the stairs, and they beat the prisoners mercilessly with their rubber truncheons. Some were made to empty the closet pails of the Nazis, in the course of which they were again brutally mishandled. One storm trooper held a prisoner's head between his legs, while another storm trooper beat him. The comrades were compelled to count the blows in a loud voice. Some of the prisoners received as many as 185 blows. In addition they were kicked and otherwise manhandled. Those treated worst were comrades Litten, Wiener, Bernstein, Kasper, Schneller and the Jewish prisoners. Our old friend Mühsam suffered terribly. Now things are a little different, but instead we have extremely severe military drill, worse than when I was a recruit. Most of the time we have to be exercising outside, marching and singing.

" The first three weeks were the worst. In the single cells we were attacked in the night and terribly beaten. The backs of many comrades were quite black. I don't know whether Litten will get through with his life. The wives of several of the Sonnenburg prisoners raised such sharp protests that Mittelbach, of the public prosecutor's department, was sent to Sonnenburg to investigate ; Litten begged him to have him shot, as he could no longer bear the brutal mishandling that was being inflicted on him."

The *Sonnenburger Anzeiger* of April 7th, 1933, reported :

" The prisoners had to march from the station to the former convict prison singing the national hymns, the rubber truncheons of the Berlin auxiliary police often helping them along."

This account by one of the Sonnenburg prisoners is confirmed by letters from Frau Mühsam and Frau Kasper, who visited their husbands in Sonnenburg. Frau Mühsam writes :

" They have beaten our husbands to the point of death. Erich—I saw him, and I did not recognise him, Therese, I did not recognise him among the others ! How they have been beaten ! They have cut off his beard and knocked out his teeth. They made him carry his trunk. . . . He fell down on the road. Then the beasts beat him terribly as he lay on the road and could not get up. When I reached Sonnenburg, there he was sitting, completely broken, and he was horrified that I had come. His first words were ' How can you have come to this hell ? You won't get out alive ! They will kill you, because you have seen us and how we have been mishandled ! ' When I saw Kasper, I had to keep control of

myself not to faint. It was all the more ghastly as I had
seen him three days before. He was standing leaning
against the wall, his face white and absolutely mutilated.
There was blood running down from one eye, which was
quite blue, to his mouth. His mouth was black and
swollen as if someone had stamped on his face. He could
hardly speak or move with the pains he had all over his
body."

The wives of the political prisoners Bernstein and Geisler
succeeded in forcing the control authorities to grant them a
permit to visit Sonnenburg. Frau Bernstein writes :

" I felt as if it was a stranger in front of me. His eyes and
the skin round them were blood-red and badly swollen.
Across his face there were broad weals from blows with
rubber truncheons. I was not allowed to get close to him,
but his whole body must be battered ; during the whole
time he stayed quite still in a strange position."

Frau Geisler writes :

" When I saw my husband he was so changed, and his
face was so terribly swollen, that I had to keep myself
in hand not to scream with horror."

A prisoner who succeeded in escaping from Sonnenburg
and getting over the German frontier reports :

" There are 414 political prisoners in Sonnenburg, among
them Carl von Ossietzky, who was arrested on February
28th. One of his fellow prisoners, who was thirteen days
in Sonnenburg and now has been able to get across the
frontier, saw Ossietzky in the hospital ward. Bent double,
sunken features, his face yellow, his hands moving
nervously, shambling gait—that is his description of
Ossietzky. The other Sonnenburg prisoners: Dr.
Wiener, whose whole body had been beaten black and

blue ; the Communist Bernstein, whose kidneys have been injured by blows and who can now only walk with a crutch ; Erich Mühsam, who with Kasper were forced to dig a grave for themselves, being told that they were to be shot the following morning. . . . One night they broke the window of Kasper's cell and pushed a revolver through, threatening to shoot him. Then they rushed into his cell and beat him with rubber truncheons.

The daily programme in Sonnenburg is :

5.15 a.m. Get up, empty the closets (there are no drains in Sonnenburg), clean the cells, wash, exercise, etc.
8.30 a.m. Breakfast.
9–10. Military drill ; singing of Hitler songs.
10.30–12. Rest and dinner.
12.30–5.30 p.m. Military drill and gymnastics.
6 p.m. Supper.
6.30–7.30. Exercise.
7.30–8.30. Free time, prisoners all together."

The mishandling in the Sonnenburg camp was so inhuman that the new police commander of the camp appointed on April 11th felt compelled to make a report on it to his superior officer. He received orders from above to destroy the copy of this letter. Most of the pieces of this torn-up copy have come into our hands.

Sonnenburg,
18 May, 1933.
Concerning certain occurrences since I took over the prison on 11.4.33.

" On taking up my post on the 11.4.33 I ascertained that no order was maintained in this prison, especially by the storm troop men. Irregularities in the main concerned :

" 1. Treatment of prisoners by the storm troopmen.

" 2. Attitude of storm troopers to the administration officials.

" 3. Conduct of storm troopers among themselves.

" 4. Conduct of storm troopers in public.

" 5. The situation with regard to pay of the storm troopers.

" In regard to point 1 : a section of the prisoners, especially the prominent ones, were extremely severely mishandled by members of the storm troops. To put a stop to this mishandling, the injured prisoners have been kept under control of (word missing) officers. I threatened the storm troop men that if (missing) were repeated, I would have the storm troopers kept under strict control day and night to put a stop to the (missing) on prisoners. In spite of this I have established two instances of prisoners being struck. In view of the way the storm troopers support each other, especially in connection with such incidents, the investigations I set on foot proved fruitless. I have therefore threatened the storm troopers that the slightest incident of this sort again will lead to my dismissing the guards on duty at the time, that is, the whole of the storm troop.

" In regard to point 2 : there is continuous conflict between the storm troop men and the administration officials on the question of pay. In spite of reasonable advances against pay the storm troop men feel that they are being prejudiced, and they hold police inspector Pelz to blame. Their attitude to police inspector Pelz was carried so far that only my personal intervention brought them to reason. When the storm troopers were withdrawn on 24.4.1933 I had to place an armed police guard at Pelz's house to prevent any violence. In regard to point 3 : there were frequent conflicts among the storm troop men, generally over trivialities . . ."

(Here the report breaks off).

Compulsory Labour. The National Socialist minister Frick stated that the prisoners in the concentration camps were to be trained to become useful citizens. In fact, the work that they are forced to do is absolutely useless. A neutral visitor to the Oranienburg camp describes what he saw as follows :

" The work—if we can call it work—is the most pointless labour, both for prisoners and warders, that it is possible to imagine. Three young workers were driving six of their fellow-unemployed to pull grass out of the ground as quickly as possible. . . . Behind the factory building water is being splashed about. Some dozens of men are busy trying to clean the old building. . . . It is even worse where the wood is being cleared. The trees have already been removed. The prisoners, under heavy guard, are trying to dig out the gigantic roots with their fingers. Storm Troop men drive on workers who are old enough to be their grandfathers : ' Old sow ! ' ' Red swine ! ' and so forth. . . ."

Compulsory Drill. After the compulsory labour comes compulsory drill. According to official statements, the time from 1.30 to 5.30 p.m. is allotted to drill. This is severe military drill and military exercises of an extremely exhausting character, which the prisoners are compelled to carry out for hours at a time.

And so for days, weeks and months the same futile work, the same futile and exhausting drill has to be carried out, on food which is entirely inadequate. Ordinary prisoners can at least count the days to their release, but the prisoners in concentration camps have no idea when they will be set free. The barbarous treatment the prisoners receive, the exhausting work and drill, the low diet, and the hopelessness of their position has driven many to suicide. The *Politiken* correspondent who visited the Heuberg camp early in April 1933 reported that :

" Captain Buck answered my question quite willingly. He admitted that attempts at suicide are not infrequent at this camp."

But there are also repeated cases which are officially reported as " shot while trying to escape." The falsity of such reports is obvious : the camps are most closely guarded, with armed patrols, police dogs, and searchlights at night. The prisoner must realise the hopelessness of any attempt to escape ; and for that reason there are few real attempts to escape from the camps. The murders in the camp, however, are systematically reported as " shot while trying to escape."

Dachau : The Murder Camp.

Fourteen cases of murder in the Dachau camp, near Munich, became known in the course of a few weeks.

In the middle of April the official Wolff Telegraph Bureau reported :

" Munich, April 14 (WTB.). In the Dachau concentration camp, near Munich, Communists made an attempt to escape. The Storm Troop police found themselves compelled to use their guns. They brought down four Communists, of whom three were killed on the spot, and one was mortally wounded."

According to the *Daily Telegraph* of April 27th, 1933, the commandant of the Dachau camp confirmed this report to the English journalist Geyde. The names were not stated in the official announcement. The victims were described as Communists. But it soon became known that they were not Communists, but middle class Jews. A prisoner who was in the Dachau camp describes the murder as follows :

" A few days ago we were going out as usual to work. All of a sudden the Jewish prisoners—Goldmann, a merchant, Benario, a lawyer from Nürnberg, and the merchants, Artur and Erwin Kahn—were ordered to fall out of the ranks. Without even a word, some Storm Troop men shot at them ; they had not made any attempt to escape. All were killed on the spot. All had bullet wounds in their foreheads. They were buried secretly, no one being allowed to be present. Then a meeting was called, and a Storm Troop leader made a speech in which he told us that it was a good thing these four Jewish sows were dead. They had been hostile elements who had no right to live in Germany ; they had received their due punishment."

We have particulars of thirteen similar murders at Dachau.

Two of the most brutal cases were the murder of the Communist members of the Diet, Dressel and Goetz ; the former was tortured to death, and the latter was shot after weeks of brutal maltreatment.

Tens of Thousands in Prison. The thirty-five to forty thousand prisoners in the concentration camps are not the only political prisoners in Germany ; in addition, there are the prisoners awaiting trial and those who have been sentenced to imprisonment and penal servitude. Their number is growing every day. Every day the Press announces new mass arrests. In the second half of June the number of new arrests was higher than in any previous period. Sometimes a thousand arrests are made in a day. Thus for example in Seftenberg, a small town in the Niederlausitzer coalfield, 267 social democrats have been arrested ; in Bremen over 80 ; and several hundreds in Braunschweig, Hamburg, Saxony, Berlin and Stuttgart, all on one day only.

The total number of prisoners awaiting trial or already serving sentences can only be guessed at ; it is certainly not less than twelve to fifteen thousand.

The prisoners awaiting trial are herded together in overcrowded prisons, sometimes four or five in a cell intended for a single prisoner. Many of the prisoners have no bedding of any kind.

Among those awaiting trial are many well-known officials of the Communist and Social Democratic Parties, as well as members of the Democratic Party, the People's Party, the Centre Party and even the German Nationalist Party. Ernst Thaelmann, leader of the German Communist Party, was arrested on March 3rd in Charlottenburg and put in prison. In all the Government papers and the Press which had been " brought into conformity " it was reported that he had been arrested in connection with the Reichstag fire.

The Arrests. It will be difficult for people in other countries to realise the arbitrary methods used by the police and Storm Troops in making arrests. One day an illegal leaflet is seen in a street ; it is reported by a policeman or an adherent of the Nazis. Police motors immediately rush up, the whole district is cordoned off, all houses are searched from attic to cellar, books and typewriters are seized, and often completely innocent citizens are carried off. Any obstruction is immediately met with violence and arrest. Every day the papers report such raids and mass arrests. Early in July the Hitler Government began to seize as hostages the relatives of workers who had escaped. The best known case is the arrest of five relatives of Scheidemann ; but this is only one case among many.

The Sentences. The public prosecutors have been busy since February 27th. Special courts have been instituted in practically every German town. Denunciations bring a continuous stream of prisoners ; and the charges are as arbitrary as the sentences. Often prisoners are kept for weeks in prison and then set free without even being tried. But even after being set free they are continuously menaced with further arrest, and in many cases have to report daily to the police.

The following are some examples of the nature of the charges and the heavy sentences passed :

" The special court of Moabit, Berlin, sentenced the unemployed workers Max Ziegler and Richard Schröter to 15 months and 18 months imprisonment respectively, because Ziegler, a member of the Communist Party, had distributed in East Berlin illegally produced copies of the *Rote Fahne* which he had received from Schröter."

" The Darmstadt special court sentenced a female member of the Young Communist League to 8 months, and a male member to 5 months imprisonment, for producing and distributing a leaflet. The prisoners are 16 years of age."

There are innumerable sentences for spreading " atrocity stories." Often the relatives of arrested persons are told that they cannot expect the case to be heard for several weeks, owing to the number of cases awaiting trial. The relatives can seldom find a lawyer prepared to undertake the defence. The position of the prisoners is made worse by the fact that the Hitler Government has prohibited the " Red Aid " organisation, which used to help the families of political prisoners. But it still carries on its work, with the help of similar organisations in other countries and the " Committees for the Relief of the Victims of German Fascism " which have been set up on the initiative of the Workers' International Relief organisations.

CHAPTER X : MURDER

MURDER stalks through Germany. Mutilated corpses are carried out of Nazi barracks. The bodies of people disfigured beyond recognition are found in woods. Corpses drift down the rivers. "Unknown" dead lie in the mortuaries.

During the world war lists were published of those who were killed. The lists were even exchanged between enemy governments. The Hitler Government is naturally not so "liberal" as to publish the list of all its victims. Only a small number of the murders ever appear in the Press, and then in the form of "shot while trying to escape" or in some similar lying form ; and if anyone were to try to get at the truth, he would suffer the same fate : torture and death.

On March 22nd a general amnesty was proclaimed for all criminal acts "committed in the fight for the national revolution." This general amnesty is a licence for all past and future murders.

Hitler's Comrades of Potempa. There is no complete list of the victims of Nazi knives and bullets even in the months preceding Hitler's entry into the Government. Certainly there must have been many hundreds murdered : Social Democrats, Communists and members of the Catholic Parties as well as non-Party workers. A wave of murderous attacks on Social Democrats, Communists and members of the Democratic parties developed in the first half of August 1932 ; in many towns these occurred on the same day, showing clearly that they were organised. In January, 1933, under the Schleicher Government, the number of crimes of violence perpetrated by National Socialists rose very rapidly, and after Hitler became Chancellor they increased from day to day. In the first half of February,

27 working men and women were murdered by Nazi storm troops.

The most notorious case in the summer of 1932 was the murder of a worker in Potempa, a village in Upper Silesia. A murder gang of Nazis, who had first drunk heavily in an inn, forced their way into a house where a Communist worker lived and literally trampled him to death in front of his aged mother. When all the bestial details of the crime had been disclosed in court and the death sentence had been passed on some of the criminals, Hitler openly came to their defence and in a letter described them as " my comrades." They were pardoned by the Papen Government.

Immediately after March 5th, 1933, that is, even before the " general amnesty," these murderers were amnestied by Hitler and again let loose upon the working class.

The Murders and how they are Hushed up.   As in all other sections of this book, we rely in this chapter only on material which has been carefully checked up : the main sources are accounts of eyewitnesses, and reports published by the Press in Germany which has been " brought into conformity." These Press reports not only reveal the murders but also show the methods used to hush them up —methods which unintentionally often provide proof of the crime.

In the month of March 1933, reports of political murders still appeared in the Press as a result of the initiative of the reporters. But in spite of the fact that the only surviving newspapers had been " brought into conformity," so many reports of murders began to appear that they became dangerous for the Hitler Government. In the course of April the reporting of murders was taken out of the hands of the Press itself, and even of the local censors appointed by the Hitler Government : the following announcement was issued by the Wolff Telegraph Bureau :

" Berlin, 2nd April. WTB. The Government has advised all news-agencies that reports on incidents in Germany, particularly reports on conflicts arising out of the Jewish boycott, must not be published without express sanction from the press department of the Reich Government. No alteration of the wording of the report as passed for publication is permitted."

As a result of this centralisation of the censorship, a concrete picture of incidents is seldom given ; and if any details appear, they are almost certain to be contradictory. There are many ways in which the incidents are dealt with so as to conceal the true facts.

In the first place, bodies found are said to be of " unknown persons." In most cases the police can immediately identify such bodies, as the dead persons have already been reported as missing or as having been taken away by force. But the reports do not disclose their identity.

Secondly, a great number of murders are represented as suicides. The following report of the murder of Councillor Kresse, of Magdeburg, shows how clumsily the truth is concealed :

"Magdeburg, 14th March (TU.). An incident resulting in bloodshed occurred late on Sunday evening at Felgeleben, near Magdeburg, at an inn which had been used as a voting station. The Social Democratic Councillor Kresse, who arrived at the inn from Magdeburg, was taken into custody by the police officers there at the request of a number of storm troop men. In another room an argument developed between Kresse and a number of storm troop men, in the course of which Kresse fired a shot at the National Socialists, severely wounding the storm troop leader Gustav Lehmann. Everyone ran out of the inn, into which several shots were then fired from outside. Shortly afterwards Kresse was found dead in the inn, with a bullet through his head. A post-mortem examination is now being carried out to establish whether Kresse, after his revolver attack, put an end to his own life, or whether he was killed by one of the shots fired into the inn from outside."

The National Socialist Party Press has a tendency to make such reports as sensational as possible. For example, the *Völkischer Beobachter* of April 25th presents one of the worst cases of lynching as suicide, in the following terms :

" Terrible suicide : smeared with tar and burnt. A man living in a bungalow on the Honer Moor has committed suicide by a terrible method. He went into the tool-house built on to his bungalow, where there was a barrel of tar. After taking off some of his clothes, he smeared himself with tar and set fire to the barrel. He died in the fire which resulted. The motive of the suicide was melancholia. The bungalow was completely burnt down. The suicide was a married man with several children."

The third method is to ascribe to natural causes deaths which take place in hospital as a result of Nazi brutalities. In a number of cases (for example, that of Dr. Eckstein, of Breslau) the report is used to slander the individuals after their death ; references to venereal diseases are made to discredit the victims.

The fourth method is to suggest that the motive of the crime was not political ; in such cases, naturally, no details of persons or motives are given, as for example the following report published in *Germania* of May 15th, 1933 :

" A police report states that on Saturday evening Henseler, a slater, was forced by several persons to accompany them to No. 21 Lessingstrasse. Shortly afterwards the neighbours heard a number of shots. H. was found in the loft, severely wounded, and taken to hospital, where he died within a short time. The criminals escaped without being recognised."

The fifth method is the use of a formula which, since the murder of Karl Liebknecht and Rosa Luxemburg, has had a quite definite and unambiguous meaning—the formula : " Shot while trying to escape." Here is a typical case, told in the officially published reports :

I

The *Frankfurter Zeitung* of April 5 publishes the following report from Düsseldorf, dated April 4 (WTB.) :

" The Communist leader Bässler, who has evaded arrest for a considerable time, was located this morning by auxiliary police officers. During the search the arrested man made use of a moment when he was not under observation to attempt an escape. As he would not stop in spite of repeated warnings, the officers made use of their weapons. B. was seriously wounded by a bullet and died after being taken to hospital."

II

The *Angriff* of April 5 publishes the following message from Düsseldorf, dated April 5 :

" The police state that on April 4, at about 4 p.m. (!) the Communist official Bässler was arrested in his flat by protective corps men. In the search of his flat two packets of dynamite were discovered. Documents were also confiscated. On the way to the police station B. made an attempt to escape. He did not stop in spite of being summoned to do so several times, and continued to run after warning shots were fired. He was severely wounded by a shot in his back, and died shortly after being taken to hospital."

In actual fact, Bässler's home was surrounded during the night ; he was brought out early in the morning and shot in the street. The contradictions in the official reports are clear. The dynamite was not found, but invented.

"Reduction in the Number of Political Murders." The *Deutsche Allgemeine Zeitung* of May 6th, 1933, published the following, under the heading : " Great reduction in the number of political murders since the National Government took power " :

> " The following statement is official : The Prussian Premier and Minister of the Interior, Goering, announces through the Chief of the Secret Police Department that there has been a marked reduction, since the National Government took power, in acts of violence with fatal results arising from political motives. . . . Almost simultaneously with the taking of power by the National Government the effective defence measures taken by the new Government, together with the relaxing of political tension as a result of the victory of the national movement, brought about a rapid fall in the number of fatal cases, which had previously been mounting steadily and has now reached its lowest point for a long time, with only two fatal cases in April of this year."

At about the same time as the Hitler Government issued this transparent announcement, it was also officially announced that during the month of April forty-six bodies had been brought to the Berlin mortuary alone, with their features mutilated beyond recognition. During the month of April the Fascist Press itself reported fifty political murders, the names being given in each case.

We now give details of a number of cases, giving the sources of information in each case.

" Shot while Trying to Escape."   We have already quoted the reports published in the *Frankfurter Zeitung* and the *Angriff* in connection with the death of Heinz Bässler. Bässler had been a member of the National Socialists and a storm troop leader ; in December 1930 he began to understand the real policy of the Nazis and left the National Socialist Party, later joining the Communist Party. This was the reason why he was murdered. The following letter shows how he was done to death :

" If only our dear Heinz was still alive ! I can't realise it. But God will revenge this crime. This crime was no German deed.

" In the morning, that is, Tuesday morning about four, we were roused by seven protective corps men and two detectives. We were kept quiet with revolvers. Heinz had to dress and go with them. We had to lock the doors and were not allowed to open the windows. O God, how roughly they treated our Heinz ! They closed off the street as early as three o'clock, and at four they came up. And then they took him with them and they shot him in the street, ' martial law.' Oh, what he must have suffered, the poor lad, I wish I had gone with him ! He had three shots through his heart, one in his arm, one in his neck, one in his pelvis, and two others besides, eight shots in all. Then they left him lying there, and some peasants found him, like a dog. I can't believe it. I went running to Herr M. in the morning, for Heinz told me, go at once to him and tell him, for Weitzel has pledged himself to help me. But what help did he give ! Heinz trusted people too much. Frau Lene, if you could have seen Heinz now, on the death bier, you would have called God to judge, they had treated him so brutally ! I can't forget what he looked like, how can anyone treat a poor harmless human being so brutally ? And then the lies in the newspapers, that Heinz had been shot while trying to escape and that they had found two packets of dynamite ! Such meanness, and it's not possible to get any justice done. Not even a pistol or a piece of paper of any importance did they find ! And then the papers write such a provocation ! But I call God in heaven to judge, for such a cruel and mean crime. . . .

" Everyone is so overwhelmed by this crime, they can't believe it, that these people should shoot down a person by himself, so mean and brutal. The funeral is Saturday afternoon at half-past one, at the South Cemetery. Heinz will be buried by the clergyman, and many,

many people will come with him on his last journey. When I went to Herr M., how he treated me ! When I said to him, how can anyone shoot a helpless man like that, he answered : ' If you say much more, I'll have you arrested too. . . . ! ' "

" I'll Shoot You Down." About 6 p.m. on March 6th, Grete Messing, a working woman, married and with two children, left her home in the Sommermühlenweg in Selb (Bavaria) and went towards the town to do some shopping. About forty yards from her home she met a National Socialist of the name of Lager, who lived in the same street. He got in front of her and provoked her by saying " Heil Hitler ! " Frau Messing rejoined " Rot Front " and tried to pass him. Lager stopped her and threatened her with his revolver, saying " I'll shoot you down ! " She answered calmly : " Shoot away ! "

Lager put his Browning to the woman's throat and pulled the trigger. Frau Messing was mortally wounded. Her husband carried her back to her home, and there she bled to death. The murderer went to the Nazi inn, drank some liquor and then handed himself up to the " auxiliary police." He was put under arrest. Ten days later he was released. A guard of honour met him at the station in Selb. Lager was not expelled from the storm troops. On the other hand, the husband and nineteen-year old son of the murdered woman are in Bayreuth penitentiary, under " protective arrest."

Police and auxiliary police carried out repeated searches in working-class houses in Selb. They were not looking for a criminal, nor for a murderer, but for a photograph which was documentary proof of the murder. This photograph is printed here.

Three Bodies in the Machnower Forest. On March 11th, 1933, the whole Press reported the finding in the Machnower Forest of three bodies of young persons who had been shot, but whose identity was unknown. In spite

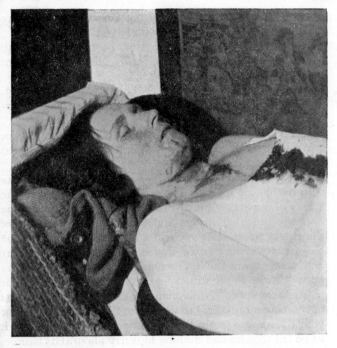

GRETE MESSING, a working woman, who was shot down in the street by a storm trooper, and bled to death.

PLATE NO. 16.

of the fact that the police had all particulars these were withheld from the public. The three youths were :

1. Fritz Nitschmann, upholsterer, born at Oldenburg, March 1st, 1909, then living in Berlin. His parents did not belong to any party, nor did he.

2. Hans Balschukat, a worker, born August 28th, 1913, in Berlin. Living in Berlin. Member of the Red Aid organisation.

3. Preuss, twenty-three years of age. Living in Berlin.

We have received the following information with regard to Fritz Nitschmann :

At 9.30 p.m. on March 8th, Nitschmann was walking with his fiancée towards his home. When they reached the corner of the Stubenrauch-Erdmannstrasse, a red car came over the Siegfried Bridge and crossed to the left side of the empty street. Two men in storm troop uniform—the chauffeur was in civilian clothes—jumped out of the car and came towards Nitschmann and his fiancée, calling out : " Halt, stand still, you must come and have your papers examined." Nitschmann said quietly : " You must have made a mistake," to which the Nazis replied : " Shut your mouth and get in ! " Nitschmann did as he was told, as he felt that he had nothing to worry about. His fiancée, who also belongs to no party, wanted to get into the car with him, but was pushed roughly away by the Nazis, who told her that Nitschmann was only being taken to be identified, and that nothing would happen to him. His fiancée, who was crying after being pushed away, did not note either the number of the car or the number on the collar of the Nazis. The car drove through the Stubenrauchstrasse and turned into the Hauptstrasse.

Immediately after his arrest Nitschmann's fiancée went to his mother and told her what had happened. From there she went to the police station in the Kriemhildstrasse and stated the facts. There she was told : " Nothing will happen to him, he will be back soon. Come again to-morrow." At 8 a.m. on March 9th, his mother went to the same police station, and was told the same thing. She was however told that during the night enquiries had been made at all police stations, and that Nitschmann had not been brought in to any. She was to come again at noon. At noon his father went to the police station and reported him as missing.

Up to March 11th, Nitschmann's parents heard nothing from the police. At 9 a.m. on that date police officers arrived with the information that the Berlin *Morgenpost* had reported that three bodies had been found in the Machnower Forest. From the description given, Nitschmann's father thought that one of these must be his son, and he went to the police station, where however he could not yet get any further information.

At noon the father went to the police headquarters and spoke to the inspector who was dealing with the case. The inspector, who did not then know that Nitschmann had been carried off by storm troop men, told the father that in all his experience he had never come across such a brutal murder. After the father had given all details, the inspector stated that he and his officers would do everything they could to discover the criminals.

The father identified his son in the mortuary, in the presence of the inspector. The body showed ten bullet wounds, eight in the back, one in the neck, and one in the jaw. Permission to take a photograph of the body was refused. Cremation also was not allowed, in view of the possibility of expert examination being necessary. Up to March 15th the Criminal Department had not yet authorised the handing over of the bodies to their families.

Two persons independently approached Nitschmann's father and gave the number of the car in which Nitschmann had been carried off as IA 78087 ; both also stated that it was a red car.

With regard to Hans Balschukat, the following information is in our possession :

" On March 8th, Balschukat was arrested at the entrance of Gotenstrasse 14 in Schöneberg by three National Socialists with drawn revolvers, who carried him off

in a dark car. On March 10th his father received a
post card with the following :

   " ' I have to-day found a purse with contents. Please
come for the purse on Saturday, March 11th, at
6 p.m.
       'HANS SCHMIDT, Bornstedt bei Potsdam,
                       ' Viktoriastrasse 26.' ''

When the card arrived, Balschukat's father was not at
home, and his mother took it to the police, who told her
that she should not in any circumstances go to Bornstedt. At the same time they telephoned to Bornstedt and
to the detectives who were then investigating the crime in
the Machnower Forest. The purse was taken charge of by
the Criminal Department. That same day the father also
went to the police, who told him that he must not go to
Bornstedt, that the man who alleged that he had found the
purse had already been arrested, as he was suspected of
the crime, in view of the fact that the purse showed no sign
of having been lying about.

On March 11th the father saw his son's body. He could
not identify him at first, as the body was terribly disfigured.
The lips were swollen and blue, the chin battered in, and
there were blue patches on the neck and larynx and chest,
apparently caused by violent kicks. The arms and chest
had a number of swollen patches, which were evidently
the result of the lad having been tied up.

From the father's superficial examination—he was not
allowed to examine the body carefully—the murdered lad
had had six or seven bullets through him, two at the
back of his head, one through his temple, two or three in
his right arm, and a shot through his chest.

No details can be secured with regard to the murder of
Preuss, as his father refuses to give any information.

Steel Rods and Spirits of Salt.   Grotohenne, a telegraph fitter, was a member of the Reichsbanner, but held

no political office of any kind. On Monday, March 27th, he was visited by storm troop men, who insisted on his coming with them to the storm troop quarters. When he did not come home after some considerable time, Frau Grotohenne went to the storm troop quarters, and just as she was asking one of the Nazis to release her husband, Grotohenne was brought out into the street, little more than a bleeding lump of flesh. Several men brought him home ; he complained of internal pains as well as external injuries. Grotohenne was able to tell what had been done to him. His clothes had been taken off and he had been beaten with steel rods for three hours, from time to time being made to wipe the blood from the floor with his own clothes. When he was lying almost unconscious the Nazis tried to pour spirits of salt between his clenched teeth. As they did not succeed in doing this, they then forced his teeth apart, tearing away a part of his upper lip in doing this. Grotohenne died on April 29th, after terrible suffering. An official post-mortem was held, and the cause of his death was certified as : " apoplexy and internal burns." The case was referred to the Criminal Department, but up to the present none of the criminals have been followed up.

Beaten, Stabbed and Trampled on. On March 28th the Communist Edom, of Robertstrasse 6, Königsberg, was carried away from his home at midnight. As it was known that he was a friend of the Communist Reichstag deputy Schütz he was beaten for two hours in such a brutal way that he lost control of himself and told the Nazis where Schütz was living. At 2.30 a.m., Schütz was brought to the same Nazi barracks and there beaten, stabbed and trampled on for twelve hours ; on the evening of March 29th, Schütz died in hospital, the cause of death being given as heart failure. On April 3rd, Schütz's body was put into the ground like a dog's. His death was not reported in any German paper ; the doctors and nurses who had attended him were forced by threats to say nothing. In the meanwhile, Frau Schütz had been arrested. After her husband had been buried she was compelled to sign an undertaking to say nothing of what had happened. The Nazis took Schütz's twelve-year-old son to see his father's mutilated body, and one of them said to him : " You will have the same fate if you follow in his footsteps."

Lynched in Prison. The three following official reports on the case of Schumm are enough to expose the methods used by the Fascist news-agencies :

I

" Kiel, 1 April (TU.) : At about eleven o'clock a dispute arose in front of the Jewish furniture shop kept by Schumm, in the course of which the son of the Jewish shopkeeper attacked a protective corps man. When one of his comrades came to the latter's help, a fight developed between the two protective corps men and the shopkeeper, who rushed up, and his son, in the course of which a shot was fired which seriously wounded in the chest the protective corps man Walter Asthalter, 22 years old, of Kiel."

(The facts were as follows : In the course of the boycott of Jewish shops a storm troop gang occupied the furniture shop kept by Schumm. The shopkeeper was molested by the Nazis, and his son, a lawyer, tried to protect him. A dispute arose, and then a tussle, " in the course of which a shot was fired "—by one of the Nazis—which seriously wounded another of the storm troop men.)

II

" Kiel, 1 April (WTB.) : The son of the proprietor of the Schumm furniture shop, who in the morning had fired some shots at a storm troop man in front of his father's shop and wounded him severely in the stomach, has been shot in the police cell to which he had been brought. It is reported that a number of persons went to

police headquarters and demanded that the door of
Schumm's cell should be opened, and when this was
done, several shots were fired which killed him on the
spot. The body was conveyed to the medical institute."

(This second report is already improved to make it appear
that Schumm, who was absolutely unarmed, had not only
fired the shot, but " some shots." The report gives the
circumstances of the murder of Schumm accurately enough,
but without expressly stating that the Nazis concerned
murdered him to get a witness of the morning's crime out
of the way.

But both these reports were so transparent that that same
afternoon the Central Press Bureau intervened and produced the following account, which is false in every particular.)

III

" Kiel, 1 April (WTB.) : The Jewish lawyer and commissioner for oaths Schumm at 11.30 this morning shot
a protective corps man of the name of Walter Asthalter
in the stomach ; according to information so far to hand,
the shooting, which took place in the Kehdenstrasse,
was without any plausible ground. The protective corps
man died in the Clinic. An enraged crowd of people
assembled in front of the police jail, before the removal
of Schumm, which had been ordered by the authorities,
could be effected. The enraged crowd forced its way
into the prison, where Schumm was killed by revolver
bullets. The whole incident developed so quickly that
the police could do nothing to stop it. The crowd also
forced their way into the shop kept by Schumm's father
in the Kehdenstrasse and destroyed the stock."

How the mineworkers' leader Albert Funk was
murdered. On April 16th the mineworkers' leader,
Albert Funk, was recognised by a National Socialist in
Dortmund and denounced to the police. Albert Funk had

for many years played a leading part in the struggles of the mineworkers ; he was formerly a Communist member of the Reichstag and leader of the United Mineworkers' Union.

Funk was put into the Dortmund police prison. He succeeded in getting out a letter reporting the terrible brutalities inflicted on seven other prisoners ; he himself was not brutally treated at first. The papers said not a word about his arrest ; this was enough to arouse the gravest fears. On April 26th, after ten days in prison, Albert Funk was murdered. His wife came to the prison to ask to see him, and was told that she could not, because he had poisoned himself in his cell. This was on April 28th.

On the next day, April 29th, the Press of the Ruhr district published " sensational disclosures " about alleged discoveries of arms, dynamite dumps, terrorist groups, etc., of the Communists in the Recklingshausen area, and in this connection it was reported that the Communist Reichstag deputy Albert Funk, who had been arrested, had made an insane attempt to escape from the Recklinghausen prison by jumping from the third-floor window into the courtyard ; that he had broken his spine, arms and legs ; that he had been taken fully conscious to hospital, where he died shortly afterwards. Nothing was said about Funk having been in prison for two weeks ; and naturally not a word of explanation was given as to how he was suddenly transported from Dortmund to Recklingshausen.

Albert Funk had been driven almost out of his mind by horrible tortures, and his tormentors then forced him to throw himself out of the window. When some of the murdered man's imprisoned comrades who were in the courtyard at the time cried out in horror, the murderers shouted down to them : " You Moscow swine can come and jump after him ! "

Literally Torn to Pieces.   A witness reports :

" Early in March, Fritz Gumpert, of Heidenau, was arrested. He was accused of ' having buried munitions and arms.' He was taken to the Königstein fortress and thence to the concentration camp at Hohenstein. There he was put in chains and tortured. He was so appallingly ill-used that he died. His wife was informed that he had died of internal hemorrhage.

" Workers in the Heidenau factories collected money to bring the body to Heidenau. This was permitted, but on the express condition that *the coffin should not be opened.* The workers did not observe this condition. None of the eye-witnesses will ever forget the sight. Gumpert's face had been completely torn to pieces. As far as they could tell, his tongue was missing. Traces of heavy chains were visible on his arms. The back of the body was a lump of flesh that had been cut in pieces and was full of holes. The spine was broken. The sexual organs were lacerated. The right thigh was torn open. The pit of the stomach had been kicked in, so that the intestines were protruding. The lips showed how the victim had bitten into them to endure the appalling tortures he had suffered.

" Horrified and enraged workers gathered round, and the storm troop men used this as an excuse to confiscate the body again. A number of police and doctors came up, and a raid was conducted on the working-class houses in order to confiscate photographic apparatus and films. All witnesses were threatened with the severest penalties if they spoke of the case. Those who were known to have seen the body were warned ' to keep their mouths shut.'

" On Friday, April 28th, the funeral took place. Some 3,000 working men and women went to take part, but all approaches were barred by storm troops armed with rifles. When the cemetery gates were reached, the Nazis attacked the procession, and only the relatives were allowed in the cemetery. A clergyman wearing the swastika spoke at the graveside."

St. Bartholomew's Night in Köpenick.   In many German towns the Nazi storm troops have carried out

the " night of the long knife " foretold by Hitler before his advent to power. On the night of June 21st–22nd the Nazis began a series of murders, which lasted several days, in Köpenick, a suburb of Berlin. The victims were officials of the Social Democratic Party, of the Reichsbanner and of the Communist Party.

On June 21st the storm troops twice searched the house of a trade union secretary, Schmaus, in Köpenick. They stated that they were looking for arms. During the night the storm troop men came a third time, arrested Schmaus's son-in-law, who was a Communist, and then stormed the house, firing a number of shots. Schmaus had a feeble-minded son twenty-two years of age who was wakened by the shooting, picked up a revolver and went to oppose the Nazis. His mother shouted to him in alarm : " Don't shoot ! " But the son shot at and mortally wounded two of the Nazis who had forced their way in.

Then the slaughter began. Schmaus's son-in-law Rakow-ski was immediately shot by the Nazis in front of the house. Schmaus's son was arrested and brutally done to death. Schmaus himself was hanged by the Nazis in his house. Frau Schmaus was accused of having told her son to shoot, and was so brutally ill-used that she died a few days later.

That night " Marxists " were arrested throughout Köpenick and Friedrichshagen. Among them were the Reichsbanner leader and former premier of Mecklenburg, Johannes Stelling ; the fifty-five-year-old Paul von Essen, who was an official in the Reichsbanner ; and Assmann, fifty-seven years of age, who had been Reichsbanner leader in Friedrichshagen. A Social Democratic eye-witness gives the following account of what happened to the prisoners in the Nazi barracks :

" We were taken by car to the Köpenick prison. The square in front was filled with storm troop men, who wanted to attack us as soon as they saw us. The storm troop leader, however, shouted : ' Stop, don't hit them in the street ! ' But we were hardly inside the building when they began to attack us. We were driven up the stairs and along a long passage. In a long cell there were ten comrades standing with their faces to the wall. The floor and wall was already spattered with blood. An old woman, with blood streaming from her mouth and nose, and her clothes spattered with blood, was forced to scrub the floor. One of the storm troop men asked me : ' Do you know this whore ? ' I looked at her more closely, and saw with horror that she was my wife's mother. Then the Nazi told Comrade Kaiser to strike another comrade in the face. When Kaiser hesitated, he hit him such a blow with his fist that he went staggering to the wall. Then the comrades were forced with blows from sticks to hit each other until they were bleeding. . . . After that we had to run the gauntlet about ten times through lines of storm troop men armed with sticks and truncheons. In the course of this some of the older comrades collapsed. Meanwhile, the fifty-five-year-old Paul von Essen was brought in, the Nazis greeting him with howls of joy. He had been unemployed for a long time, and had just come out of hospital ; he was blind in one eye ; he took part in the war, and he had four children. They first hit him in the face, then pulled down his trousers and beat him with really insane fury with sticks and truncheons until he lost consciousness. Comrade von Essen has since succumbed to the terrible injuries his torturers inflicted on him. . . .

" Then we were each taken to a cell and beaten. The brutalities were repeated regularly every hour. Finally I was taken to the leader for examination, and in my despair I denied that I was a Marxist. He then ordered that I should not be beaten meanwhile, but if it turned out that I had told a lie I was to be shot.

" Shortly afterwards the door of my cell was flung open, and a storm troop leader rushed in with other storm troop men and beat me, shouting : ' You scoundrel, we'll finish you off to-day ! ' I was then dragged along the passage to my mother-in-law's cell, and while two of the Nazis held me, the old woman, who was fifty-three years of age, was beaten with sticks until she lay quiet on the floor. She is now out of her mind and in an asylum. . . ."

This eyewitness did not recognise either Stelling or Assmann among the prisoners. Some days later Stelling's body, covered with wounds, and sewn up in a sack, was taken out of the Finow Canal. At the same time two other unknown bodies were recovered. Eleven other men were missing. On July 12th people in Friedrichshagen heard that Assmann's body had also been found.

And so also throughout Germany, at the time when Hitler was more and more openly acting on behalf of the rich capitalists of Germany, the number of murders was rising.

Chapter XI: THE GERMAN WORKERS' FIGHT AGAINST FASCISM

On April 21st, 1933, the police press bureau in Stuttgart issued the following :

" Although the seizure and confiscation of all Communist printed papers was ordered as far back as March 1st, Communist sheets are still circulating. . . ."

On April 28th the police press bureau of Berlin stated :

" In the course of the search a considerable quantity of printed matter and numerous stencils for the production of leaflet material for May 1st were found in Steglitz and Friedenau."

That the attempt to stop the organisation of the anti-Fascist fight had not succeeded is shown by the following announcement made by the police press bureau of Cassel on May 5th, 1933 :

" In continuation of the measures taken against the illegal district leadership of the German Communist Party in Cassel, early on Thursday morning the political police carried out searches in secret offices and in the houses of the leaders of the district committee. . . ."

On May 26th, 1933, the Bremen police announced that :

" In spite of the police warning issued a few days ago in connection with the distribution of illegal Communist sheets, and the reference to the severe penalties attached, on Thursday evening the illegal *Arbeiter Zeitung*, six pages in size, was circulated by the Communists. . . ."

Hitler aimed at carrying out the destruction of all political parties. But there is one party that he cannot destroy : the German Communist Party, which is carrying on the fight against Fascism illegally. The statements issued by the Hitler Government are every day proving that this party's active opposition cannot be broken. Reports are coming in from every part of Germany showing that groups of workers belonging to the Social Democratic Party and to the Reichsbanner, the League of Socialist Youth and the Christian organisations are joining with the Communists in this fight.

In the days following the burning of the Reichstag, anti-Fascist sheets issued by the Communists were already circulating among the workers. Workers' homes and the cellars and roofs of blocks of flats were transformed into secret printing works. Although hundreds of active agitators were arrested, thousands of newly trained and determined workers took their place. In spite of the extension of torture and ill-treatment, the fight for freedom against Fascism continued even more vigorously and with increasing effect. Each line of the illegal papers issued by the Communists is literally written in blood. New horrible acts of torture are perpetrated wherever each issue of these papers appears.

Before the end of March an illegally printed pamphlet on the burning of the Reichstag was produced, and was distributed in every part of Germany. Its external appearance is that of an advertisement of the film *In the Sign of the Cross*.

Goering, the organiser of the Reichstag fire, was compelled to pay a glowing tribute to the " disintegrating work " carried out by the Communists when, at the end of June 1933, he dissolved the organisation of young German Nationalists on the official ground that it had been completely permeated by Communists. Early in July the threatening statements issued by Hitler and Frick against a " second revolution " showed that the work of unmasking the Hitler Government was achieving success even among large numbers of the storm troops and of the National Socialist factory cells.

The following pages give only a brief and partial statement of the " underground " work which is being carried on in Germany.

The Illegal "Rote Fahne."

One of the most vital sections of the fight against Fascism is the production and distribution of illegal newspapers. The *Rote Fahne*, the central organ of the German Communist Party, has been appearing regularly since the burning of the Reichstag. Police activities, raids, the allocation of thousands of spies, nightly patrols of storm troop men through printing works have been unable to prevent the production of this paper. It continues to appear as a two-or four-page paper, and to find its way into the blocks of flats in Wedding, into the A.E.G. and Siemens factories and into the railway stations. Though the technical production of the paper may be worse than before, it is certain that none of its former issues have ever been read by so many people as the present issues.

The Christian Socialist paper *Reichspost*, issued in Vienna, on May 27th, printed the following interesting story :

" At first the *Rote Fahne* appeared in an illegally printed edition of 300,000 copies, and this was followed by a number of duplicated editions. Secret presses—previously prepared for such purposes—duplicating machines and typewriters began their work. Soon the greater part of the local, cell and industrial papers—though most of them only duplicated—were again in circulation, and hundreds of thousands of leaflets were being passed from hand to hand in the factories and at the Labour Exchanges."

In twenty different areas in Greater Berlin, in addition to the printed *Rote Fahne*, duplicated papers produced from wax or metal sheets are regularly distributed weekly, experienced, long before the Hitler dictatorship was and sometimes twice weekly. They all bear the heading *Rote Fahne*. These papers are edited by workers.

Red Papers Throughout Germany.   Early in May the Hamburg police announced that :

" In spite of the strongest counter-measures taken by the authorities, again and again treasonable publications of the Communist Party of Germany, and particularly papers such as the prohibited *Hamburger Volkszeitung* and other Marxist productions, are being produced and sold on the streets and in the houses."

In the Ruhr district the *Ruhr Echo* has appeared several times, in large editions. The May 1st number was even printed in two colours. In Essen, although whole districts of the town have been searched through by storm troops and police, and although courageous distributors of the papers have been most horribly tortured, duplicated editions of the *Ruhr Echo* continue to appear.

A letter received from a Munich worker reports that every week a hectographed newspaper is issued in an edition of 3,000 copies. Immediately after its production it is distributed to the separate anti-Fascist groups and brought by them to the workers in a number of different ways. Six Reichsbanner groups are helping in the distribution.

The Bremen police refer to the illegal, six-page paper, the *Arbeiter Zeitung*. In Stuttgart the South German *Arbeiter Zeitung* appears in printed form, and illegal papers are also distributed in Leipzig and Frankfurt-am-Main. During April and May several numbers of the Düsseldorf journal *Freiheit* were distributed. In Mannheim several issues of the *Rote Fahne Badens* have been published. In Erfurt the *Thüringer Volksblatt* appears in duplicated form.

In the Factories.   The only party which had made pre-parations for carrying on underground activity in the factories was the Communist Party. Its members were already established, in the secret production and distribution of factory papers. And because of this experience, it has been possible for numbers of such papers to be distributed in the factories during the period of the Hitler dictatorship. For example, a worker in the A.E.G. works in Berlin reports as follows in the *Antifascistische Front* of July 2nd, 1933 :

" Our last leaflet appeared in a format 10 x 20 cm. We produced it in the following way : We first worked out the slogans and cut them in linoleum ; then we put the strips of linoleum over an inked blotter and printed off copies one by one. During the night we posted a great number of these copies on various gates of the factory, and we scattered the remainder in the streets round. Our fellow workers, who are really starving for material of this kind, picked up the leaflets as they came to work in the morning and showed great enthusiasm, each single leaflet passing through dozens of hands."

The illegal papers *Hafentelegramme*, *Funksprüche* and *Der Sturm* are being published in the port of Hamburg. From one Hamburg office it is reported that the rolls of paper in the closets contain small leaflets or cuttings from illegal papers. In the Siemens works in Spandau, Berlin, anti-Fascist young workers have up to now succeeded in producing their paper regularly. In the Bielefeld works the *Rote Wacht* is being produced and distributed by a joint group of Communist, Social Democratic and Reichsbanner workers.

" Lightning Demonstrations." During the months of March, April and May there were large and small anti-Fascist demonstrations in hundreds of places ; most of them took the form of so-called " lightning demonstrations." In such demonstrations the workers assemble at an agreed point at a given signal, carry out a demonstration lasting only a few minutes, shouting slogans against the Hitler dictatorship and singing anti-Fascist songs. These demonstrations as a rule succeed in dispersing again before the police or storm troops are able to intervene ; these mobile methods are adopted to prevent a large number of arrests.

During April such demonstrations were held—in addition to very many others of which we have no reports—in Remscheid, Cleve, Krefeld, Siegen, Stettin, Worms, Osterode, Düsseldorf, and Linden near Hanover.

A report from Hamburg states that early in May the Young Communist League distributed 10,000 printed leaflets, posted up 80 posters prepared by hand, and painted anti-Fascist slogans on walls and pillars in every part of the town. Four lightning demonstrations were held, in each of which an average of 300 young workers took part.

A Danish anti-Fascist reports that during a visit to Germany he saw a street choir of four workers, who suddenly shouted : " Who set fire to the Reichstag ? The Nazis ! "—and then separated and disappeared.

Early in March a streamer was found across a working-class street in Dortmund, bearing the words : " Nero set fire to Rome and put the blame on the Christians—Hitler set fire to the Reichstag and blames the Communists ! " The same slogan, printed from a linoleum cut, was posted on walls all over Dortmund at the end of April.

The *Vossische Zeitung* of May 3rd reports :

" The Wolff Telegraph Bureau reports from Barnau that in the night of April 30th–May 1st a red banner bearing the hammer and sickle was fastened to the top of the steeple of the Marienkirche. Early in the morning of May 1st it was taken down by storm troop men at the risk of their lives. That morning, which was the festival of national labour, Nazis who went to hoist the swastika banner at the Town Hall discovered that it had been stolen during the night. The excitement in Bernau arising from this double act of provocation was indescribable. During the night of May 1st–2nd about forty suspected persons were arrested by the storm troops and police, and removed to the concentration camp at Oranienburg."

In addition to torture and murder, starvation is used by the Hitler Government as a method of fighting the anti-Fascists ; the following quotation from the *Frankfurter Zeitung* of July 10th, 1933, illustrates the methods used in the attempt to force the unemployed to denounce anti-Fascist agitators :

" Cassel, July 8th. In Schmalkalden, which is in the administrative district of Cassel, intensified Communist propaganda among the unemployed has been in evidence during the last few days. Several Communist leaflets have been distributed, and their producers and distributors have not yet been discovered. The Mayor of Schmalkalden has therefore ordered that relief is to be withheld from *all* recipients who are of Left tendencies until the criminals have been caught."

Anti-Fascists who are charged before the courts are not allowed witnesses or any other opportunities of defence. Before the charge is heard, the penalty has already been decided on. But in spite of everything many of the accused have made a heroic stand in court against the Fascist dictatorship. A report from Altona dated June 2nd, 1933, for example, states that during the trial of 20 anti-Fascist workers :

" The Communist worker Lütgens, against whom the Government attorney demanded the death penalty, stated that he regarded this demand put forward by the prosecution as an honour, as there could be no higher honour for a revolutionary worker than to be sentenced to the death penalty by a capitalist class court, and prison clothes were robes of honour."

In the middle of May a typist, Fräulein Jürr, was sentenced to imprisonment for eighteen months for having passed on leaflets. The Berlin journal *Der Tag* reported that :

" The accused stated in court that she still remained loyal to Communist ideas, to which prosecuting counsel replied : ' Attention must be called to the audacity and shamelessness displayed by Communists, who dare to proclaim their views even here in front of the special tribunals.' "

Similar cases are reported from all parts of Germany.

Only a very small percentage of the sentences passed on anti-Fascist agitators is ever reported in the Press ; but the increasing severity of the sentences has done nothing to stop the anti-Fascist work which is being carried on unceasingly. It has only been possible, within the limits of this book, to give a few examples of this work. The organisation of political and economic strikes, the hundreds of separate movements within the factories, and the revolts in the compulsory labour camps must be left to the second volume of the *Brown Book*.

The story of the heroic stand made by anti-Fascists in the struggle for German freedom has still to be written : the story of fighters who stood their ground in spite of the menace of murder ; the story of prisoners who met the death sentence with a proud declaration of their loyalty to Socialism ; the story of tortured victims who sang the " International " in spite of steel rods and truncheons ; the story of heroes like the teacher Wilhelm Hamann in Hessen, who was ordered to raise the swastika banner and hout : " Long live the leader of the German people, Adolf Hitler ! "—but who hurled the banner to the ground and amid the blows of the storm troop men shouted : " Long live the revolution and comrade Thälmann ! "

Tens of thousands of nameless heroes are fighting to free Germany and the world from the shameful barbarism of the Brown Shirts. They are facing courts martial and the gallows, torture and concentration camps. Their loyalty and courage cannot be broken. And their ceaseless activity is fanning the spark which will burst forth into the flame of Socialist freedom.

Appendix: LIST OF MURDERS

THE FOLLOWING is an extract from our list of murdered workers and intellectuals. We have definite information relating to over 500 murders carried out by the Nazis since March 3rd, and below we give the detailed particulars of 250. Our sources of information are official German announcements, press reports which have not been denied, and authenticated reports of witnesses.

It must be borne in mind that the list is only a small selection of the total number of murders, most of which are concealed by the rigorous censorship and the threats made by the Nazis to relatives and friends and witnesses.

1933

March 3rd. GERDES, Communist Member of the Diet, Oldenburg. Shot in the street. (*Wolff Telegraph Bureau.*) UNKNOWN COMMUNIST, Homberg, killed by a revolver shot. (*WTB.*) UNKNOWN REICHSBANNER MAN, Bremen, shot in the street. (*WTB.*) UNKNOWN WORKER, Bernburg, shot by National Socialists. (*WTB.*) GUSTAV SEGEBRECHT, Berlin, shot in the Stephan Inn, Liebenwalderstrasse 41. (Report from witness.) BERNHARD WIRSCHING, Berlin, Petristrasse 8/9, shot by Nazis in his flat. (Report from witness.) EBELING, a Magdeburg worker, killed in the Breckenstrasse by a shot through his stomach. (Witness.) WEISS, caretaker of the Social Democratic People's House, Worms, shot. (Witness.) UNNAMED GIRL, Worms, killed in the raid on the People's House. (Witness.) FABIAN, a Communist worker, Kellinghusen, shot at and died in hospital. (*WTB.*)

March 4th. TWO UNNAMED WORKERS, Cologne, severely wounded by shots and subsequently died. (*WTB.*) UNNAMED MEMBER OF THE "IRON FRONT," Thalesschweiler, shot in the street. (*WTB.*) FRIEDRICH MARQUARDT, Düsseldorf, Behrenstr. 14, no party, killed by blows. (Witness.)

March 5th. KLASSEN and DE LONGUEVILLE, Oberhausen (Rhine Province), killed in a school courtyard "while attempting to escape." Both had bullet wounds in the front of their bodies.

(Witness.) WARNICKE, Quickborn, near Pinneberg, shot. (*WTB*.) UNNAMED REICHSBANNER MAN, Central Germany, stabbed to death. (*WTB*.) TWO BROTHERS BASSY, Bankau, Upper Silesia, murdered by storm troopers. (Witness.) KARL TARNOW, Berlin, beaten to death in Knesebeckstrasse, Neukölln. (Witness.)

March 6th. GRETE MESSING, working woman, Selb, shot in the street. (*WTB*.) HANS BAUER, worker, no party, never returned from the Nazi barracks in the Hedemannstrasse, Berlin. (Witness.) FRIEDLÄNDER, a baker's apprentice, 19 years old, murdered in the Nazi barracks in the Hedemannstrasse. (*Berliner Tageblatt*.)

March 7th. BERNHARD KRAUSE, Communist worker, Wiesenau, near Frankfurt-on-the-Oder, shot by storm troops. (*WTB*.) TWO UNNAMED WORKERS, Hamburg, killed in Nazi raid. (*WTB*.) UNNAMED WORKER, Düsseldorf, killed in the Levetzowstrasse. (*Telegrafen-Union*.)

March 8th. UNNAMED COMMUNIST WORKER, Billstedt, near Hamburg, shot "while trying to escape." (*WTB*.) PHILIPP, caretaker at Trade Union House, Breslau, shot when Nazis occupied the building. (*WTB*.) HEINRICH SPARLICH, building worker, Breslau, killed by a bullet and a knife stab in the back. (*Deutsche Allgemeine Zeitung*.) BALSCHUKAT, NITSCHMANN and PREUSS, Schöneberg, Berlin. Bodies found in Machnower Forest. (*Vossische Zeitung*.) UNNAMED COMMUNIST WORKER, Bochum, found shot in the street. (*TU*.) UNNAMED WORKER, Bochum, shot in his flat by six unknown men. (*TU*.) BLESS, member of the Reichsbanner, Offenbach, mortally wounded in a Nazi attack, since died. (Witness.)

March 9th. UNNAMED MEMBER OF THE REICHSBANNER, Munich, mutilated corpse found in the Munich Trade Union House, which had been occupied by Nazis on March 1st. (Witness.) LANDGRAF, director of publishing house, Chemnitz, shot when the *Volksstimme* building was occupied. (*TU*.) HELLPUCH, Communist worker, Duisburg, found shot. (*WTB*.)

March 10th. FRAU BICKS, 70 years of age, Berlin, mortally wounded by storm troopers who fired through her door. (*WTB*.) HERMANN, a watchmaker, Dresden, member of International Workers' Relief, beaten to death in his house. (Witness.) HANS SAILE, circulation manager, shot when the *Volksfreund* offices in Braunschweig were occupied. (Witness.) ULLRICH, leader of the Hessen Social Democrats, beaten to death. (*Berliner Tageblatt.*) TWO UNNAMED WORKERS, Zschopau, shot by storm troopers. (Berlin *Lokal Anzeiger.*) ALFRED PETZLAFF, Communist worker, Schöneberg, Berlin, taken by Nazis from his home; body found mutilated at Priesterweg station. (Witness.) SCHEUNFLÜGEL, a worker, Bernau, Chemnitz, killed by a " chance bullet." (Berlin *Lokal Anzeiger.*)

March 11th. ERICH MEYER, a young worker, Spandau, beaten to death. (*Frankfurter Zeitung.*) ROBERT DITTMAR, a worker, Karlshorst, near Berlin, found shot. (Berlin *Lokal Anzeiger.*) UNNAMED WORKER, Breslau, stabbed to death. (*TU.*) FÖRSTER and TANDLER, Communist workers, Limbach, near Chemnitz, " shot when trying to escape." (Witness.) PAUL KRANTZ, a young worker, Limbach, near Chemnitz, " shot when trying to escape." (*WTB.*) UNNAMED MAN, no party, Oppeln, shot on the steps of the Town Hall. (Berlin *Lokal Anzeiger.*)

March 12th. COUNCILLOR KRESSE, Social Democrat, Magdeburg, shot at election station in Felgeleben. (*TU.*) EICHHOLZ and KATHER, workers, Tolkemith, " shot while trying to escape." (*TU.*) SPIEGEL, Social Democratic lawyer, Kiel, attacked at his home and killed. (*WTB.*)

March 13th. UNKNOWN WORKER, Elbing, found shot. (*TU.*) HEINZ WESCHE and ERNA KNOTH, Communist councillors, Chemnitz; the first shot in the prison courtyard, the second beaten to death in his cell. (Witness.)

March 14th. KRUG, Schweinfurth, shot " in self-defence " by a Nazi. (*TU.*) UNNAMED WORKER, Hamburg, shot by detectives. (*WTB.*)

March 16th. DR. ASCHER, Berlin, Swinemunderstrasse, beaten to death. (Witness.) LEO KRELL, editor, Berlin, beaten to death. (Witness.)

March 17th. TWO UNKNOWN PERSONS, Elbin, " shot when trying to escape." (*Nachtausgabe.*)

March 18th. WALTER SCHULZ, Communist worker, Wittstock, murdered in prison. (Witness.) HANS SACHS, manufacturer, Chemnitz, shot. (*WTB.*) SIEGBERT KINDERMANN, Charlottenburg, Berlin, taken to the Hedemannstrasse, beaten to death, and thrown from the window. (*Berliner Tageblatt.*) UNNAMED WORKER, Wedding, Berlin, beaten to death at Nazi quarters. (Witness.)

March 19th. KREBS, Communist worker, Moabit, Berlin, shot by storm troopers in the street. (Witness.)

March 20th. GÜNTHER JOACHIM, lawyer, Berlin, tortured, died in Moabit Hospital. (*Vossische Zeitung.*) KURT POSSANER, Berlin, shot. (*Wiener Blatter.*)

March 21st. OTTO SELZ, Sträubing, shot. (Witness.)

March 22nd. WALTER BOEGE, Ebersbach, shot " while trying to escape." (*Vossische Zeitung.*) WILHELM WENZEL, Communist worker, Essen, shot in the street. (*WTB.*) DRESCHE, Dresden, found murdered. (Witness.) PAUL REUTER, Selchowerstrasse, Berlin, beaten to death by storm troopers. (Witness.)

March 23rd. ERICH LANGE, ex-member of the Nazi protective corps, Gelsenkirchen, shot by storm troopers. (Witness.) FRANCK, member of the Reichsbanner, Worms, said to have committed suicide. (*Unsere Zeitung.*) HERBERT PANGERITZ, worker, Bergstrasse 78, Berlin, brutally treated and died in hospital. (Witness.)

March 24th. FRAU ARBETS, a working woman, Gladbach, " shot while trying to escape." (*TU.*) ERICH PERL, 17 years old, Leipzig, shot in the street after release from a Nazi barracks. (Witness.) HAUS, retired Social Democratic councillor, found shot in Eichlingshofen. (*Frankfurter Zeitung.*)

March 25th. SOCIALIST, Wedding, Berlin, maltreated and died in hospital. (Witness.) FRAU MÜLLER, Aue, Saxony, maltreated, said to have committed suicide. (Witness.)

March 27th. NEUMANN, shopkeeper, Königsberg, beaten and used as target. (*TU.*) GROTOHENNE, telegraph fitter, Braunschweig, beaten to death. (Witness.) DR. MAX PLAUT, lawyer, beaten to death in a Nazi barracks. (Witness.) MAX BILECKI, Schöneberg, tortured in Nazi barracks and died in hospital. (Witness.)

March 29th. WALTER SCHUTZ, Communist member of the Reichstag, Königsberg, trampled to death. (Witness.)

March 30th. FRITZ ROLLE, worker, Siemensstadt, found stabbed. (*WTB.*) LEIBL VOLLSCHLÄGER, Skalitzerstrasse, Berlin, murdered and thrown into the river. (Witness.) UNKNOWN JEW, in Oberhessen, hanged by the feet, and died. (*Manchester Guardian.*)

April 1st. WILHELM POTTER, baker, and KARL GORMANN, Communist worker, Woldenberg, shot " while trying to escape." (*Vossische Zeitung.*) WILHELM DENGMANN, steel-worker, Duisburg, shot in the street. (*Vossische Zeitung.*) UNNAMED WORKER, Munich, shot "while trying to escape." (*Münchner Neueste Nachrichten.*) FRITZ SCHLUMM, lawyer, Kiel, beaten to death in prison. (*TU.*) PRESSBURGER, cattle dealer, Munich, shot, described as suicide. (*Münchner Neueste Nachrichten.*)

April 2nd. H. WERTHEIMER, Kehl, alleged stroke before arrest. (*WTB.*)

April 3rd. PAUL JAROS, smith, Limbach, near Chemnitz, shot "while trying to escape." UNNAMED WORKER, Augsburg, alleged stroke before arrest. (*TU.*) GEORG BELL, shot by storm troop men in Austria. (*Conti-WTB.*)

April 4th. HEINZ BÄSSLER, Düsseldorf, shot "while trying to escape."[1] (*WTB.*) WILHELM DREWS, worker, Berlin, found shot. (*Vossische Zeitung.*) DR. PHILIPPSTHAL, Biesdorf, Berlin, beaten to death. (*Berliner Tageblatt.*)

April 5th. RENOIS, Communist councillor, Bonn, shot "while trying to escape." (*TU.*) SAUER, Zubachwitz, member of Social Democratic Party, beaten to death in concentration camp. (*Neue Welt.*) WILHELM DREWS, Communist worker, Hamburg, shot in the street. (*TU.*)

April 6th. MAX NIEDERMAYER, Communist councillor, Johann Georgenstadt, Saxony, beaten to death in Zwickau prison. (Witness.) KURT FRIEDRICH, Communist worker, same town, shot. (Witness.)

April 7th. HANUSSEN, Berlin. (*TU.*) See report.

April 8th. UNNAMED WORKER, Neukölln, Berlin, beaten to death by storm troops. (Witness.)

April 9th. WALTER KASCH, Hamburg, shot.

April 10th. FRITZ ENGLER, hairdresser, no politics, Chemnitz, tortured and killed in the Zeisig Forest. (Witness.)

April 11th. MAX RUPF, Reichsbanner member, Chemnitz, found shot. (*TU.*) DR. ARTHUR WEINER, lawyer, Chemnitz, found shot. (*Frankfurter Zeitung.*) ALWIN HANSPACH, Communist worker, Friedersdorf, Zittau, shot in prison. (*TU.*)

April 12th. BENARIO, a lawyer, ARTHUR KAHN and ERWIN KAHN, and GOLDMANN, merchants from Nürnberg, shot "while trying to escape," Dachau concentration camp. (*WTB, Deutsche Allgemeine Zeitung.*) FRITZ KOLLOSCHE, Charlottenburg, tortured in Nazi barracks, died in hospital. (Witness.)

[1] See photograph at end of book.

April 13th. ALBERT JANKA, Communist member of the Reichstag, alleged suicide. (*WTB*.) GUSTAV SCHÖNHERR, worker, Hamburg, tortured to death. (Saarbrück *Arbeiter Zeitung*.)

April 15th. SPIRO, a Jew, aged 17, Berlin, murdered in Nazi barracks in the Hedemannstrasse. (Witness.)

April 16th. BRETSCHNEIDER, Siegmar, Saxony, found shot. (*WTB*.)

April 18th. BEYER, Krefeld, found shot. (*Vossische Zeitung*.) RICHARD TOLLEIT, Communist worker, Königsberg, shot "while trying to escape." (*Frankfurter Zeitung*.) UNKNOWN COMMUNIST WORKER, Königsberg, shot "while trying to escape." (*TU*.)

April 19th. UNKNOWN RAILWAYMAN, Munich, stabbed in the back, described as suicide. (*Münchner Neueste Nachrichten*.) ALFRED ELKER, a Christian, beaten to death by storm troopers because of his Jewish appearance. (Witness.)

April 20th. KAMINSKI, Dortmund, member of anti-Fascist League, beaten to death in prison. (Witness.)

April 21st. FRITZ DRESSEL, Chairman of Communist fraction in the Diet, described as suicide (*Münchner Neueste Nachrichten*), but reported by witness to have been murdered in Dachau camp.

April 22nd. MAX CASSEL, dairyman, Wiesbaden, shot in his flat. (*Deutsche Allgemeine Zeitung*.) SALOMON ROSENSTRAUCH, merchant, Wiesbaden, shot in his flat. (*Deutsche Allgemeine Zeitung*.) PAUL PAPST, worker, alleged suicide in Nazi barracks. (*Germania*).

April 23rd. KURT BENKE, a storm trooper, Berlin. (*Angriff*.) FRANZ SCHNEIDER, anti-Fascist worker, Goch, Rhineland, alleged suicide in prison, (*Vossische Zeitung*.) KONIETZNY, Communist worker, Oelsnitz, Erzgebirge, alleged suicide in prison. (*Vossische Zeitung*.)

April 24th. UNKNOWN MAN, Honer Moor, tarred and burnt, alleged suicide. (*Völkischer Beobachter*.) CORDES and SON, merchants, Wittmund, near Bremen, shot in a pogrom. (*WTB*.)

April 25th. MENDEL HABER, merchant, Dortmund, shot, and his body thrown into the river. (*Dortmunder General Anzeiger*.) TWO UNNAMED WORKERS, Heil, Lippe, found dead. (*Völkischer Beobachter*.) GRANITZA, worker, Königsberg, shot "while trying to escape." (*Nachtausgabe*.)

April 26th. WILLY PLONSKE, worker, Berlin, found dead. (*Angriff*.)

April 27th. ERWIN VOLKMAR, Neukölln, Berlin, alleged unpolitical murder, shot in the street. (*Angriff.*)

April 28th. UNNAMED MAN, Wollenberg, Oberbarnim, shot and burnt. (*Frankfurter Zeitung.*) FUNK, Communist member of the Riechstag, Dortmund, murdered in prison, alleged suicide. (*Angriff.*) FRITZ GUMBERT, Communist worker, Heidenau, beaten to death after weeks of torture. (See report.)

April 29th. UNKNOWN MAN, found murdered near Werneuchen in the Mark. (*WTB.*)

April 30th. HACKSTEIN, Communist worker, Gravenbroich, shot " while trying to escape." (*Kölnische Zeitung.*) ANDRES VON FLOTOV, German Nationalist landowner, arrested by Nazis and shot " while trying to escape." (*Conti.*)

End April. UNNAMED WORKER, Ebersdorf, Saxony, and HEINZ GOLDBERG, member of Red Sports organisation, shot in the cellar of *Hermann-Goering House*, Lobau. (Witness.)

May 2nd. RODENSTOCK, Social Democratic secretary of the Municipal Workers' Union, and TWO UNKNOWN TRADE UNION OFFICIALS, tortured and beaten to death in Nazi barracks in Duisburg. (Witness.) DANZIGER, Jewish merchant, Duisburg, attacked by Nazis and so brutally treated that he died. (Witness.)

May 3rd. DR. ERNST OBERFOHREN, chairman of German Nationalist fraction in Reichstag, found dead in his Kiel house. Described as suicide. (See report.)

May 4th. UNNAMED MEMBER OF STAHLHELM, Berlin, shot in Nazi quarters. (Saarbrück *Arbeiter Zeitung.*)

May 5th. SIMON KATZ, worker, Polish citizen, beaten to death. (Witness.) UNNAMED MAN, Potsdam, tied up and thrown into the river. (*Vossische Zeitung.*) SPANGENBERG, Communist worker, Bredereiche, Templin, alleged suicide in prison. (*Vossische Zeitung.*) UNNAMED DYE-WORKER, Sagan, alleged suicide, murdered in prison. (*WTB.*)

May 6th. UNNAMED GIRL, Grossen, found dead. (*Angriff.*)

May 8th. DR. ECKSTEIN, leader of Socialist Labour Party, Breslau, tortured to death. (*WTB.*)

May 9th. DR. MEYER, Jewish dentist, Wuppertal, mutilated by Nazis and drowned. (Witness.) GALINOWSKI, worker, Allenstein, shot " while trying to escape." (*WTB.*)

May 10th. UNNAMED YOUNG WORKER, member of Red Sports organisation, Wedding, Berlin, murdered in Nazi barracks in the Hedemannstrasse. (Witness.)

May 11th. BIEDERMANN, Social Democratic member of the Reichstag, Hamburg, described as suicide. (*Frankfurter Zeitung.*) GLÜCKOW, Communist worker, Berlin, tortured, died in hospital. (Witness.)

May 12th. SEPP GOETZ, Communist member of the Diet, maltreated and murdered in Dachau concentration camp. (Witness.)

May 13th. UNNAMED NAZI AUXILIARY POLICEMAN, Kiel, found shot ; he had asked when the Government was going to carry out its promises. (*Frankfurter Zeitung.*) HENSELER, Communist worker, Düsseldorf, shot. (*Germania.*)

May 15th. DR. ALFRED STRAUSS, Munich, a lawyer, aged 30, a German Jew, beaten to death. (Witness.) UNNAMED MEMBER OF STAHLHELM, Berlin, attacked by Nazis and stabbed to death. (Witness.) PALETTI, Schöneberg, Berlin, tortured to death. (Witness.)

May 17th. HERMANN RIEDEL, Gladbeck, alleged suicide. (*Der Tag.*) JOHANNES and WILHELM BARDT, Duisburg, beaten to death. (*Der Tag.*)

May 18th. UNKNOWN MAN, Berlin, alleged suicide. (*Vossische Zeitung.*) HONKSTEIN, Grevenbroich, shot " while trying to escape." (*WTB.*)

May 19th. LEONHARD HAUSMANN, Communist official, shot " while trying to escape " in Dachau concentration camp. (*WTB.*)

May 20th. ARTHUR MÜLLER, a worker, member of Reichsbanner, beaten to death in Nazi barracks, General Papestrasse, Berlin. (Witness.)

May 25th. SCHLOSS, a merchant, Nürnberg, shot. (Witness.)

May 26th. GROMANN, an artist, Duisburg, shot by protective corps men in Kalkumer Wood. (Witness.)

May 27th. FRANZ LEHRBURGER, Nürnberg, shot " while trying to escape in the Dachau concentration camp. (*Frankfurter Kurier.*)

May 29th. WILHELM ARON, of Bamberg, member of Reichsbanner, shot in Dachau " while trying to escape." (*Bamberger Zeitung.*)

End of May. TWO COMMUNIST WORKERS shot in Siegburg concentration camp. (Witness.)

June 8th. STORM TROOPER, Düsseldorf, shot for distributing opposition leaflets. (Dortmund *General Anzeiger*.)

June 10th. KARL LOTTES, Communist worker, shot " while trying to escape." (*WTB*.) FRITZ KOKORENZ, a storm trooper in opposition, found shot in his home, Berlin. (Witness.) WALTER ERNST, found half buried in Hennigsdorf Cemetery, Berlin. (*WTB*.)

June 12th. UNNAMED WORKER, Essen, shot " while trying to escape." (*TU*.)

June 20th. WALTER KERSING, worker, member of German Nationalist youth organisation, Frankfurt-on-Oder, shot by Nazis in a " dispute." (*WTB*.)

June 21st. PAUL URBAN, worker, Brandenburg, alleged suicide in prison. (*Nachtausgabe*.) THREE UNKNOWN MEN, found dead in a pool, with their arms and legs bound, at Neustädtel near Zwickau. (12-*Uhr Mittagsblatt*.)

June 22nd. ALTENBURG, Communist worker, Arnswalde, Neumark, shot " while trying to escape." (*Deutsche Allgemeine Zeitung*.) SCHMAUS FAMILY, FATHER, MOTHER and SON, murdered by storm troopers. (See report.) RAKOVSKI, worker, Köpenick, shot by storm troopers. (See report.) JOHANNES STELLING, former premier of Mecklenburg, murdered. (See report.) PAUL VON ESSEN, member of Reichsbanner, Köpenick, beaten to death. (See report.)

June 24th. ARTHUR MAY, Communist official, Aachen, shot " while trying to escape." (Police report, Aachen.)

June 26th. UNKNOWN COMMUNIST WORKER, Braunschweig, murdered in prison, alleged suicide. (*WTB*.)

June 29th. DR. ROSENFELDER, lawyer, Nürnberg, murdered in Dachau concentration camp. (Witness.)

End of June. GLÄSPER, local leader of Red Aid organisation, Elberfeld. GOTTSCHALK, town councillor. OTTO DATTEM, Communist councillor, Elberfeld, murdered shortly after release from concentration camp, body thrown into a river. ERWIN DÄHLER, a young worker, found dead, mutilated. GORSMEIER, Elberfeld, shot by Nazis after arrest and thrown into a pool. UNNAMED WORKER, Elberfeld, found shot in the Bremerstrasse. UNNAMED WORKER, Elberfeld, found shot. (All of these Elberfeld murders are authenticated in reports from witnesses.) HUNGLINGER, police officer, Munich. SEBASTIAN

NEFZGER, Munich. MICHAEL SIGMAN, Social Democrat, murdered in Dachau concentration camp. (Reports from witnesses.)

July 1st. MAX MARGOLINER, merchant, Breslau, maltreated in the Brown House during April, died in hospital two months later. (Witness.)

July 10th. JOSEPH NIES, journalist, member of Freethinkers' League, Erfurt. ALFRED NOLL, Communist official, Jena. UNNAMED COMMUNIST WORKER, Erfurt. All three shot by storm troopers when the illegal printing-press used for the *Thüringer Volksblatt* was discovered. (Witness.)

July 12th. ASSMANN, member of Reichsbanner, Köpenick, killed in the Köpenick "St. Bartholomew's night." (See report.) VAN TENDE, Communist worker, Essen, political prisoner since October 1931, shot "while trying to escape." (*Conti-WTB.*) SCHULZ, Communist member of Diet, Berlin, died in hospital after maltreatment. (*Temps.*) FRITZ LANGE, Communist worker, Königsberg, lynched. (*Angriff.*) JOSEPH MESSINGER, Communist worker, Bonn, murdered in prison, alleged suicide. (Havas agency.)

July 14th. FRANZ BRAUN, editor of *Volkswacht*, Stettin, murdered in his cell the day after he was arrested. (*Conti-WTB.*) THREE UNKNOWN COMMUNISTS, Schwerin, shot "while trying to escape" on their way to Sonnenburg concentration camp. (*Vossische Zeitung.*) UNKNOWN COMMUNIST WORKER, Stettin, shot. (*Conti-WTB.*) UNNAMED COMMUNIST OFFICIAL, Bochum, shot "while trying to escape." (*Vossische Zeitung.*)

July 15th. SPEER, a tailor, Berlin, found with his throat cut through. (Witness.) KLARA WAGNER, typist, Treptow, Berlin, shot. (Witness.)

July 17th. DR. WILHELM SCHÄFER, Frankfurt, ex-Nazi, found shot. (*Frankfurter Zeitung.*)

July 20th. UNNAMED WORKER, Berlin, found dead at Hirschgarten. (Witness.) MAN, 50 years of age, found dead near Berlin. (Witness.) HUGO FEDDERSEN, Communist worker, Hamburg, murdered in prison, alleged suicide. (*WTB.*) STORM TROOPER, Obermenzig, near Munich, found shot ; he had adopted an opposition standpoint. (*Conti-WTB.*)

July 24th. ERICH and GUSTAV RUDOLF, Dühringshof, shot "while trying to escape." (*Frankfurter Zeitung.*) THREE STORM TROOPERS of opposition tendency found shot, Grünewald, Berlin. (Witness.) JASKOWIAK, Nazi of opposition tendency, Leverkusen, shot by a protective corps man " in self-defence." (Dortmund *General Anzeiger*.)

July 29th. SOLECKI, Communist worker, Iserlohn, shot by auxiliary police " in self-defence." (*WTB*.) HEINRICH FOERDING, Communist worker, Coesfeld, thrown from window of police station, Recklinghausen, alleged suicide. (*WTB*.)

August 1st. Four workers, LÜTGENS, TESCH, WOLFF and MÖLLER, executed in Altona.

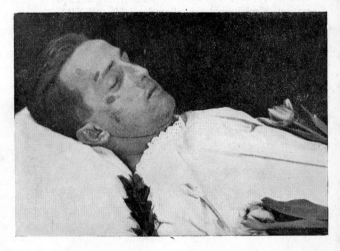

HEINZ BÄSSLER, " shot while trying to escape."
(Note the bullet wounds in the face.)

PLATE NO. 17